Generative Processes in Music

Generative Processes in Music

The Psychology of Performance, Improvisation, and Composition

Edited by

John A. Sloboda

Department of Psychology
University of Keele

CLARENDON PRESS · OXFORD
1988

Oxford University Press, Walton Street, Oxford OX2 6DP
Oxford New York Toronto
Delhi Bombay Calcutta Madras Karachi
Petaling Jaya Singapore Hong Kong Tokyo
Nairobi Dar es Salaam Cape Town
Melbourne Auckland
and associated companies in
Beirut Berlin Ibadan Nicosia

Oxford is a trade mark of Oxford University Press

Published in the United States
by Oxford University Press, New York

British Library Cataloguing in Publication Data
Sloboda, John A.
Generative processes in music: the psychology
of performance, improvisation and composition.
1. Music—Psychology
I. Title
781'.15   ML3830
ISBN 0–19–852154–5

Library of Congress Cataloging in Publication Data
Generative processes in music.
Bibliography: p.
Includes indexes.
1. Music—Performance—Psychology.
2. Improvisation (Music)—Psychology.
3. Composition (Music)—Psychology.
4. Cognition. 5. Developmental psychology.
I. Sloboda, John A.
ML3838.G38 1988   781.6'01'9   87–12369
ISBN 0–19–852154–5

Set by Hope Services, Abingdon, Oxon
Printed in Great Britain by
St Edmundsbury Press Limited,
Bury St Edmunds, Suffolk

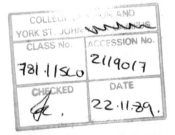

Preface

JOHN SLOBODA

This book was conceived to remedy an imbalance in the Psychology of Music literature. The vast majority of serious psychological research has been devoted to an analysis and understanding of the processes involved in listening to music. This is reflected in the existence of a major journal with the title *Music Perception*. There could not be a journal entitled *Music Performance*, because there just would not be enough research to fill it.

The reasons for the relative neglect of generative processes (including performance, improvisation, and composition) are various. I wish to comment briefly on three of these: cultural bias, measurement problems, and problems of control. I shall then turn to some general comments about the contributions to this volume.

Through a long social and historical process contemporary Western art culture has become characterized by functional specialism. In the case of music, as with most other art forms, a gulf has emerged between producer and consumer. Adult producers are typically few in number, often institutionally trained. Adult consumers are typically large in number, usually untrained, and often unskilled in most forms of music production. With the advent of sound recording and other forms of mechanical transmission it has become possible for the various functions to be completely separated in both time and space. Consider, for instance, a Beethoven symphony. A group of performers construct their interpretation in necessary isolation from the composer, and also from the audience for whom the performance is intended (for example in a recording studio). A member of the audience may then 'receive' the interpretation in social isolation from both composer and performer as a disembodied aural experience. This is particularly true of the domestic listener who may, through use of headphones and darkened room, create the impression of being totally and exclusively enfolded by sound. Even at the concert there are usually strong social and geographical factors which separate listeners from performers. Performers and listeners go in and out by separate doors; they do not interact with one another. Any form of audience interruption is usually violently resisted. Such constraints tend to reinforce an 'illusion' which projects the sound of the music away from the realities of its origins in human work, both physical and mental. As in the puppet theatre, the modes of production become veiled in mystery, and we may have no particular wish to venture behind the proscenium arch.

In such a culture it is, perhaps, inevitable that the listener's response to music should become the primary focus of the psychology of music. This focus would, however, be less than fully comprehensible in cultures (maybe the majority of the world's musical cultures so far) where functional specialism had not gone so far. In many cultures it would be strange to hear music without joining in in one way or another. The separation between performer and composer is also necessarily less clear. Especially when the music is without notation, the originator of the music must necessarily perform it to communicate it. Also, composition/improvisation is often a social process, with several individuals in a group contributing substantially to the form of the music.

One of the recurrent themes of the contributions to this book is inextricable connection of generative and receptive processes. Their separation can only ever be partial. The reality is that all music must reflect the psychological propensities and capacities of humans as composers, performers, and listeners. To an extent, each type of involvement with music includes the others. Composers temper their compositional processes against their own aural judgements (see Lerdahl, Chapter 10) and their understanding of the performance characteristics of various instruments. Performers refine their performances against both their own aural awareness and their ability to image alternatives (see Pressing, Chapter 7). Listeners grasp a work of music by attempting to sing or hum parts of it, or by engaging in some form of rhythmic movement. They may also 'compose' variants or elaborations of the music in informal (but not necessarily overt) behaviour. Sagi and Vitanyi (Chapter 8) go so far as to propose that the ability to receive music is constrained by the extent to which people are capable of generating variants within a particular genre. In a similar vein, Dowling (Chapter 6) shows that young children's ability to discriminate tonal from atonal melodies is dependent on the level of singing ability that they have achieved.

We may suppose, in fact, that the impulse to generate and perform music is as inherent a part of the human constitution as is the impulse to generate language. The research reviewed by Dowling (Chapter 6) shows that very young children produce spontaneous songs which incorporate but by no means mimic elements of adult productions. Just as in language development, song development seems to go through a set of ordered, rule-governed stages. It may be that the failure of early generativity to flower into full-scale compositional ability is a result of both the ubiquitous concern of the 8–11 year old with 'correctness' and also traditional educational styles which undervalue experimentation and self-discovery. Where opportunities are given for self-directed musical productivity (for example Swanwick and Tillman 1986), children demonstrate an impressively varied yet ordered progression of compositional strategies right through the school ages. Davidson and Scripp (Chapter 9) support this picture by an intriguing study of children's spontaneous notations for music.

A second reason for the neglect of generative processes relates to problems of measurement in psychological science. It is always easier to collect one's data in the form of responses from a limited and pre-ordained set (for example yes–no decision, same–different decisions) than it is from relatively unconstrained and multidimensional behaviour. This concern for precision and simplicity in measurement has led to a concentration within the psychological community on rather simple laboratory tasks. Claxton (1980, p. 13) paints a humorous but not altogether inapposite picture of the typical study in cognitive psychology:

cognitive psychology does not, after all, deal with whole people, but with a very special and bizarre—almost Frankenstinian—preparation, with consists of a brain attached to two eyes, two ears, and two index fingers. The preparation is only to be found inside small, gloomy cubicles, outside which red lights burn to warn ordinary people away. It stares fixedly at a small screen, and its fingers rest lightly and expectantly on two small squares of black plastic—microswitches. It does not feel hungry or tired or inquisitive; it does not think extraneous thoughts or try to understand what is going on. It simply processes information.

In terms of music psychology, this 'Frankenstinian' orientation has led to many studies in which subjects hear short computer-generated fragments through headphones and then are required to make some (usually binary) judgement about them, whose accuracy and reaction time may be measured relatively simply. The advantages and limitations of this approach are well known and discussed (for example Sloboda 1985; Longuet-Higgins 1987) and need not be rehearsed again here. Suffice to say that every single empirical contribution to this volume has, at one stage or another, adopted a different approach to measurement. In general, subjects have been allowed to produce responses of some complexity and length, free from excessive experimental constraints. This approach is essential is one is to make any meaningful contribution to the psychology of performance or composition.

The problems of recording and analysing these responses have been approached in a number of ways. Some researchers rely on auditory transcription into conventional (or amended) notation, and then perform formal or informal anayses on the transcripts (for example Gruson, Chapter 5; Dowling, Chapter 6; Sagi and Vitanyi, Chapter 8; Davidson and Welsh, Chapter 10). The advantages and disadvantages of the transcription method have been discussed at length by Sloboda and Parker (1985). Whilst transcription produces a record which is easily understandable by literate musicians, it runs the risk of making the performance seem more coherent than it actually was (by the transcriber's 'intelligent' cleaning up of inherently messy data). It is also necessarily selective, and cannot reliably record information about expressive parameters of the performance. There also remains the problem of how to turn such transcriptions into quantitative form, for the application of statistical techniques. The contributors to this volume solve this problem in a number of ways, ranging from highly elaborate coding schemes (Gruson, Chapter 5) to informal stylistic analyses (Sagi and Vitanyi, Chapter 8).

Other researchers have used mechanical and electronic means of recording performance parameters in a precise quantitative fashion (for example Clarke, Chapter 1; Gabrielsson, Chapter 2; Sundberg, Chapter 3; Rasch, Chapter 4). This allows for more sophisticated statistical analysis, the testing of precise models with quantiative predictions, and the capturing of highly important expressive dimensions of performance. The disadvantages of this method arise largely from the data overload that is generated, and from the fact that it is much more difficult (although not impossible) to apply informed musical intelligence to the interpretation of data. The ubiquity of the computer has made the first problem more manageable and has, one suspects, been largely responsible for the modest upturn in the quantity of this work in the last ten years.

A third set of researchers have used tasks which require subjects to write down the end-products of their cognition in notation, traditional (Davidson and Welsh, Chapter 10) or otherwise (Davidson and Scripp, Chapter 8). This is a particularly useful method of studying composition, especially when coupled with verbal protocols. The disadvantage of the method is that schemes of quantitative measurement are hard to devise, and are usually descriptive in nature. They are, however, particularly rich sources of ideas and insights.

The third reason for the neglect of generative processes is linked to the second, and relates to the difficulties of devising suitable experimental controls over generative behaviour. Without some form of control over the conditions under which subjects exercise their generativity it becomes very difficult (but not entirely impossible) to extract any generalities about the processes involved; and without generality there is no science. The range of controls deployed in this volume varies from the very broad (in the case of improvisation and composition) to the very tight (in the case of some performance studies, where note, speed, and fingerings are specified). For instance, Sagi and Vitanyi (Chapter 8) offer the minimum constraint of a text. Subjects of varying abilities and backgrounds are required to improvise any tune they like to that text. Davidson and Welsh (Chapter 10) adopt a similar but rather more constrained tactic. They offer their subjects a rhythm, and ask them to assign pitches to the rhythms so as to produce a melody which must modulate in a certain way. Again, subjects of varying levels of ability are tested. Gruson (Chapter 5), in her study of piano practising, simply specifies the piece to be practised, and leaves everything else up to the subjects.

Clarke (Chapter 1) is at the other extreme in his studies of expressive performance. He studies piano performance so as to control (by exclusion) the possibility of subjects using pitch and timbral variations, and then devises melodies with special qualities to test very specific hypotheses (such as that sliding the bar line along a single melodic fragment will affect expressive performance of it in systematic ways). Subjects are required to produce accurate performances of these melodies. Control is also obtained in another way by several authors. Instead of gathering data by looking at many different subjects, they obtain relatively large amounts of data from one or few subjects, looking for generalities *within* the behaviour of individual subjects (for example Clarke, Chapter 1; Gabrielsson, Chapter 2; Rasch, Chapter 4). It may be more important to show that the behaviour of an individual is systematic and rule governed, than to show that many individuals are systematic in precisely the same way. Indeed, in the study of artistic behaviour one may argue that one would neither expect, nor wish for, high degrees of uniformity between subjects.

The final part of this preface is concerned to make some general points about the contributions to the volume, and to highlight some specific aspects of individual contributions.

The first thing to say is that most of these contributions report pioneering work. There is no long tradition of research into most aspects of music generation. Thus, to my knowledge, Gruson (Chapter 5) is the first person ever to have subjected rehearsal behaviour to systematic quantitative analysis. Davidson and Welsh (Chapter 10) are the first to apply systematic analysis to a compositional task undertaken by groups chosen to represent differing ability levels. Sagi and Vitanyi (Chapter 8) have created the first large-scale corpus of improvisations by untrained people. With the pioneering comes an element of risk. It is not clear which of these approaches and ideas have a future. Some of the work is necessarily exploratory, and without the substantial backing of related research. It is not clear that all the theorizing contained here will actually be confirmed by data. Lerdahl makes a provocative and highly original claim about what constitutes a viable relationship between methods by which composers compose and how listeners listen. Will composers be able to use Lerdahl's constraints to guide them towards composing structurally rich yet comprehensible pieces? We do not yet know. Can Pressing's impressive theory of improvisation be tested against actual improvisations? The ideas are rich and plausible, but do they have predictive value? Such issues are raised but not resolved here.

The second point about the contributions is that they are truly interdisciplinary in nature. The contributors are roughtly equally divided into those working in psychology departments or other scientific setings, and those working in music or socio-cultural studies. The individaul contributions draw on ideas from linguistics, sociology, neurophysiology, acoustics, artificial intelligence and computer science, as well as psychology and music. This diversity of approach is welcome, particularly when similar ideas recur in contributions from quite different sources. It does mean, however, that several languages and perspectives rub shoulders with one another, and this sometimes makes for tensions. Psychologists may well find the contributions of the musicians unsatisfactory because of their apparent disconnection from the task of data gathering. Experimentalists may well find the rather informal analyses in some of the papers disappointing. On the other hand, musicians may well find the interpretative caution of some psychologists irritating and pedantic. Others may find the cultural narrowness of the types of music discussed less than satisfactory. Neither I nor the contributors should have to apologize for this. As a reflection of the 'state of the art' this volume represents the growth pains of a young discipline, full of ideas and enthusiasm, but not wholly co-ordinated in approach or methodological priorities.

Chapters 1 to 3 form a relatively coherent group of contributions, all focusing in slightly different ways on the question of what makes a musical performance. It is abundantly clear that a mechanical performance reproducing exactly what is contained in the notation rarely makes a satisfactory performance. Clarke (Chapter 1) emphasizes the role of performance in exemplifying structural aspects of the music through expressive gradients, discontinuities, and contrasts. He embeds several ingenious experimental studies within a theoretical framework that emphasizes the importance of hierarchical mental representations as a means of controlling performances. Gabrielsson (Chapter 2) supplements Clarke's study with some naturalistic data on rhythmic performance. This data confirms that performers make systematic and significant deviations from strict metricality, but also that it is hard to make generalizations about the nature of the deviations. The same figure may be played differently in different contexts, or by the same performer on different occasions. Sundberg (Chapter 3) describes some ingenious studies where a computer 'learns' to play expressively by being supplied with a set of rules for modulating timing and loudness in certain musical contexts. These rules are modified by playing the results to a panel of human judges and asking for judgements of appropriateness. Sundberg amplifies the interesting point that 'apt' expressive devices are very often not explicitly identified as such by judges, but simply contribute to a sense of 'rightness' about a performance.

Rasch (Chapter 4) summarizes his painstaking and elegant work on synchronization in ensemble performance. He is one of a tiny number of researchers who have examined any aspect of ensemble playing. He reports many intriguing results, including the finding that musicians achieve better synchrony at faster speeds than at slower speeds. It also seems that a degree of asynchrony increases the perceptual clarity of individual lines, even though listeners are not consciously aware of quite large degrees of asynchronization in musical performance. Finally, Rasch provides an elegant mathematical justification for the fact that ensemble of more than 10 players tend to need a conductor while smaller groups do not.

Gruson (Chapter 5) reports a pioneering study on rehearsal strategies of musicians at different levels. She finds that people at any given level do not change their strategy much over the course of learning a given piece, but that significant strategy differences do exist between different levels of expertise. For instance, experienced players are more likely to repeat musically coherent sections of the piece. Beginners are much more likely to repeat individual notes. The general drift of her evidence is that experienced rehearsers are more aware of the structure of what they are rehearsing, and that this makes rehearsal more efficient.

Dowling (Chapter 6) explores the strong links between perception and production in the development of musical competence in young children. He reviews the literature on developmental aspects of song production and reports two new empirical studies. The first shows that children as young as three years old can reliably discriminate tonal from atonal melodies so long as their song performance is relatively advanced. The second study explores the structure of nursery songs as opposed to folk-songs and art songs. The analysis shows that nursery rhymes very rarely depart from strict diatonicity, and Dowling argues that such songs are optimal for children extracting and internalizing rules of tonality. This chapter is, in a sense, the pivot of the book, since it reminds us that children's song has elements of reproduction and improvisation inextricably intertwined. The preceding chapters deal exclusively with reproductive performance. Those to follow deal exclusively with the creation of new music through improvisation or composition.

Pressing (Chapter 7) provides a monumental survey of concepts from a number of disciplines that are relevant to an understanding of improvisation, and outlines a theory of improvisation that concentrates on the psychological bases for moment-to-moment choices within an improvisational structure. The theory is associationistic in nature, and proposes that improvisation proceeds by means of choices of elements which either *continue* or *interrupt* some aspect of the immediately preceding context. In its concern with the note-by-note structure of an improvisation it contrasts with the contribution of Sagi and Vitanyi (Chapter 8). Here, the emphasis is on global features of structure and style in the spontaneous improvisations of ordinary Hungarians. A principal finding of the study was that the majority of untrained subjects were able to use *some* coherent strategy to provide a melody, often based on forms available in their culture, but to some extent affected by the nature of the words they were required to set.

Davidson and Scripp (Chapter 9) present intriguing data from children aged five to seven who were asked to notate various musical fragments without explicit instruction. What is particularly impressive about these data is the coherence of the schemes devised by children. Even at age five, many children devise abstract symbols to represent particularly the rhythmic structure of the music. By age seven, pitch becomes an increasing focus for notational attention. Interestingly, at age five performance skill and notational skill seem largely uncorrelated; but by age seven the two seem to have become 'yoked' together into a unified domain of musical intelligence.

The final two chapters in the book turn to the skill of composition. Lerdahl (Chapter 10) draws some logical yet provocative consequences from his influential work with Jackendoff (Lerdahl and Jackendoff 1983). If a listener understands music by constructing a hierarchical mental representation of it, then effective compositions will abide by constraints which allow listeners to do just that. Lerdahl identifies a number of specific constraints, and shows that serial music falls foul of several of them. This, he argues, is the reason why such music is so impenetrable.

Davidson and Welsh (Chapter 11) adopt a data-driven approach, in contrast to Lerdahl's theory-driven one. They look at the processes by which music students of differing expertise construct a melody given certain conditions that the melody must fulfil. Their analysis yields some tempting pointers as to the nature of compositional expertise. The more expert group worked with larger units (as shown by the size of section they would play over). They also engaged in more reflection, while the less experienced group worked in an enactive fashion (for example trying out possibilities at random until hitting on one that 'worked'). The study also highlights the dissociation of skills at this level. Even very gifted performers can be 'poor' composers without specific practice.

It is customary for the editors of multi-author volumes to draw some general overarching conclusion from the set of studies he or she has gathered together. I am reluctant to do this. My reluctance stems from the fact that the unity of a set of papers is often to be found, not in their outcomes, but in the shared assumptions that motivated them. In the case of this volume, many of the contributors attended an international conference on Psychology and the Arts held in Cardiff in 1983 (Crozier and Chapman 1984). It was primarily as a result of conversations there, and a sense of shared purpose, that the idea for this book was born. To find, therefore, that the contributions point in the same general direction is as little of a surprise as it would be to discover that the occupants of a given aeroplane are all headed for the same destination.

In the case of this volume, I would identify five core assumptions which run explicitly or implicitly through the majority of contributions:

(1) Music generative capacity is inherent in all human beings, although it may be developed to a greater or lesser extent.

(2) The capacity to generate any but the most primitive musical sequences is based on the ability to derive sound sequences from higher-order structures or rule systems.

(3) These rule systems have some universal constraints on them (arising from general facts about human cognitive capacity) but incorporate specific constraints picked up from the prevailing musical culture.

(4) Specific instruction is not necessary for skill acquisition, but practice is. Through practice, and possibly through general developmental changes, similar stages in skill acquisition can be observed in the several generative domains.

(5) Many aspects of skill become partly automated, and not open to conscious introspection. Their nature must therefore be elucidated by observation and analysis of generative behaviour rather than (or in addition to) verbal self-report.

The papers in this volume all attempt to put flesh on the bare bones of one or more of these assumptions through theorizing and/or empirical observation. Their success may be judged by the degree to which the reader is more inclined to assent to these assumptions after reading the book than he or she was before. If the reader wishes for elucidation on different but equally important issues, such as the role of motivation and emotion in sustaining and shaping generative behaviour, or the nature of effective training in these skills, then he or she must search elsewhere. If the search is successful then I would certainly like to know about it.

References

Crozier, W. R. and Chapman, A. J. (eds) (1984). *Cognitive processes in the perception of art*. Elsevier, North-Holland.

Claxton, G. (1980). Cognitive Psychology: a suitable case for what sort of treatment. In *Cognitive psychology: new directions* (ed. G. Claxton). Routledge Kegan Paul, London.

Lerdahl, F. and Jackendoff, R. (1983). *A generative theory of tonal music*. MIT Press, Cambridge, Mass.

Longuet-Higgins, H. C. (1987). Music and the psychologists; or the poet and the peasant. *Psychology of Music* 15 (1), 3–7.

Sloboda, J. A. (1985). *The musical mind: the cognitive psychology of music*. Oxford University Press, Oxford.

Sloboda, J. A. and Parker, D. H. H. (1985). Immediate recall for melodies. In *Musical structure and cognition* (eds. P. Howell, I. Cross, and R. West), Academic Press, London.

Swanwick, K. and Tillman, J. (1986). The sequence of musical development. *British Journal of Music Education* 3, 305–39.

Contents

Contributors

Eric F. Clarke, Music Department, The City University, Northampton Square, London EC1V 0HB, UK.

Lyle Davidson, Project Zero, Harvard University, Longfellow Hall, Appian Way, Cambridge, MA 02138, USA.

W. Jay Dowling, Program in Human Development and Communication Sciences, The University of Texas at Dallas, Richardson, TX 75083–0688, USA.

Alf Gabrielsson, Department of Psychology, Uppsala University, Box 227, S–75104 Uppsala, Sweden.

Linda M. Gruson, 28 Vesta Drive, Toronto, Ontario M5P 2Z5, Canada.

Fred Lerdahl, School of Music, The University of Michigan, Ann Arbor, MI 48109–2085, USA.

Jeff Pressing, Department of Music, La Trobe University, Bundoora, Victoria 3083, Australia.

Rudolf A. Rasch, Instritute of Musicology and Institute of Phonetics, University of Utrecht, Drift 21, 3512 BR Utrecht, The Netherlands.

Maria Sagi, Research Institute for Culture, H–1251 Budapest, Corvin Ter 8, Hungary.

Lawrence Scripp, Project Zero, Harvard University, Longfellow Hall, Appian Way, Cambridge, MA 02138, USA.

John A. Sloboda (editor), Department of Psychology, University of Keele, Keele, Staffordshire ST5 5BG, UK.

Johan Sundberg, Department of Speech Communication and Music Acoustics, Royal Institute of Technology, S–10044 Stockholm 70, Sweden.

Ivan Vitanyi, Research Institute for Culture, H–1251 Budapest, Corvin Ter 8, Hungary.

Patricia Welsh, Project Zero, Harvard University, Longfellow Hall, Appian Way, Cambridge, MA 02138, USA.

1

Generative principles in music performance

ERIC F. CLARKE

Introduction

The aim of this chapter is to give an account of generative principles involved in music performance at two levels. One level concerns the representation of musical structure in a form that gives a coherent and intelligent input into a motor system. The word generative is understood here in the same descriptive and analytic sense as in Chomsky (1957), and in the more recent music theory of Lerdahl and Jackendoff (1983). The second level at which generative principles are identifiable is in the production and control of the expressive aspects of performance, which function so as to convey a particular interpretation of a musical structure. This sense of the word generative is much closer to the idea that something is actually generated, rather than simply being describable in terms of generative principles. These two usages of the term correspond to rather different psychological orientations, and while there are certain circumstances in which the two become closely associated, one purpose of this chapter is to illustrate the distinction between them.

The generative structure of musical knowledge

Playing music is an activity that is comparable in cognitive complexity to speaking a language, and comparable in its demands on motor control to playing a sport like tennis. It has thus been a focus of attention for psychologists interested in issues of motor control (for example Gates and Bradshaw 1974; Shaffer 1981), and for those interested primarily in musical cognition (for example Bengtsson and Gabrielsson 1983; Sloboda 1983). The motor programming perspective adopted in most recent work on motor control has, however, diminished the separation between these two lines of enquiry by emphasizing the importance of cognitive structures in the control of movement. Continuous reference to a large body of musical knowledge is required in music performance if the result is to be fluent and intelligent, making it difficult to maintain a definite distinction between the cognitive structures of abstract musical understanding and those embodied in a motor programme for musical performance. This discussion of the knowledge structures that form the basis for musical performances therefore starts at a comparatively high level of abstraction by considering first some aspects of music theory.

Although the relationship between music theory and psychology is rather loosely defined, most music theory not only incorporates psychological principles of one sort or another (for example gestalt principles in Meyer 1973), but also takes the explanation of musical experience as one of its primary aims. It is, in other words, a theory of how people hear music, as well as a theory of how music is formally structured.* The structures described by music theory can therefore be taken as reasonable indicators of the nature of cognitive structures for music, particularly since recent work (for example Shepard 1982) has tended to confirm the perceptual significance of these structures.

The most widespread characteristic of musical structure embodied in music theory is its hierarchical nature (see Narmour 1983 for a recent review). In the parameters of both pitch and rhythm, structures are represented almost without exception as being organized in a series of levels, between which relationships of reduction or elaboration operate. Although hierarchical structures should not simply be equated with generative structures, they are nevertheless closely related, and as a number of authors have shown (for example Longuet-Higgins 1976; Sundberg and Lindblom 1976; Lerdahl and Jackendoff 1983) truly generative theories can be shown to have considerable explanatory power.

All of these studies make use of tree diagrams as representations for a generative structure, although it is not a requirement that a generative structure be represented in this way. Since a tree diagram is a useful shorthand that conveys generative relationships, I will make use of it for illustrative purposes in the following discussion. In considering the generative structures of musical knowledge, my aim is to examine their more global characteristics, rather than the precise nature of the generative principles themselves. It is the topology of generative relationships that is of interest, or put another way, the pattern of hierarchical structures that constitutes musical knowledge.

The issue can be tackled only in relation to specific performance conditions. It is inevitable that the knowledge structures that underlie a performance of a piece from memory will be different, at the highest levels at least, from those associated with a free improvisation, or a sight-read performance from notation. Starting at one extreme, performances of

* Note that this is not the case with all music theory. For example many of the structures discussed in Forte (1973) are of a level and type of abstraction that makes it extremely unlikely that they could be perceived in any direct fashion.

classical music from memory appear to offer the most deeply embedded generative structures. Though something of an idealization, we can imagine a performer who, at the start of a performance, has a complete knowledge of the generative structure of the piece, from the very highest level, where the whole piece is represented as a unity, down to the lowest level, where each individual note is represented. Figure 1.1 is a schematic representation of such a knowledge structure. Evidence for the highest level in this structure is rather sparse, and is confined to statements by a number of composers (Mozart, Beethoven, Hindemith) which indicate that they were able to hear (or imagine) their own compositions in a single 'glance'. Since these composers were also performers, the unified conceptions of which they claimed to be capable can be regarded as the basis of performances as well as compositions.

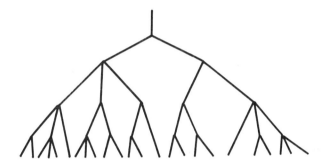

Fig. 1.1. Schematic representation of an idealized knowledge structure for a memorized musical performance.

The evidence for totally unified structural knowledge is a little tenuous, but does not affect the essential point that high-level musical structures acquire unified cognitive representations. It is easier to accept that a performer may have a unified conception of each of three large sections, for instance, that together make up a movement. These units connect with all the individual events of the piece through the multi-levelled branching structure that a tree diagram illustrates. It is difficult to know quite how one might experimentally test the existence of these very high levels of generative structure, but tonal structures of a fairly abstract nature (and hence at a fairly high hierarchical level) such as the concept of key, or tonal area, have been demonstrated to have psychological reality as well as theoretical value (see Krumhansl 1983).

The idea that a performer who has memorized a piece of music has a complete generative representation is an idealization not only because the structural depth of the representation is uncertain, but also because it seems implausible that a complete structural representation of the complexity required for a piece of even moderate length could be activated. It is more likely that only a part of the entire structure is active at any time, the remainder being in a latent state, or active only in broad outline. At any particular moment the generative structure is incomplete or only partially activated, the active region shifting as the performer progresses through the music, revealing different areas and levels of the structure. For instance, in the middle of a deeply embedded musical phrase, only a region of low-level generative connections might be active, since there is little need for a performer to have access to high-level structural information; his or her main concern is the detailed structure of connections within the phrase itself. At a phrase boundary, however, it may be important for the performer to know how the previous and subsequent phrases are related to one another and to the overall structure of the piece. At these moments a small area of low-level structural connections may be active, sufficient to specify the immediate succession of events to be played, together with a section of the higher levels of generative structure specifying larger-scale relationships. Figures 1.2(a) and 1.2(b) illustrate schematically these two conditions. This suggests that in the course of a performance, a player's structural awareness constantly

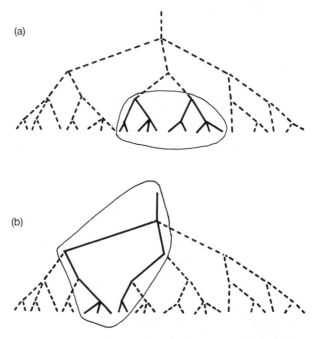

(a)

(b)

Fig. 1.2. Schematic representations for partially activated knowledge structures in a memorized performance: (a) illustrates active parts of the generative structure (ringed) in mid-phrase; (b) illustrates active parts approaching a phrase boundary.

shifts between regions of activated structure that vary in durational extent and generative depth. As a general rule, the depth to which the generative structure is activated is directly related to the structural significance of phrase boundaries lying close to, or at, the player's current musical location.

The second type of performance whose representational structure I wish to consider is music played from a notated source. Unless the performer already knows the music extremely well, and is simply looking at the notation for reassurance, a variable amount of uncertainty surrounds his or her anticipation of how the music may develop, and the relationship between current and future events. The future course of musical events is not, of course, completely unknown, since listeners and performers continually make projections on the basis of acquired stylistic knowledge (see Meyer 1956; Narmour 1977); but it seldom turns out that the music exactly matches these projections for a number of reasons: (1) performers and listeners may envisage a number of different possible continuations; (2) stylistic knowledge, on which projection is based, is never perfect and complete; (3) it is in the nature of music to depart from stylistic norms in the interest of creativity. Figure 1.3, which represents the knowledge structure of a piece performed from notation midway through the music, indicates these uncertainties with dashed connections and question marks.

The significance of the mismatch between projection and outcome lies in its effect upon the continuous construction of a generative representation during a performance. With memorized performance, the generative structure is known entirely (or at least to a high level) in advance, and is simply unpacked during a performance. Thus misrepresentation of the generative structure on the part of the performer is essentially restricted to memory lapses at various levels. By contrast, in an unmemorized performance it is likely that incorrect projections will result in inappropriate attributions of structual significance, failure to grasp long-term connections,

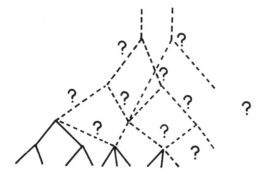

Fig. 1.3. Schematic representation for the knowledge structure of a musical performance from a notated score.

and so on. It is a feature of generative structures that they can be perfectly represented only when all the information has become available. In the course of assembling a representation from the raw data of notation, mistaken assumptions and oversights will inevitably result in a flawed structure that must be continually reassessed and retrospectively modified in the light of new evidence. Such re-evaluations are jeopardized by memory limitations, and may also lead to constructive rationalizations which distort the true structure of the music. In short, a performer playing unfamiliar music from notation is viewed as working from a generative representation that is incomplete in certain respects, almost certainly limited in the depth to which it extends, and subject to continuous modification in response to unfolding musical developments.

As a final example, let us consider the knowledge structures of improvised performance. Improvisation itself varies from the comparatively constrained conditions found in traditional jazz, where a harmonic sequence and metrical structure must be closely adhered to, to the almost entirely undetermined format of free improvisation. Taking the freer end of this spectrum, an improvising performer is necessarily working from a structural representation that is radically incomplete, since s/he does not yet know how the structure will turn out. A performer may start out with a more or less clear idea of the overall shape of the piece, but will typically have only the vaguest idea of how that shape will be realized. Alternatively, s/he may have no preconceived ideas whatsoever concerning the overall outline and may simply start off from a comparatively low-level structure —a motivic germ for a piece.

The questions are therefore how some sort of structure is developed (if it is), and whether that structure is generative in nature. Sudnow (1978, 1979) has provided an account of some of the processes involved in playing improvised jazz on the piano, based on an introspective analysis of his own playing. He takes the view that improvised piano playing should be viewed as the creation of 'an improvisatory hand' (Sudnow 1979, p. 14) and the logic and necessity of its movements, rather than as the outcome of abstract musical thought, with the hands acting simply as executive agents.

In accounting for the way in which these movements are structured, Sudnow questions the extent to which a hierarchical, generative process is involved, particularly at high levels of skill. Three stages of skill acquisition can be identified in Sudnow's account, differing in the extent to which they involve generative structure. At an early stage, his improvisations consist of relatively rigid routines that are executed in an invariant fashion, and which are structured together either according to the dictates of a predetermined framework, or simply by virtue of what comes most easily to the fingers. Such improvisations are therefore hierarchical up to a certain level (the level of the individual routine), and then either predetermined (and usually hierarchical in the case of jazz 'standards') or regulated by manual dexterity at higher levels. However, the rigidity of the individual units, and the problems of accommodating them to a variety of overall frameworks, cause Sudnow considerable problems in performance, and result in a rather frantic and discontinuous style.

The second stage is to break down the preformed gestures of the first stage into their individual elements so as to recover the flexibility that his performance lacks. This is relatively easy to achieve, but presents a problem which the final stage must overcome: a method of structuring the elements together that achieves coherence without rigidity. Sudnow implies that the strategy he adopts is principally associative, or if hierarchical then only to a very limited extent. His aim is to start an improvisation with few preconceptions as to how it will develop, and to allow the hand to explore new consequences and ramifications of its current activity in an unfolding exploration of the keyboard. The impetus to continue comes not from an overall scheme into which the material must fit, but from a continual monitoring of the events just completed that generates ideas for events just ahead. The style is thus characterized by a precarious, unpredictable, associative structure.

a single voice at the tips of the fingers, going for each next note in sayings just now and then, just this soft and just this hard, just here and just there, with definitions of aim throughout, taking my fingers to places, so to speak, and being guided, so to speak. (Sudnow 1978, p. 152)

A note of caution, however, must accompany Sudnow's account. It has been demonstrated by many authors that complex motor skills cannot achieve fluency and accuracy if they do not develop the hierarchical structures of motor programmes. Shaffer (1981) cites the example of moving a stylus to a number of targets with and without advance information, the former condition leading to hesitant, slow, and inaccurate performance when compared with the latter. Similarly, in his own work (Shaffer 1976), Shaffer showed that a copy-typist given no text preview (and thus unable to construct a motor programme) was reduced to a low level of speed and fluency when compared with her performance when she was given an eight-character preview. As far as motor control is concerned, typing is very similar to playing music, and it demonstrates that a literal interpretation of Sudnow's claims is untenable. An improviser must construct a representation for at least a short sequence of events in advance, and cannot operate at speed or with any fluency on an event-to-event level. Sudnow may have become unaware of these hierarchical structures, and the structures themselves may be no more elaborate than the eight-character preview of Shaffer's typist, but they undoubtedly exist.

The associative structure that Sudnow describes corresponds to a particular style of jazz improvisation, and in a different stylistic context a more considered approach is often required. This can either take the form of carefully constructed and rehearsed schemes, involving complex extended melodic and harmonic strucutres—in others words hierarchical/ generative structures—or can be characterized by a process of selecting patterns from a fixed repertoire. With this latter genre in mind, Sudnow comments that:

Some musicians do no more improvising than the stand-up comic who decides only in which order to tell the same jokes the same way at each performance. (Sudnow 1979, p. 43)

The various representations underlying an improvised performance can be brought together by considering the abstract representation of an improvised performance in its very earliest stages, as shown in Fig. 1.4. All

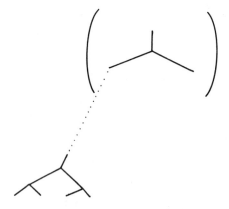

Fig. 1.4. Representation of the musical knowledge structure at the start of an improvised performance.

that exists is a low-level musical unit, characterized here as a small-scale, hierarchically organized event. A complete performance will consist of a large collection of such events, organized in different ways, and related to this first event according to three possible principles:

(1) The first event may be part of a hierarchical structure, to some extent worked out in advance, and to some extent constructed in the course of the improvisation. Figure 1.5 (a) is a schematic illustration of a complete piece formed according to this principle.

(2) The first event may be part of an associative chain of events, each new event derived from the previous sequence by the forward transfer of information. Figure 1.5(b) illustrates a complete piece formed on the basis of this principle.

(3) The first event may be selected from a number of events contained within the performer's repertoire, the rest of the improvisation consisting

(a)

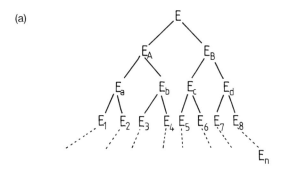

(b)

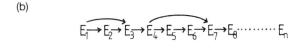

(c)

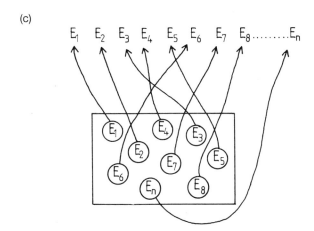

Fig. 1.5. The idealized knowledge structures for improvisations structured in three different ways: (a) hierarchically; (b) associatively; (c) by repertoire selection.

of further selections from this same repertoire, with a varying degree of relatedness between selections. Figure 1.5(c) illustrates this principle.

In any real performance all three principles will contribute to the improvisation. As we have seen, performance structures are never entirely associative, or perfectly hierarchical, and the selection of patterns from a repertoire of possibilities will necessarily take place within an overall framework (associative or hierarchical) of some sort, however vague. It may be, however, that different improvising idioms can be characterized by the balance of the three principles, and the interactions between them. The improvising style known as free jazz is principally characterized by associative structure, since it eschews the constraints of a pre-planned structure, and attempts to avoid the use of recognizable 'riffs'. More traditional jazz improvisation tends towards the hierarchical principle, in its adherence to a fairly strict harmonic outline. And be-bop improvisation illustrates the selective principle in the way in which a performer may try to construct an improvisation so as to include as many 'quotes' from other sources as possible (ranging from other jazz pieces to national anthems).

To summarize the main points of this section, the representational structure of musical knowledge can be shown to have a generative component in all performance contexts. However, the strength of that generative component differs considerably when the variety of performance contexts (memorized performance, performance from notation, improvisation) is considered. Memorized performance illustrates the most pervasively generative representational structure, though it seems likely that at any moment during a performance only a part of that structure is active. Performance from notation demonstrates a less complete generative structure which, in the case of music that is poorly known or sight-read, is constructed from the projections of a player's stylistic knowledge coupled with the continuously unfolding input of detailed information derived from the score. The result is a hierarchical structure that is incomplete in certain respects at high levels, and perhaps at odds with the music's formal structure. These are the errors and omissions which are rectified through extended practising and general musical training. Finally, improvisation illustrates a performance context in which musical representations of a variably generative character are constructed on the spot, or with an element of pre-planning, according to the principles of hierarchical, associative, and selective elaboration. The balance of these three may offer a succinct way in which to characterize improvising idioms.

As stated at the outset, no radical discontinuity need be imagined between the abstract, and essentially static, representational structures discussed here and the representations for action contained within a motor program. Indeed, Shaffer (1976, 1981) has shown that in both typing and musical performance abstract properties play a vital role in the control of performance. None the less, motor programs result in the generation of real activity in a way that abstract knowledge structures do not. At a certain point declarative knowledge becomes procedural, and the term generative comes to mean not description, but production. One area of particular interest in which such a process is crucially implicated is the control and shaping of the expressive properties of a performance.

Generative processes in performance expression

Whenever a skilled performer plays music, whether at sight or after years of practice, alone or in an ensemble, s/he plays with expression. Continuously variable modifications of the timing, dynamic, articulation, vibrato, and timbre of notes and note groups are identifiable and can be preserved with astonishing precision from one performance to another, sometimes separated by years. On the other hand dramatic changes in these expressive parameters can be observed between successive performances of the same piece of music separated by only a few minutes. These observations prompt the following questions: how is it possible for a performer to introduce expression into a performance when the music is unknown, to preserve an interpretation over long periods of time, and to alter an interpretation at a moment's notice?

The options available that account for these facts are limited. Either one must assume that a performer has simply learned a fixed expressive pattern that is applied to each piece of music, and exists in a number of fixed variants; or one must assume that the expressive profile is generated at the time of performance from information specified in the musical structure. The first option is not really a serious possibility since expressive profiles have been shown by a number of authors (Shaffer 1981, 1984; Sloboda 1983; Clarke 1984) to be closely related to musical structure. Given the structural differences between pieces of music even within the same style, it is inevitable that a mismatch between structure and expression would result from the application of a fixed expressive profile to different pieces. There is no plausible alternative, therefore, to the idea that expression is derived from structure.

Structure and expression

Some aspects of the relationship between structure and expression can be illustrated with two different studies of piano performance. The first (Clarke 1982) is primarily concerned with the interaction between rhythm and performance tempo, and demonstrates that the changes in expressive timing structure that accompany changes in tempo relate to structural properties of the music. The performances (of a highly repetitive piece by Erik Satie called 'Vexations') show consistent deviations from strictly metrical timing that produce a profile of partially periodic timing curves. Maxima in these curves indicate boundaries which segment each performance into a number of groups. Significantly, these group boundaries correspond to positions in the musical structure at which formal breaks can be identified, using analytical principles similar to those of Lerdahl and Jackendoff (1983). At faster tempi there are relatively fewer groups in the timing profile, and at slower tempi relatively more, the additional boundaries being formed at positions where the music indicates a structural discontinuity of some sort. Thus the expressive changes that accompany changes in performance tempo are based on structural properties of the music, and can be characterized as the transformation of latent expressive possibilities into manifest expressive features in accordance with the dictates of tempo and musical structure.

A second study investigated the expressive changes that result from modifying the relationship between a constant rhythmic structure and its metrical context. The metre of a piece of music is a regular framework of accented and weak beats, existing at a number of levels of structure, around which individual notes and groups of notes are organized. A partial representation of metrical structure is contained in the time signature, bar lines, and beams connecting notes that are used in conventional music notation. In the study a single-line melody was constructed, which was written so as to start in a variety of positions within the bar while keeping all the note values and pitches constant. The result was a complete cycle of orientations between the metrical framework and the note sequence, such that the sequence started on each of the available beats in the bar. Experienced pianists were asked to play each of these variants a number of times, in random order. Figure 1.6 shows two of the variants as examples.

Fig. 1.6. Two of the metrical variants of a constant pitch/duration sequence used in the study of interactions between rhythm and metre.

The study showed that significant changes in the expressive profile of the sequence accompanied the cycle of metrical reorientations, and could be identified in all three of the expressive parameters available (timing, dynamic, and articulation). The expressive changes are, however, related to the metrical changes in a manner that is rather more complex than might be expected, for the following reasons.

(1) Changes in the notated metre of the sequence precipitate other

structural changes. These include changes in the position of group boundaries and changes in the melodic/harmonic function of notes brought about by an altered relationship to the main metrical accents. Figure 1.7 shows two of the tunes used in the study which illustrate this point. The metrical change is simply specified and is directly observable in the notation, while changes in group structure and melodic/harmonic function (see Fig. 1.7) are more concealed since they are not directly represented in the notation. Expression is related to a whole range of structural features, and will reflect these second-order structural changes no less than the metrical changes. Added to this are further structural effects brought about by what may be termed the functional resistance of notes: a short note, for instance, resists functioning as a group ending simply by virtue of its brevity, and similar resistances can be identified for long notes.

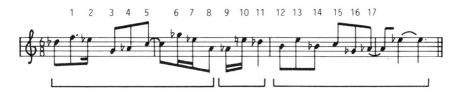

Fig. 1.7. Two tunes from the rhythm/metre study showing changes in group structure (indicated by brackets) and melodic/harmonic function that are triggered by metrical changes. Note 3 functions as an appoggiatura to note 4 in tune 2, but not in tune 1; and note 16 functions as an appoggiatura to note 17 in tune 1, but not in tune 2.

(2) Within each of the three expressive parameters (timing, dynamic, articulation) expressive gestures can perform a number of different functions: these include altering the relative proportions of events within a rhythmic group, indicating the position of a group boundary, marking a metrical accent, and creating an expressive gradient towards a focal point (that is, a pattern of directed motion). As a result expressive gestures are functionally ambiguous, in the sense that they specify a number of alternative interpretations. It is only through interactions with the underlying musical structure that these ambiguities are resolved.

(3) The three expressive parameters interact with one another in at least two ways: first, they may substitute for one another, so that, for instance, an accent may be conveyed by making a note longer, or louder, or more legato, or delaying its entry; and second, they may combine to form expressive complexes that possess a compound function that is not simply the sum of the individual expressive components. For example, in the appropriate context a note that is played loud and staccato will receive a particularly emphatic accent, despite the fact that staccato articulation is usually associated with metrical weakness. The combination of dynamic intensity and staccato articulation appears to convey an expressive meaning that is not explicable in terms of a summation of the individual components.

In the study described here, most expressive changes could be explained on the basis of changes in the position of metrical accents (those points being played louder, or longer, or more legato) and group boundaries (indicated by points of discontinuity in the timing, dynamic, and articulation curves), a more minor role being the emphasis of peaks in the melodic contour. With more complex musical material, the subtlety and complexity of the relationship between expressive features and the associated structure would undoubtedly increase.

What this study demonstrates, however, is that a performer generates an expressive strategy for a musical extract on the spot. This is evident from the brevity of the preparation time that the players needed for the study; from the way in which the players were able to activate an appropriate expressive strategy almost immediately when going from one variant of the sequence to another randomly selected sequence; and finally from the evidence that in many cases a player used a number of different expressive strategies for the same sequence on different repetitions, each strategy nonetheless conveying the main structural characteristics of the material. This suggests strongly that a performer is aware of a number of interpretative options in his or her approach to the music, which might emphasize different structural aspects, but which are in some sense equally adequate. In order to understand how this range of options is structured and controlled, the nature of an interpretation and the general function of expression must first be considered.

Interpretation and the function of expression

Shaffer (1984) has described an interpretation as a compact coding of expressive forms, from which an expressive performance can be generated when required. Two qualifications, or additions, can be made to this. First, the expressive forms which constitute the interpretation are rather abstract. This is evident in the way in which performers use a variety of different expressive strategies to project essentially the same interpretation, as mentioned in connection with rhythm and metre. This suggests that an interpretation consists of a set of abstract expressive markers that can take a material expressive form within any of the parameters available. Second, an interpretation is not only an expressive coding, but also a structural coding. A performer must form an understanding of the musical structure, or decide between structural alternatives offered by the music, and encode that in some stable and compact manner. The structural component then acts as a framework around which the expressive markers are organized.

Pieces of music are invariably open to a number of different structural interpretations, and the primary role of expression is to limit the extent of this ambiguity by emphasizing certain structural interpretations at the expense of others. This does not mean that expression necessarily operates in the service of clarity, since a performer may choose to emphasize either those structural characteristics that are most obvious, or to extract more hidden and disruptive features of the music. Similarly, although a performance must aim to be expressively coherent, that aim does not entail the resolution of all structural ambiguity, since a performance may intentionally attempt to manipulate conflicting aspects of the music.

At a detailed level, however, each expressive act operates so as to project a particular functional meaning for a given musical structure. This is achieved in a variety of ways, the most general underlying principle being the intensification of gestalt properties of the musical structure that are already evident, or the establishment of gestalt features when the music is structurally neutral. Examples of this are the establishment of boundaries in the grouping structure of the music by means of changes in dynamic, articulation, or timing; the imposition or emphasis of a sense of direction towards a structural focal point by means of dynamic, articulation, or timing gradients; or the modification of the accentual status of events (that is, changes in figure/ground relations) by means of dynamic or agogic emphasis. (Agogic emphasis is the accentuation of a note by prolonging its inter-onset duration.)

In a majority of these examples the relationship between the expressive aim and the expressive means is very direct: boundaries are indicated by relatively large parametric changes, directed motion is indicated by graduated parametric increase, and accentual strength is indicated by relative parametric intensity. Within at least two of these parameters (timing and articulation), however, the directness of this expressive function is threatened by ambiguity. The lengthening of a note can indicate that it is accented, that it finishes a structural unit at some level, or that the following (delayed) note is of structural importance. Similarly, although an underlying correlation between structural significance and increased legato articulation appears to hold, structural significance can also be indicated by means of emphatically staccato articulation.

This uncertainty concerning the meaning of an individual expressive gesture is usually clarified by two considerations. First, the expressive sequence in which a particular gesture is incorporated will frequently resolve any ambiguity, and second, the structural context in which the gesture occurs may clarify its meaning. Figure 1.8 shows a short musical extract with a hypothetical expressive profile in three parameters. The penultimate note receives an expressive treatment (long, legato, loud) which in isolation might indicate that it was a strong beat. In reality the correct interpretation of the note as an emphasized upbeat (weak beat) is virtually guaranteed by the previous expressive profile, which helps to establish the metre, and by the structural context, which makes the note weak and unstable. Under conditions of structural clarity, and for listeners well-versed in the musical idiom, expressive characteristics function as responses to, or refinements of, the immanent properties of the music.

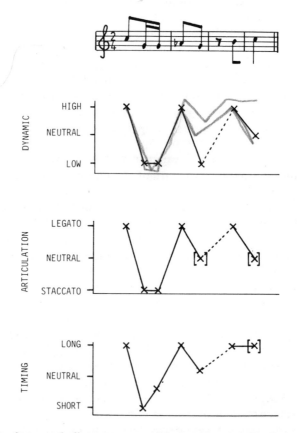

Fig. 1.8. A short melodic sequence with associated hypothetical expressive features, illustrating the way in which the expressive and structural context affect the meaning of an individual expressive gesture (on the penultimate note). See text for details.

When the musical structure is weak or indeterminate, however, expressive effects may function primarily to impose a particular structural interpretation onto a neutral structural base.

The distinction betweens strong and weak musical structures may also affect the way in which listeners distinguish betwen expressive deviations and mistakes. A strong structure may be sufficiently stable that if a feature of the performance conflicts radically with the structural implications of the piece, it is perceived as a mistake, or, if less prominent, simply ignored. In an ambiguous piece, on the other hand, a listener is likely to be more strongly influenced by expression and is more or less forced to take at face value anything that a performer does. Strong structures therefore act selectively to filter out inappropriate expressive features, which are then labelled as mistakes by a listener, or not noticed. Weak or unfamiliar musical structures, on the other hand, provide a listener with no clear reference against which to judge performance features, which must therefore be accepted as structural indicators, with all the ambiguities that have been discussed. In these circumstances the performer is under particular pressure to pay the most acute attention to details of expression, since an unintended deviation may jeopardize a listener's understanding of the music. It may be for this reason that the performance of contemporary music puts such great expressive demands on performers, since both listeners and performers are on the whole unfamiliar with its structural principles.

The generative source of expression

The close relationship between structure and expression embodied in an interpretation forms the basis for an account of the source and systematic construction of expression. Using the structural component of an interpretation as its input, a set of generative rules derives an expresive strategy as output. A range of studies (for example, Shaffer 1981, 1984; Clarke 1982, 1984; Sloboda 1983) indicate that the generative rules for expression in piano performance can be summarized as follows. Within the domain of timing three principles operate:

(1) Graduated timing changes can be used to indicate the group structure of the music, group boundaries being marked by maxima in the timing profile. This principle can be described by a quadratic function, with the position of the minimum point in the curve specified by a variable parameter, allowing a range of related curves to be generated that differ in the balance of upbeats and afterbeats. When the minimum point is displaced to the left in a group, upbeats predominate, and the internal dynamic or directed motion of the group is towards its ending. When displaced to the right, afterbeats predominate and the internal dynamic or directed motion of the group is a dissipation away from its beginning.

Figure 1.9 illustrates this principle with three schematic curves which differ in the balance of upbeats and afterbeats. Todd (1985) has formalized this function using a parabolic curve, and has shown that with only a single function at one level of structure a reasonable approximation to some of the piano data can be obtained which also reflects structural properties of the music being performed. More recent attempts at elaborating this formalization, using hierarchically nested levels of the function (Shaffer 1985), indicate that even better approximations can be achieved with only a minimal increase in formal complexity. It appears that the amount of timing modification is directly related to the structural significance of a musical segment. By displacing the minimum point of the parabola relative

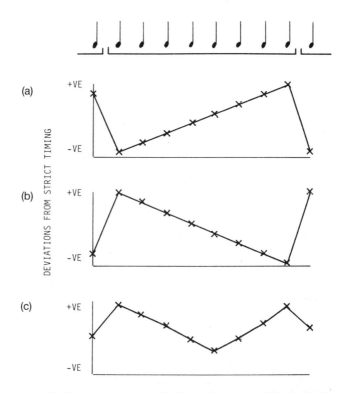

Fig. 1.9. Schematic diagram of three related timing curves differing in their pattern of upbeats and afterbeats, and produced by displacement of the minimum point in the curve to left or right. The top of the figure shows a succession of notes with group structure indicated by brackets. In (a) the minimum is displaced to the left, resulting in a predominance of upbeats and a sense of end-oriented direction. In (b) the minimum is displaced to the right, resulting in a predominance of afterbeats and a sense of dissipation away from the beginning of the group. In (c) the minimum is positioned roughly in the middle of the group, giving a balance of upbeats and afterbeats, and a centred focus of direction.

to the segmental boundaries according to criteria of structural significance, a timing curve of appropriate slope and degree of rubato is generated.

(2) A note may be lengthened so as to delay a following note, the function of the delay being to heighten the impact of the significant delayed note. This function is frequently associated with the first principle, since the delayed note is often the start of a new group, the previous note being lengthened both for reasons of delay and because it falls at a group boundary. Delay is therefore only observably distinct when it occurs mid-group, or when applied to isolated notes that are not part of a graduated timing curve.

(3) A note that is structurally significant may be emphasized by increasing its inter-onset interval (agogic accent). Since significant events usually occur towards the beginning of musical groups (see Lerdahl and Jackendoff 1983), the principle balances the predominantly end-effects of the first principle.

Within the domain of dynamics, three principles can be identified:

(1) Graduated changes in dynamic may be used to indicate a pattern of upbeats and afterbeats, and directed motion, within the group structure of the music. This is essentially a translation of the first timing principle into the dynamic domain and should be formalizable in the same way, namely by a quadratic function fitted to the group structure of the music, with the position of the dynamic minimum specified by a variable parameter that alters the balance of upbeats and afterbeats. Figure 1.10 illustrates the principle with performance data from the rhythm and metre study discussed earlier. The figure shows two performances of the same tune, in which the positions of the dynamic maxima remain the same (positions 1, 4, 6, 11, 13 and 16), but the positions of three minima change. This has the effect of transforming notes 3, 9, and 10 from upbeats in the first performance into afterbeats in the second, and notes 14 and 15 from afterbeats in the first performance to upbeats in the second.

(2) Dynamic contrast may be used to articulate group boundaries, employing an association between dynamic discontinuities and underlying structural discontinuity. As an illustration, Fig. 1.11 shows dynamic data from performances of another tune in the rhythm and metric study. The sharp change in dynamic level between positions 8 and 9 coincides with the first clear opportunity in this tune of establishing a group boundary.

(3) Significant structural events (for example metrical accents, melodic peaks, harmonic changes) may be dynamically intensified, a principle equivalent to the third timing principle.

Within the parameter of articulation, three principles can once again be identified, equivalent to those of dynamic usage:

(1) Graduated changes in articulation may be used to indicate a pattern of upbeats and afterbeats, and directed motion, within the group structure of the music. This appears to be rather less distinct as a principle than its

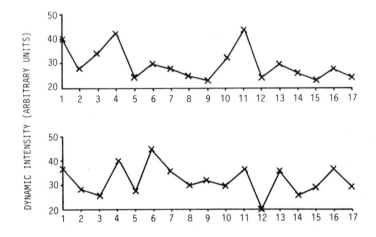

Fig. 1.10. Dynamic data from two performances of the same tune showing changes in the pattern of upbeats and afterbeats reflected in displacements of three dynamic minima.

dynamic equivalent, and cannot be formalized with the same quadratic function. It is more often associated with upbeats, a pattern of increasing staccato indicating the approach to a downbeat, though it can also be used to indicate afterbeats.

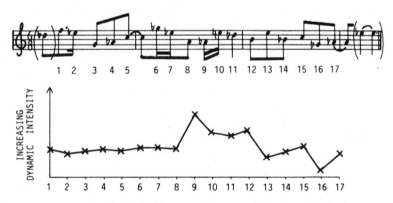

Fig. 1.11. Dynamic data illustrating the use of dynamic contrast to mark a group boundary between notes 8 and 9.

(2) Group boundaries may be indicted using discountinuities of articulation. This can either take the form of sustained articulatory contrasts that define different groups, or the use of an isolated staccato (or detached note) at a boundary as a separating device. This is illustrated in Fig. 1.12, where the isolated staccato articulation at note 8 serves to establish a group boundary. Conversely, an exaggerated legato articulation can be used as a device to hold together the components of a group.

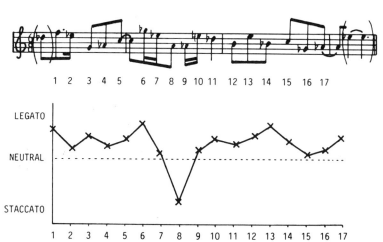

Fig. 1.12. Articulation data illustrating the use of an isolated staccato note (data point 8) to mark a group boundary.

(3) Individual events may be accentuated by articulation. There appears to be an underlying association between structural significance and legato articulation, although this association is rather weak, and in the correct structural context staccato articulation may serve to accentuate a note (Clarke 1984).

These, the essential principles of expression in piano performance, demonstrate three underlying expressive functions:

(1) The indication of structural direction by means of parametric gradients.

(2) The indication of group structures by means of parametric continuities and discontinuities.

(3) The accentuation of individual events by means of local parametric intensification or contrast.

A number of factors influence choices within this system of expressive options. To begin with there are the resources of the chosen instrument, which vary considerably in restrictivenesss. At one end of the spectrum only timing and articulation can be varied on a harpsichord, whereas the voice, for instance, offers expressive opportunities that include timing, dynamic, articulation, timbre, verbal content, vibrato, and the continuum between speech and song. The piano falls towards the restricted end of this range, offering systematic control over only timing, dynamic, articulation, and pedalling. Since the same piece of music may be played on different instruments, a performer who switches from one instrument to another may have to make a considerable readjustment to the resources that the instrument offers. Quite apart from the different tone qualities of the two instruments, the differences in the use of timing in harpsichord and piano performances of Bach's keyboard music illustrate this adjustment. Performers who play both instruments confirm that they must make a conscious stylistic modification to suit the instrument. On a more refined level, changes in instrument design and construction affect performance expression: the range of dynamic contrast offered by a modern grand piano was not possible on the pianos available to Mozart or Haydn, and expressive effects are consequently obtained in different ways on the instruments of that period.

The second factor affecting expressive options is the influence of performance style. Just as instruments show historical development in their design and construction, so also do conventions of performance expression show significant historical (and geographical) variation. These may be linked to instrument technology, but are by no means simply the consequence of such changes. Writings on performance practice have a long history (see Donington 1977), but it is only in the last 30 years or so that the study of historical changes in performance practice, and the attempt to reconstruct stylistically authentic performances, have become established.

Writings on performance practice vary from prescriptive statements to rather more considered and closely argued discussions of particular problems. Whether well-informed or not, performers certainly have opinions about the manner in which different styles of music should be played, and adapt their expressive usage accordingly. The debate over the use of rubato and vibrato in performances of baroque music exemplifies the differences of opinion among performers over the need for, and nature of, historical authenticity.

We can regard a stylistic convention as a particular configuration of the expressive principles set out above, that brings about a certain type of expressive characterization. In Baroque performance practice, for example, group-final lengthening (the first of the three timing principles) is used very little, while the second and particularly the third principles (delay and agogic accent) are used more extensively. This results in an overall absence of ritardandi and a more widespread use of agogic accents, coupled with delay, particularly of the final tonic at cadences. By contrast, the nineteenth-century Romantic style placed enormous emphasis on the first timing principle, and the first dynamic principle (by contrast with Baroque and Classical layered dynamics, which correspond to the second dynamic principle). It should be possible to charactize the performance practice of any period in this manner, as well as the personal style of a performer whose performance practice is sufficiently consistent.

Matters of stylistic convention may be broadly considered part of the performance context—in this case historical context. The details of expression are, however, also sensitive to contextual features of a far more local and immediate kind. It is this detailed context that constitutes the third factor operating on the range of expressive options. Sloboda (1983) has pointed out that it is implausible to assume that the expressive features of a performance are triggered by individual notational symbols. This means that structural information must be integrated from a collection of notational symbols before it can form the basis for an expressive strategy. It must also be supplemented by information about the current expressive context, and any logistical constraints that might apply: it is, for example, impossible to play notes legato that do not lie within the hand's span (without using the sustaining pedal).

Although performers make use of a variety of expressive strategies in the same structural context, this does not mean that expressive features can therefore be freely substituted. Each parameter has certain intrinsic qualities that make it more or less suitable for use in any given context. While articulatory differences may be good indicators of grouping properties, they are less effective than dynamics for outlining the shape and direction of large-scale melodic processes by virtue of their disruptive and divisive characteristics. On the other hand, when playing in an ensemble it may be more effective for a soloist to project an individual line by means of articulation than with dynamics, which might result in an unacceptable overall dynamic level or a muddy texture. Similarly, rubato is effective in solo performance, but in ensemble performances must be more constrained if overall synchrony is to be preserved, although Shaffer (1984) has shown that considerable rubato can be used in piano duet performances. Furthermore, even in solo performances, rubato must be used with discretion when the music involves a high level of rhythmic complexity, so as to avoid obscuring the structure.

The final factor influencing the choice of expressive options is the manner in which a player choses to perform. Seashore (1938/1967) demonstrated that a performer could play the same piece of music with an expressive profile that differed according to whether he was instructed to play artistically or metronomically. The differences were principally in the degree of rubato, rather than the pattern of rubato, but there is every indication that a performer can choose to alter the pattern as well. Sloboda (1983) showed that a professional performer who was experienced in playing exam dictations conveyed the metre of a short tune to listeners more effectively than a performer of similar calibre who did not undertake such duties, apparently by adopting a more didactic approach to the relationship between metre and expression. This suggests that performers can choose to play in a manner that emphasizes the metre of the piece, or some other basic structural feature, or may subtly contradict those structural features for artistic effect.

Clearly a performer must not contradict the structure to such an extent that the music becomes incomprehensible to a listener, but a performer must also avoid playing music in a trite and obvious way. The choice of a 'mode' of performance is therefore influenced by the audience and occasion, as well as the performer's artistic intentions. The style of performance in a concert recital is likely to be rather different from the same performer's style at a children's concert, or during a melodic dictation exercise.

At a more subtle level, an individual interpretation can be regarded as a personally selected patterning of the expressive principles that may persist over a long period of time, or may be quite ephemeral. The expressive principles will be set in a particular configuration according to considerations such as the desire for contrast or continuity, and novelty or consistency. In a rondo movement, for instance, a pianist may choose either to retain the same expressive configuration at each return of the rondo theme, if the aim is to achieve continuity and consistency, or to make use of as wide a variety of expressive characteristics as possible, if the aim is to convey the potential novelty of the theme on each of its appearances. In a sonata form movement, on the other hand, it is usual to play the recapitulation with essentially the same expressive characteristics as the exposition, in order to make clear the significance of the return to material that has already been heard. As a third example, in a highly contrapuntal piece of music with a number of distinct motivic elements, it would be appropriate to give each an identifiable expressive profile if motivic clarity and identity are to be achieved. The structural 'archetypal schemata' that Meyer (1973) proposes may therefore have their expressive parallels.

Finally, the broad aims of a performance must be considered. Sloboda (1983) has pointed out that a performance can be considered to have primarily artistic or primarily communicative aims. If communication is the primary aim, then it is not too difficult to prescribe a successful configuration of the expressive principles outlined above. If, on the other hand, artistry is the primary aim, then prescription is both impossible and inappropriate. The essential characteristic of artistic activity (and aesthetic objects) is a radical form of ambiguity and creativity, and while the expressive resources may be outlined, their precise disposition on any occasion can be accounted for only in retrospect, not predicted. Were this not the case, and our curiosity in these ambiguities and possibilities not boundless, we might all have given up going to concerts long ago.

References

Bengtsson, I. and Gabrielsson, A. (1983). Analysis and synthesis of musical rhythm. In *Studies of music performance* (ed. J. Sundberg). Publications issued by the Royal Swedish Academy of Music 5 No. 39.

Chomsky, N. (1957). *Syntactic structures*. Mouton, The Hague.

Clarke, E. F. (1982). Timing in the performance of Erik Satie's 'Vexations'. *Acta Psychologica* **50**, 1–19.

Clarke, E. F. (1984). Structure and expression in the rhythm of piano performance. Unpublished Ph.D. thesis. University of Exeter.

Donington, R. (1977) *The interpretation of early music*. Faber and Faber, London.

Forte, A. (1973) *The structure of atonal music*. Yale University Press, New Haven.

Gates, A. and Bradshaw, J. L. (1974). Effects of auditory feedback on a musical performance task. *Perception and Psychophysics* **16**, 105–9.

Krumhansl, C. (1983). Perceptual structures for tonal music. *Music Perception* **1**, (1), 28–63.

Lerdahl, F. and Jackendoff, R. (1983). *A generative theory of tonal music*. MIT Press, Cambridge, Mass.

Longuet-Higgins, H. C. (1976). Perception of melodies. *Nature* **263**, (5579), 646–53.

Meyer, L. B. (1956). *Emotion and meaning in music*. University of Chicago Press.

Meyer, L. B. (1973). *Explaining music: essays and explorations*. University of California Press.

Narmour, E. (1977), *Beyond Schenkerism: the need for alternatives in music analysis*. University of Chicago Press.

Narmour, E. (1983). Some major theoretical problems concerning the concept of hierarchy in the analysis of tonal music. *Music Perception* **1**, (2), 129–99.

Seashore, C. E. (1938). *Psychology of music*. McGraw-Hill, New York (Reissued 1967 by Dover, New York).

Shaffer, L. H. (1976). Intention and performance. *Psychological Review* **83**, (5), 375–93.

Shaffer, L. H. (1981). Performances of Chopin, Bach and Bartok: studies in motor programming. *Cognitive Psychology* **13**, 326–76.

Shaffer, L. H. (1984). Timing in solo and duet piano performances. *Quarterly Journal of Experimental Psychology* **A36**, 577–95.

Shaffer, L. H. (1985). The expressive component in musical performance. Paper delivered at the Third International Conference on Event Perception and Action, Uppsala, Sweden.

Shepard, R. (1982). Geometrical approximations to the structure of musical pitch. *Psychological Review* **89**, (4), 305–33.

Sloboda, J. A. (1983). The communication of musical metre in piano performance. *Quarterly Journal of Experimental Psychology* **A35**, 377–96.

Sudnow, D. (1978). *Ways of the hand: the organisation of improvised conduct*. Routledge and Kegan Paul, London.

Sudnow, D. (1979). *Talks body*. Alfred Knopf, New York.

Sundberg, J. and Lindblom, B. (1976). Generative theories in language and music description. *Cognition* **4**, 99–122.

Todd, N. P. (1985). A model of expressive timing in tonal music. *Music Perception* **3**, (1), 33–58.

2

Timing in music performance and its relations to music experience

ALF GABRIELSSON

Performance and notation of music

Our experience of music and our ideas about music mainly derive from listening to performed music. The characteristics of musical performances are therefore of fundamental importance. The performance of a piece of music represents the overt, auditory manifestation of the composer's and/or the performer's intentions, ideas, feelings, and whatever is being communicated in music. It is the direct stimulus to the listener and will profoundly affect his way of perceiving and understanding this piece of music. His impression from the performance may remain for years to come, perhaps for his whole lifetime. However, another performance of the same piece may make him revise his ideas about it in different directions. Music critics excel in discussing the merits of different performances, for example, how conductors such as Toscanini or Furtwängler shape a Beethoven symphony, how pianists such as Backhaus or Kempff play a Mozart sonata, or how Glenn Gould performs music by Bach. The relations between the composer's idea, the actually performed music, and the listener's impression are complex, indeed.

In Western art music as well as in much popular music there is also a visual manifestation of the music, the score. However, the 'translation' from the score into sounding music is obviously made very differently by different performers. The notation has to be supplemented by various implicit rules, which relate to the type of music and associated performance practice (for example, church music, dance music, Baroque music, music from the Romantic era), with which different performers are more or less familiar. Of course, they are also influenced by teachers, other performers, their own earlier performances, and their ideas about the meaning of the music they are going to play. The musical score is only a starting point for the performer. It provides him with a skeleton, which he should bring to life with sound. It is one of the fascinating aspects of music that the result of this creative process may become so varied for different musicians and in different situations.

Music may thus be said to exist at different levels and in different forms: as an idea (in a wide sense) in the composer's and performer's mind, in the written score, in sounds, and in the listener's experience. The communication between the composer/ performer and the listener is meant to be realized by the *sounding* music, not by reading of a score. In fact much music (such as folk music over the whole world, and certain jazz music) never appears in notation but relies totally on performance and aural tradition to spread and survive. Nevertheless most thinkers and writers about music take musical notation as the starting point for their discussion. They even provide notations of music which has never appeared in that form (for example, transcriptions of folk music).

There are several reasons for this emphasis on notated, rather than performed, music. The musical notation is in many respects very convenient and efficient. It is also easily reproduced in print, while the handling of phonograph records or magnetic tapes to provide sound illustrations is more clumsy and requires special equipment. Certainly many writers also point out the limitations of musical notation and make due reservations as to its appropriateness. Still, I think that it is very easy to be led astray, even unconsciously, by the properties of notation; they may affect our experience and conceptualizing of music in a similar way that words may do in other areas, encouraging us to 'force' pitches into a limited number of pitch categories, to write down a rhythm using the most common note values, etc. The results from many studies of performances provide further support for this opinion.

Analysis of performances

The characteristics of different performances may of course be studied by simply listening to them. It is often easy to hear differences and changes in tempo, in dynamics, in intonation, articulation, and phrasing. For closer study of certain points you can use simple tricks; for instance, you can play tape-recorded music at half-speed, or even slower, to have more time for listening. However, many characteristic features of a performance elude our perceptual analysis and require accurate physical registrations. Here we meet one important explanation of the relative scarcity of performance studies: to make detailed registrations of sounding music is very difficult, even with the technology available today. I have elsewhere (Gabrielsson 1985) reviewed earlier attempts in this direction, including registrations of organ playing (Sears 1902), of piano performance stored on 'player rolls' for mechanical pianos (Hartmann 1932; Vernon 1937) or studied by filming the action of the hammers (Hendersson 1937; Skinner and C. E. Seashore 1937), of singing (H. Seashore 1937), and of violin playing (Small 1937). The last-mentioned researchers belonged to a very active group gathered around C. E. Seashore at the Iowa University. Their techniques and results, summarized by C. E. Seashore (1938), are still very impressive. Later advances in registrations of piano performances were presented by Wagner (1971, 1974) and Shaffer (1980, 1981). The methods used in the Uppsala studies of performances are described below.

From a physical point of view the variables manipulated by the performer are durations, intensities (amplitudes), frequencies ('pitch'), and the spectral composition of the sounds. On some instruments (for example, the whole violin family) and in singing one may vary all of them over a considerable range, and continuously. In other instruments, such as the piano and the organ, pitch can be varied only in discrete steps, and once the tone is struck one has no, or very limited, possibilities of affecting its properties any longer. Each instrument presents its own possibilites and limitations. In the above-mentioned investigations on singing and violin playing there were numerous examples of more or less continuous variations in pitch and intensity, for example, pitch and intensity vibrato, sharp or flat intonation before reaching the 'proper' pitch, dynamic swelling and shrinking within tones or phrases, glidings between successive tones, etc. In the piano studies the interest was focused on durations and intensities. Striking variations of tempo and different types of deviations from expected durations of various tones appeared, and it was noted that there was no consistent relation between intensity and (perceived) accent. Of course, none of these phenomena in the actual performances were indicated in the corresponding musical scores; they were truly outside the notation.

Timing in performance

The only variable over which the performer has practically complete control, regardless of which instrument he uses, is the duration of the sound events, as well as of 'non-sound' events (rests or silences). This circumstance is one of the explanations for why the manipulation of various durations, here generally called *timing*, is often considered to be the most important tool available to the performer. If there is a score, this prescribes, of course, the timing in many respects, but there is still a great freedom within these constraints. In the case of non-notated or improvised music this freedom is even greater.

In writings and research on music, timing is usually related to rhythm. This connection is self-evident, but other factors should also be mentioned. Since there is no melody without rhythm, timing is important for melody as well; and since a melody is often harmonized, timing influences the harmonic progression. It may also affect the single chord, since tones within a chord are often played asynchronously (Hartmann 1932; Vernon

1937) or even *arpeggio*. It is known that the time course of different partials in a tone is critical for the perceived timbre (Risset and Wessel 1982). Rasch (1978, 1979, 1981; see also Chapter 4 in this volume) showed that the tone onsets from different instruments performing polyphonic music are usually asynchronized, and that this may facilitate the perception of the different parts.

These hints are enough to show that timing, in one way or another, influences practically every aspect of the music. Instead of using the traditional musical terminology, we may also refer to such categories as the *structural*, the *motional*, and the *emotional* aspects of music experience (Gabrielsson 1973a, b, c; 1982a, b; 1985; 1986). It is clear that timing affects the way we experience the structure of a piece of music, as a whole and at different levels (Sloboda 1983; Gabrielsson 1986; Clarke in Chapter 1 of this volume). However, little is said about the effects of timing upon the experienced motion character of the music and the related emotional qualities. These two aspects will be briefly discussed before proceeding to different examples of timing.

Motion and emotion in music

Music is often said to be 'the language of emotions', which 'bypasses the intellect' and takes over, when words do not suffice any longer. Sweeping statements like these require much critical analysis, but this will be left for another occasion. On the other hand music is also often considered to reflect various kinds of motions or gestures. That music often elicits overt movements is obvious and sometimes explicitly intentional, as with dance music. However, one can also experience motion in music without moving oneself. A simple example of that is again dance music: there are striking differences in the experienced motion character of, say, waltz, foxtrot, rock 'n' roll, samba, and tango. The concept of 'swing', often referred to in jazz, is an example of a specific motion character. A march should certainly have a special motion character, and so should a properly performed Viennese waltz. The motion character of Baroque music is different from that of music in the Viennese Classical style. Becking (1928) took the difference in motion character between Mozart's and Beethoven's music as the starting point for his speculative but interesting attempts at using 'accompanying movements' (*Begleitbewegungen*) to catch such differences between different composers; see also Truslit (1938). Clynes (1977, 1980) and Clynes and Walker (1982) proposed to use the sentograph (a device for registering the strength and direction of finger pressure in studies of emotion and motion) as a means of finding out the 'inner pulse' in the music of different composers.

Music as expression of emotions and music as expression of motions are not competing, but rather complementary ideas. The close psychological connection between emotion and (overt or inner) motion is already suggested by the common origin of those two words (from Latin *movere*) and amply supported by commonplace observation: to jump for joy, fight in anger, sink down in despair, etc. To find a suitable method for studying the motional-emotional aspects of music experience is difficult, however. In my earlier research (Gabrielsson 1973*b*) I mainly used conventional verbal methods and identified motion characters such as 'rapidity', 'forward motion', 'dancing', 'walking', 'rocking', 'swinging', and many others, as well as emotional qualities including 'vital vs. dull', 'excited vs. calm', 'rigid vs. flexible', etc. It is obvious, however, that words are clumsy tools for describing these phenomena in all their continuously varying shades and shapes. The increased interest in non-verbal methods (cf. Scherer and Ekman 1982) suggests other possibilities. Clynes's (1977, 1980; Clynes and Nettheim 1982) theory of emotion and its expression primarily relies on a non-verbal method, registration of finger pressure on a 'sentograph'; it has also been used for studying experienced motion in music. Nielsen (1983) used a similar device, pressing a pair of tongs to reflect experienced tension in two pieces of symphonic music. We can expect further developments of these and other methods to facilitate the study of the ongoing processes in music listening and not remain confined to retrospective verbal reports.

This excursion has been motivated by my belief that many types of timing in music performance aim at eliciting various motional-emotional reactions in the listener. Because of the lack of proper methods to study these questions in enough detail there is, of course, little empirical evidence to rely upon. Nevertheless it seems possible to make some reasonable suggestions. They will be discussed in relation to four categories of timing; tempo, different classes of duration, articulation, and deviations from mechanical regularity.

Tempo

Tempo is a common and seemingly simple concept in connection with music. The tempo of a piece is usually indicated either by designations such as allegro, moderato, adagio, etc., or more precisely by stating a metronomic value, for example, MM ♩ = 120, that is, 120 crochets per minute. Musicians differ much in their ability to judge the absolute tempo and changes in tempo: while Madsen's (1979) and Wapnick's (1980) subjects were not especially good in this respect, Wagner (1974) found extreme accuracy in a study with the conductor Herbert von Karajan.

However, how fast the music seems to go depends not only on the metronomic tempo but on other factors as well. A piece with many 'short' tones (say, semiquavers) seems faster than another piece with the same metronomic tempo but containing only 'long' tones (say, crotchets). The number of tones per unit of time is thus important. Sometimes the situation may be ambiguous. For instance, in certain parts of a Nocturne by Chopin the left hand may have a slow pace, while the right hand performs extremely rapid passages (see Fig. 2.1). In this case the motion may be felt as rapid, or slow, or rapid and slow at the same time (a rapid motion within a slow motion), depending on how you direct your attention.

Fig. 2.1. Excerpt from 'Nocturne' Op. 15 No. 2 by Frédéric Chopin. Tempo designation: Larghetto. (Reproduced with permission from *Frédéric Chopin, Nocturnes and Polonaises*, Dover Publications, Inc., New York, 1983.)

With perceived tempo we usually mean the *rapidity of the beat* or pulse. This often coincides with the indicated metronomic tempo but not necessarily. Moreover, since the beat often can be alternatively felt at different rates (say, at the crotchet level *or* at the quaver level in a certain piece), the perceived tempo depends on which beat rate is meant. In either case, however, the perceived tempo is only one aspect, although a very important one, of the listener's impression of the speed of the piece. The experienced 'overall rapidity', as well as the rapidity of different parts, also depends on such factors as the number of tones per unit of time (already mentioned) and various melodic and harmonic factors. For instance, a melody with many large leaps may seem faster than a melody which proceeds stepwise (see data on coherence and fission in tone sequences, van Noorden 1975), and a piece with frequent harmonic shifts may appear more rapid than a piece with fewer shifts. There are thus many problems of definition and of influencing factors. No single work covers all these aspects, but data and instructive discussions on various related points appear in Behne (1972), Motte-Haber (1968), Bengtsson (1974), Longuet-Higgins (1979), Longuet-Higgins and Lee (1982), and Steedman (1977).

Even if an exact metronomic tempo is given, the performer often deviates from that, consciously or unconsciously, depending on his idea of the piece, his present psychic state, acoustical conditions, etc. During the piece there is usually much more variation in tempo than is realized or consciously perceived. The tolerance for such variation is, of course, different in different music, for example, small tolerance in a march but large in a Chopin Nocturne. One common type of variation is where a phrase begins somewhat slowly, accelerates towards the middle, and then retards towards the end. This contributes, together with other means (for example, dynamic increase and decrease), to the phrasing. Numerous examples appear in the early performance studies mentioned above and in Bengtsson and Gabrielsson (1980, 1983) (see also in Fig. 2.8 below). The exact shaping and the extent of the variation differs, of course, with each single piece and each performer. If you measure the performance of a phrase and calculate its average tempo, you may find that this average tempo in fact never appears at any position in the phrase—it is an average of a continuous variation. But as a listener you find it quite natural and adequate. You would, rather, react (negatively) if the tempo *was* perfectly constant.

A detailed study of the tempo variations in a Viennese waltz (from *Die Fledermaus* by Johann Strauss, Jr.) was presented in Bengtsson and Gabrielsson (1983). Although usually not indicated in the score, a genuine performance of a Viennese waltz includes sizeable, sometimes extreme, variations of tempo, the details of which vary with the structure of different pieces. The calculated mean tempo for the 32 bars in this case was about 170 crotchets per minute, but the actual tempo varied between 148 and 196; in the initial bar of the second period it was in fact only 90.

In such a case the mean tempo is of very limited interest. (How boring the waltz sounds when the tempo is kept constant was illustrated by a synthesized example appended to the paper.) From this, and other, examples it was concluded that

four different meanings of tempo should be distinguished: (a) the abstract *mean tempo*, calculated as the total duration of a music section divided by the number of beats in the same section, (b) the *main tempo*, being the prevailing (and intended) tempo when initial and final retardations as well as more amorphous caesurae are deleted, (c) *local tempi*, maintained only for short periods but perceptibly differing, and (d) *beat rate* . . . for describing minor fluctuations, which may not be perceptible as such.

(Bengtsson and Gabrielsson 1983, p. 50)

How does the tempo affect the listener's impression of the music? If there is a relatively stable tempo (regular beat), this provides a fundamental temporal framework for the whole piece, a structural basis for whatever else is happening. By appropriate variations of the tempo the performer can contribute to make the structural subdivisions clear to the listener: where a new motive, a new phrase, a new period, etc., begins, and where each ends. The extent of these variations often corresponds to the size or hierarchical level of the respective structural entities, for example, a certain retardation at the end of a phrase, a more pronounced retardation at the end of a period, and most pronounced of all at the very end of the piece.

However, tempo first of all relates to *experienced motion*. Although the original Latin word *tempus* means time, in music tempo designates the experienced rapidity of motion or flow. When there is a stable tempo, the listener feels a regular motion forwards. And when the tempo is varied, one feels how the motion is accelerated or retarded, how it might be brought almost to a stop now and then—but is resumed and carries on until the definite stop at the end. The performer's way of indicating the structure of the piece by variations of tempo is thus made by affecting the speed of the ongoing motion.

When one compares different performances of a piece, the first thing one notices is in fact often differences in tempo, as well as in the ways of varying the tempo. In this are also included other components of perceived rapidity, such as those discussed above in connection with Fig. 2.1 The 'total' impression of rapidity is thus a more or less complex function of various motions. In a completely homophonic texture the situation is rather unproblematic (Fig. 2.2(a)), while it is more intricate in polyphonic music (Fig. 2.2(b)), and in a piece without a regular beat at all (Fig. 2.2(c)). Whatever the case may be, there are usually considerable possibilities for the performer to manipulate various factors influencing the listener's impression of speed and motion, for the whole as well as for different parts.

With regard to the emotional effects several studies (Hevner 1937; Rigg 1940; Motte-Haber 1968; Behne 1972; Wedin 1972; Gabrielsson 1973*b*) indicated that higher tempo/rapidity was associated with judgements like 'vital', 'happy', 'exciting', 'light', 'restless', and others, while slower tempos got roughly opposite descriptions. However, the authors also point out that because of the complex structure of music, it is very difficult to ascribe such effects to differences in tempo alone—they may result from constellations of various factors, such as dynamics, pitch level, articulation, mode, etc. Although the above results certainly seem plausible and can be easily associated with various types of rapid motion, much work remains to make the picture more complete and accurate.

Fig. 2.2(a). The beginning of the German chorale 'Lob sei dem allmächtigen Gott'. *(b)* Excerpt from a choral prelude, 'Was mein Gott will, das gscheh allzeit', by Wilhelm Friedemann Bach. (From *Choralvorspiele alter Meister*, Edition Peters, No. 3048. Copyright 1951 by C. F. Peters Corporation, New York. Reproduced by permission of Peters Edition Limited, London.)
(c). The beginning of 'Les Anges' by Olivier Messiaen. (From *Oliver Messiaen, La nativité du seigneur, neuf méditations pour orgue*, Alphonse Leduc, Paris, 1936. Reproduced by permission from Alphonse Leduc & Cie.)

Different classes of duration

In the score the duration of the tones is indicated by the prescribed tempo and the note value of the respective tone. Note values (semibreve, crotchet, quaver, etc.) are defined in simple ratios to each other, such as 2:1 (for example, semibreve to crotchet) or 3:1 (dotted semibreve to crotchet). Of course, it is realized that there is a certain tolerance around these ratios in actual performance. However, it is rarely understood how extreme and varying the deviations really are, as found in empirical investigations of performance (see p.41 onwards).

Disregarding this for the moment, it is self-evident that the specific sequence of note values given in the score provides a primary structural characteristic of the piece in question. But in the same sense that the tempo reflects experienced motion, the various tone sequences also have *motional-emotional properties*. Due to the practically infinite number of possible sequences, these qualities are almost innumerable. They provide an endless variety of means for the composer and performer to shape the ongoing flow in the music (also including the use of 'non-tones', rests). As a few, extremely simple, examples consider the short patterns in Fig. 2.3. The motional characters of these certainly vary and may here be loosely described by expressions such as 'even flow', 'rocking', more or less 'jerky', 'galloping', and the like. The last, 'galloping' pattern has a very pronounced 'moving forwards' quality, as used, for instance, in the overture to *Guillaume Tell* by Rossini.

Fig. 2.3. Five short patterns illustrating different motion characters. The music example is taken from the overture to *Guillaume Tell* by Rossini, tempo designation Allegro vivace.

However, there have been few empirical attempts at elucidating these fundamental questions. Suggestions may be found in Motte-Haber (1968) and Gabrielsson (1973a, b). Clynes and Walker (1982) used a sentograph to study the responses to two-tone patterns, which were varied in the duration and amplitude of the tones. The multitude of different responses obtained even for these simple cases indicates something of the enormous possibilities available in composing and performing music to elicit various motional and emotional reactions in the listener—even richer when including variations of pitch, intensity, timbre, etc. as are found in most music.

In a certain contrast to the statements above, Fraisse (1956, 1982) claims that in a piece of music there are essentially only two classes of durations: 'long times' and 'short times' (*temps longs, temps courts*). In his excellent monograph *Les structures rythmiques* (1956), Fraisse described the results of many experiments on motor production or reproduction of rhythm patterns. His subjects' tappings of these patterns indicated the existence of two separate duration regions, the 'long times' and the 'short times', in an approximate ratio of 2:1 or higher. The absolute duration of these classes varied in different contexts, but generally 'short times' were associated with perception of 'grouping' and 'long times' with perception of 'duration'. Rhythm perception was seen as a play between those two qualities, collection and duration.

Fraisse also finds the two classes of time in the 'long' and 'short' syllables in prosody and in the dashes and dots of the Morse alphabet. With regard to music he studied excerpts from 15 pieces of piano music and found that in each piece two note values, in a ratio of 2:1 or 3:1, were dominant. Of course, there were other note values as well, but they were seen as somehow 'occasional'. The shorter note value corresponded to a duration of 135–410 ms in different pieces, which agrees well with the 'short times' in the above-mentioned experiments; the longer note value corresponded to 270–860 ms ('long times'). Fraisse (1981) further argued that the limitation to two durations relates to our inability to 'discriminate in an absolute way more than two durations in the range of perceived durations (from 10 to 200 centiseconds) (1981, p. 220).

However interesting this may sound, the theory seems simplistic from a musical point of view. There are certainly many pieces dominated by only two note values, but to make a generalization from only 15 pieces is unwarranted. To provide only one counter-example, consider another piano piece, the beginning of Beethoven's Piano Sonata Op. 14 No. 1 (Fig. 2.4). In the exposition of the first movement at least four note values (semibreve, crotchet, quaver, and semiquaver) play an important role in the themes and in the elaborations and transitions between them. A listener should have no difficulties in recognizing them as four different categories.

To reduce timing in music to be a matter of essentially only two classes of duration is not very convincing. And no empirical evidence is given to support the statement that we are unable to discriminate in an absolute way more than two durations within 10-200 cs.

Articulation

Legato and staccato are contrasting forms of articulation. In legato (or even legatissimo) the sounding tone goes on all the way until the beginning of the next tone with no perceptible break between the tones. In staccato (and even more in staccatissimo) the sounding part of the tone is very short and is followed by silence until the onset of the following tone. The silent part is often considerably longer than the sounding part. Between legato and staccato there are various intermediate levels such as non legato,

Fig. 2.4. The beginning of Beethoven's Piano Sonata Op. 14 No. 1. (From *Beethoven, Klaviersonaten, Band I*, G. Henle-Verlag, München-Duisburg, 1952. Reproduced by permission from G. Henle Verlag.)

portato, and marcato; for string instruments there are also other terms such as *detaché* and martellato.

In the score the type of articulation is indicated by the above labels and/or by various graphic signs at the notes, such as points (staccato), dashes, wedges, bows, and various combinations of these. The silent part of the tone may be written as a rest, for example, ♩ (staccato) might instead be written as ♪ ; ; .However, a frequent use of rests makes the score hard to read and is usually avoided. When there is no indication at all of the articulation, this may be interpreted as legato, or that the articulation should be as is usual for this kind of music, for this type of musical ensemble etc. Sometimes the title of the piece or other designations suggest the proper articulation. Composers differ very much with regard to how accurately they prescribe various articulations.

Whatever the case may be, the articulation is achieved by timing in performance—timing to get the intended or proper proportion between the sounding and non-sounding parts of the tone(s). From an acoustical point of view the situation is very complex, since the performer's control of this timing is affected by the properties of different instruments and by the acoustics of the room. For instance, articulation on the violin is different from articulation on the organ, and playing in a small room is different from playing in a cathedral. Moreover, a perceptual distinction between the sounding and non-sounding part may not reflect acoustic reality: the tone may be sounding all the time, first loud and then soft (for example, in reverberation)— however, so soft that it is masked or otherwise perceptually silent.

The importance of the articulation is well known by performers and is given much attention in musical training. However, there have been few empirical investigations of the performance of articulations in various situations. Even if careful physical registrations are made of the performance, they have to be supplemented by judgements from listening in order to clarify the relations to the perceived articulation. One way of approaching these problems is by means of synthesized sound sequences, which are judged by listeners. An example is given in Fig. 2.5, which contains four bars of a usual form of waltz accompaniment (see the notation at the top). Eight versions were synthesized to represent (almost) legato performance in all three beats of the bar (version 1), staccato performance in all three beats (version 8), and various combinations of legato and staccato in versions 2–7 (for example, legato in the first and second beats but staccato in the third as in version 2). The example is taken from Bengtsson and Gabrielsson (1983), and the sound example appears on an appended phonograph record. Lacking this, you may perform or try to imagine the eight versions yourself.

The perceptual effects of these manipulations are striking. The basic tripartite structure of the bar is felt the same way in all cases, but there is a tremendous difference in the motional-emotional character of the eight versions. Some of them are completely 'impossible' and sound ridiculous (nos. 1 and 5), while the others represent more or less plausible alternatives, each of them with a specific character.

This example was in fact not primarily made to discuss waltz accompaniment, but to demonstrate the effects of different articulations in a systematic way. Considering the possibilities available in real music

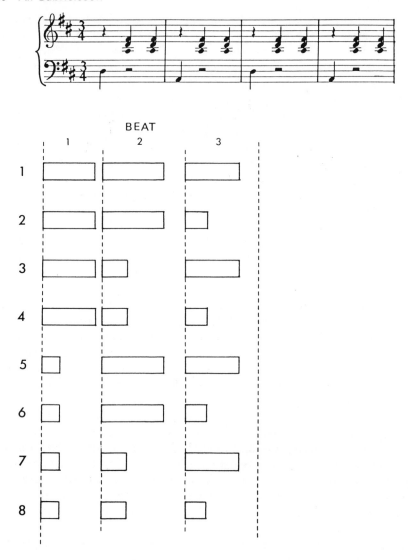

Fig. 2.5. Different articulations of a common accompaniment to waltzes, see further in text. (From Bengtsson and Gabrielsson 1983, p. 45. Reproduced by permission from the The Royal Swedish Academy of Music, Stockholm.)

performance—using even more legato or staccato, or intermediate levels such as non legato or portato (and still finer gradations for which we lack words), and combining them with dynamic means, etc.—we begin to realize the scope of the articulation repertoire available to the performer, and how he may use it to generate so many different and subtly varied experiences, which we feel so well but which elude our attempts at verbalization.

Deviations from mechanical performance

A spontaneous response to music boxes, rhythm machines, and the like is that they sound mechanical, dead, and boring. The main reason for that is the mechanical regularity in their 'performance': absolutely constant tempo, and perfect ratios (1:1, 2:1, 3:1, etc.) between successive sound events. It is generally known that human performance is not like that, and various types of deviations from mechanical regularity were described in the early investigations by Sears (1902), Hartmann (1932), and the research group around C. E. Seashore (1938); these are summarized in Gabrielsson (1985).

Extensive studies of music performance have been made in Uppsala, Sweden, in collaboration between musicologists and psychologists (Bengtsson 1974; Gabrielsson 1974, 1982a, 1982b, 1985, 1986; Bengtsson and Gabrielsson 1977, 1980, 1983; Gabrielsson et al. 1983; Gabrielsson and Johnson 1985). The general purpose has been to investigate timing in performance, especially with regard to deviations from mechanical regularity in different types of music and with different performers. In most cases the performances were especially for this research project, but performances stored on phonograph records or magnetic tapes are used as well. They are analysed by means of special electronic equipment (Tove et al. 1966), which simultaneously displays the variations of fundamental frequency ('pitch') and total amplitude (intensity). By adequate filtering and calibrations it is possible to get very accurate representations of monophonic performances and in many cases also of polyphonic music. The durations may be measured with an accuracy of ± 5 ms. An example of a registration is given in Fig. 2.6.

More recently the equipment has been supplemented by a computerized synthesizer and a sampling system. This allows digital recording and storing of performances, live or recorded earlier. They can be studied in extreme detail with a time resolution of 20 μs and can be manipulated in various ways; for example, any parts(s) of the performance can be extracted for detailed listening and analysis of transitions between tones, for spectral analysis, etc. (see Fig. 2.7 for some illustrations).

Despite the high accuracy there are still problems in certain cases, especially regarding physical and perceptual tone onsets as well as decays. While Wagner (1974) and Shaffer (1980, 1981) make registrations of piano performance directly at the sound source, our techniques mainly rely on registrations by microphone, for any instrument, placed at a distance in the room. The acoustical events thus registered are often complex. Tones

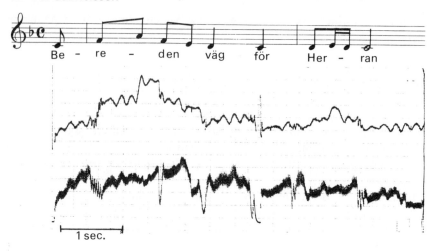

Be - re - den väg för Her - ran

1 sec.

Fig. 2.6. Registration of a professional singer performing in the first phrase of a Swedish folk chorale. The upper curve shows the fundamental frequency, the lower curve the intensity (calibration values not given here). Note the continuous variation in both curves, including vibrato and various glidings. The notes in the notation have been put to positions approximately corresponding to the onsets of the respective tones as seen in the registrations below. For further description, see Gabrielsson and Johnson (1985).

appearing after another in the score overlap each other in the acoustical reality and make us wonder exactly when, and because of which specific feature in the ongoing stimulus, the listener detects the onset of the next tone. This is one reason why performance studies have to be supplemented by studies of the listener's experience. Other, more general, reasons for that are discussed later.

On the other hand the deviations from strict regularity in performance are usually so obvious that they are detected by any reasonable technique in spite of the above-mentioned difficulties. The results described below come from monophonic performances on the flute, the clarinet, and the piano, and from orchestral performances. The music is Western art music, popular music, and folk music; many of the pieces are of Swedish origin. The statistical analysis of the data obtained for each performance generally proceeds as follows:

(1) Calculate the total duration of the performed piece (however, often omitting the very last tone, since its duration may be difficult to measure accurately).

(2) Transform the duration of each tone (from its onset to the onset of the next tone) to per mille of the total duration.

(3) Take the difference between this per mille value and the per mille value the tone would have had in a completely mechanical performance.

The last step thus gives the difference (deviation) for each tone, between the real performance and a mechanical performance. The deviation values are tabulated and/or displayed graphically as in Fig. 2.8 below. Then follows:

(4) Perform adequate statistical operations to get measures of central

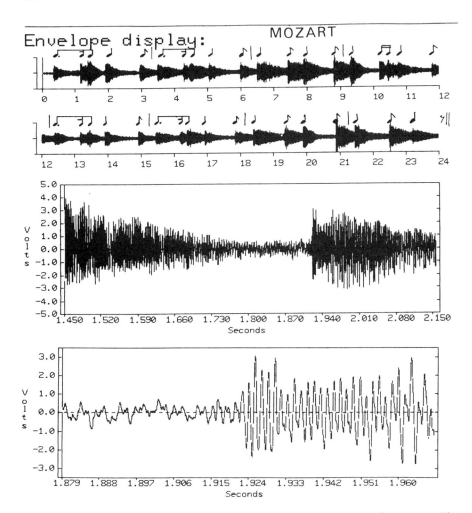

Fig. 2.7. Examples of registrations obtained from a sampling system (Synclavier II) for the pianist Ingrid Haebler's performance of the initial eight bars of Mozart's Piano Sonata in A major (K. 331; see the notation in Fig. 2.8 below). The *upper* figure shows the amplitude envelope; the onsets of the chords are clearly seen (the rhythmic notation is added here to facilitate the understanding of the figure). The numbers represent time in seconds. The *middle* figure shows the decay of the third chord and the onset of the fourth. The *lower* figure displays this in more detail: the very end of the third chord and the beginning of the fourth.

tendency and dispersion for various entities, calculate proportion values for neighbouring tones, etc., within the single performer and over several performers.

(5) Perform factor analysis on the deviation values from different performers or versions to see if there are some characteristically different ways of performing the piece.

This is only a very condensed description, and many other calculations are made, depending on the specific results for each piece or performer (see Bengtsson and Gabrielsson 1980 for details). However, the principle is to find out the deviations from mechanical performance, and to see whether they are the same for all performers, or if there are different types of deviations.

As expected, frequent deviations appear in all investigated cases. However, they are different in different pieces of music and also often between performers. A detailed description can thus only be made in connection with a certain piece and performer, for which the reader is referred to the original papers. Here we will only briefly describe some fairly common tendencies, proceeding from smaller to larger entities.

Sequences of equally long tones (according to the notation in the score), for example ♩ ♩ or ♫ , often show a long-short (LS) or short-long (SL) relation between the two tones; that is, the first tone is longer than the second (LS), or the converse is true (SL). Which alternative appears depends on the context as well as, sometimes, on the performer. In a sequence like ♫♫ the pattern is often LSSL, that is, the first and the last quavers are lengthened, the two middle ones shortened; but LSLS or SLSL patterns may also occur. In a pattern such as ♩ ♫ the quavers are often performed SL, while the relation at the crotchet level may be LS (the crotchet is longer than the two quavers together) or SL. The corresponding phenomena appear in the analogous ♫♩ sequence. In patterns such as ♩ ♩ in 3/4 metre and ♩ ♪ in 6/8 metre there is usually a much lower proportion than the mechanical 2:1 ratio between the two tones; it is often between 1.7:1 and 1.9:1 (cf. the example in Fig. 2.8) and may approach 1.5:1 in certain cases. But there are exceptions: for instance, in a march notated in 6/8 metre the ♩ ♪ sequence was performed close to the 2:1 ratio. This suggests that the general motion character of a piece is a decisive factor for the performance of various sequences within it.

The performance of dotted note values such as in ♩. ♪ or ♫. varies very much depending on context and performer. The mechanical ratio is 3:1, but the real ratio may be higher than ('sharp dotting'), lower than ('soft dotting'), or close to 3:1. It seems obvious that a ratio higher than 3:1 gives a more marked and 'jerky' character, while a ratio lower than 3:1 tends to sound 'softer'. If there are several sequences with the same type of dotting , it may happen that the dotting is made progressively 'softer' during the course of the phrase. A double dotting like ♫.. has a mechanical ratio of 7:1 but may deviate very much from that in actual performance, sometimes down to about 4:1 or even lower.

At the beat level a well-known example of deviations is the accompaniment in Viennese waltzes. The first beat is considerably shortened, and the second beat thus comes 'too early', which (together with other factors) gives an unmistakable motion character to these waltzes. A synthesized sound example, which demonstrates the perceptual effects of the second beat coming earlier and earlier, is given in Bengtsson and Gabrielsson (1983). There are numerous other examples of deviations at the beat level, more or less specific for each piece; we found, for instance, that in the popular tune 'Oh my darling Clementine' the third beat was generally lengthened.

At levels corresponding to half-measures, measures, and to still larger entities there are deviations of various types, which have to be described in connection with the performed piece. Some results were mentioned under 'Tempo' above. In order to have at least one concrete example of several phenomena mentioned above, we may look at Fig. 2.8. It shows the performance of the first eight bars of Mozart's Piano Sonata in A Major

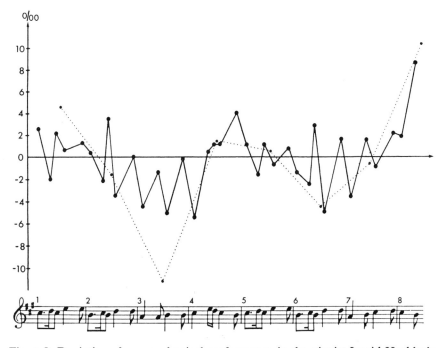

Fig. 2.8. Deviations from mechanical performance in the pianist Ingrid Haebler's performance of the beginning of Mozart's Piano Sonata in A Major (K. 331). The deviations are expressed in per mille of the total duration (until the last tone); one per mille corresponds to approximately 23 ms. See text for further explanations.

(K. 331) by the pianist Ingrid Haebler, renowned interpreter of Mozart. The horizontal line marked o represents a mechanical performance. The deviation for each tone is given by the black circles joined by the whole-drawn profile. A position above the zero line means that the corresponding tone is lengthened, a position below this line says that the tone is shortened, in relation to mechanical performance. The profile for the ♩. ♪ ♪ in the beginning of bars nos. 1, 2, 5, and 6 is V-shaped, that is, the dotted quaver and the last quaver are (relatively) lengthened, the semiquaver shortened. The sequences of ♩ ♪ are performed with the crotchet shortened or slightly lengthened; the quaver is mostly lengthened or less shortened than the crotchet. The ratio between the crotchet and the quaver is thus lower than 2:1. In average over all cases it is 1.76:1, but it varies from 1.92:1 down to 1.50:1. The dotted profile shows the deviations at the measure level. It is seen that the relation between the four bars in each half-period is LSSL, that is, the first and the fourth bars are longer, the second and third shorter. In other words, the tempo varies: somewhat slow start, accelerating in the second bar to reach the fastest tempo (= largest deviation downwards) in the third bar, then retarding towards the end of the half-period in the fourth bar. A similar profile is seen in the second half-period (the marking for the eighth bar refers to the first half of this measure). Many further observations can be made, but this may suffice to illustrate the general idea. Of course, the amount of data and interpretation grows considerably for analysis of longer examples.

Relations to the listener's experience

Results from performance studies must be interpreted with caution for several reasons. They may be more or less specific for the individual performer. The aforementioned factor analyses usually indicated two or three different ways of playing even very short pieces, and the variation among different performers' interpretations of a musical work is well known from general musical experience. There may be intra-individual variations as well. The musician changes his performance from time to time, sometimes deliberately in order to present a 'new' interpretation, sometimes unconsciously and for obscure reasons, still other times for adapting to the acoustical conditions (for example, changing the tempo).

  To find truly general results in performance data is therefore difficult. The generalities should rather be sought in the *relations between performance and* (the listener's) *experience*. The performance is the overt manifestation of the composer's and/or the performer's idea, and it is the stimulus for the listener's experience of the music. However, the performer is also a listener—he continuously checks that there is a correspondence between his intentions and the music he produces. He strives to convey his experience of the music as truly as possible to his listeners—so that they should experience the music as he does. The performance is a link joining the performer's experience and the listener's experience.

Of course, various individual characteristics (life history, attitudes towards music, personality traits etc.) affect the experience and make it more or less different for the performer and any individual listener. But there is usually also much in common, and we may assume that this communality is based on 'natural' relations between performance and experience—in other words, that *certain properties of the performance elicit certain qualities in the experience.* Long ago H. Seashore (1937, p. 118) expressed this opinion in the following words:

The psychophysical relations between the performer and the listener must be worked out; the data presented will contribute to such studies and also will depend for their final interpretation upon such investigations.

However, practically nothing has been done in the direction suggested by H. Seashore. We still discuss the relation between performance and experience in very general terms, as when C. E. Seashore stated that deviation from the regular is a general principle of art, or that 'deviation from the exact is . . . the medium for the creation of the beautiful—for the conveying of emotion' (quoted from H. Seashore 1937, p. 155). My repeated suggestions that various performance characteristics may affect structural and motional-emotional aspects of the experience is another example of such general propositions.

A basic difficulty is that we have no clear identification of the numerous dimensions which constitute our experience of music, nor do we have adequate methods to study them in a reliable way. It is my guess that non-verbal methods will play a greater role in future work on these questions. To study the relations between performance and experience we furthermore need a kind of iterative interplay between analyses of performed music and systematically varied syntheses of 'music'. A beginning of such a programme, with special reference to performance and experience of musical rhythm, is sketched in Gabrielsson (1985).

Meanwhile I again suggest that the frequent deviations from mechanical performance have structural as well as motional-emotional consequences. The experienced structure is certainly affected by variations of tempo, various other deviations, articulation, etc. (see Sloboda 1983). At the same time, however, these phenomena have obvious motional and emotional qualities: to accelerate or retard the experienced flow of the music, to provide a march or a Viennese waltz their proper motion characters, to make a dotting feel 'jerky' or 'soft', etc. For instance, the 'early second beat' in the Viennese waltz does not essentially change the basic tripartite structure of the bar—but it does change the experienced motion character.

Listening to synthesized, systematically varied sound sequences reveals that the ratio between the durations of adjacent tones may vary a lot without obscuring their structural relations (experiments to be reported). This indicates, among other things, that rhythm perception is categorical, and that considerable variation is available within the categories to affect various motional-emotional qualities. Similar results are obtained for synthesized melodies. Some of the variation in performance data may be accounted for in terms of such effects.

Concluding remarks

In this chapter timing has been treated in isolation from other means used by the performer, such as dynamics (in a wide sense), intonation, and spectral variations. Moreover, different aspects of timing (tempo, classes of duration, articulation, deviations from mechanical regularity) have been discussed separately from each other. In reality, however, all these means occur together in a complex, ever-changing interaction, depending on the instrument, the performer, and the situation. It is for the purpose of understanding the ingredients of this interaction that the present analytic approach may be justified. I hope it has also made clear the importance of studying the *sounding* music and its relations to the listener's experience rather than staying content with the simplistic picture given in musical notation. Studying the relations between performance and experience means coming very close to the musical reality, and is a fascinating challenge to all of us.

Acknowledgements

The author wants to express his gratitude to Ingmar Bengtsson, Barbro Gabrielsson, Dan Malmström, Peter Reinholdsson, and Bo von Schéele for invaluable collaboration in discussions and experiments. The investigations were supported by The Swedish Council for Research in the Humanities and Social Sciences, The Bank of Sweden Tercentenary Foundation, Knut and Alice Wallenberg's Foundation, and Uppsala University.

References

Becking, G. (1928). *Der musikalische Rhythmus als Erkenntnisquelle.* Benno Filser, Augsburg.

Behne, K. E. (1972). *Der Einfluss des Tempos auf die Beurteilung von Musik.* Arno Volk, Köln.

Bengtsson, I. (1974). Empirische Rhythmusforschung in Uppsala. *Hamburger Jahrbuch für Musikwissenschaft* 1, 195–220.

Bengtsson, I. and Gabrielsson, A. (1977). Rhythm research in Uppsala. In *Music, room, and acoustics*; Publications issued by the Royal Swedish Academy of Music, No. 17, pp. 19–56. Stockholm.

Bengtsson, I. and Gabrielsson, A. (1980). Methods for analyzing performance of musical rhythm. *Scandinavian Journal of Psychology* 21, 257–68.

Bengtsson, I. and Gabrielsson, A. (1983). Analysis and synthesis of musical rhythm. In *Studies of music performance*, Publications issued by the Royal Swedish Academy of Music, No. 39 (ed. J. Sundberg), pp. 27–60. Stockholm.

Clynes, M. (1977). *Sentics, the touch of emotions*. Anchor Press/Doubleday, New York.

Clynes, M. (1980). The communication of emotion: theory of sentics. In *Emotion: theory, research, and experience* (ed. R. Plutchik and H. Kellerman), Vol. 1, *Theories of emotion*. Academic Press, New York.

Clynes, M. and Nettheim, N. (1982). The living quality of music: neurobiologic basis of communicating feeling. In *Music, mind, and brain: the neuropsychology of music* (ed. M. Clynes). Plenum, New York.

Clynes, M. and Walker, J. (1982). Neurobiologic functions of rhythm, time, and pulse in music. In *Music, mind, and brain: the neuropsychology of music* (ed. M. Clynes). Plenum, New York.

Fraisse, P. (1956). *Les structures rythmiques*. Editions Universitaires, Louvain.

Fraisse, P. (1981). Multisensory aspects of rhythm. In *Intersensory perception and sensory integration* (ed. R. D. Walk and H. L. Pick), pp. 217–48. Plenum, New York.

Fraisse, P. (1982). Rhythm and tempo. In *The psychology of music* (ed. D. Deutsch). Academic Press, New York.

Gabrielsson, A. (1973a). Similarity ratings and dimension analyses of auditory rhythm patterns. I and II. *Scandinavian Journal of Psychology* 14, 138–60, 161–76.

Gabrielsson, A (1973b). Adjective ratings and dimension analyses of auditory rhythm patterns. *Scandinavian Journal of Psychology* 14, 244–60.

Gabrielsson, A. (1973c). Studies in rhythm. *Acta Universitatis Upsaliensis: abstract of Uppsala dissertations from the faculty of social sciences*, No. 7.

Gabrielsson, A. (1974). Performance of rhythm patterns. *Scandinavian Journal of Psychology* 15, 63–72.

Gabrielsson, A. (1982a). Perception and performance of musical rhythm. In *Music, mind and brain: the neuropsychology of music* (ed. M. Clynes). Plenum, New York.

Gabrielsson, A. (1982b). Performance and training in musical rhythm. *Psychology of Music, special issue: Proceedings of the Ninth International Seminar on Research in Music Education* , 42–6.

Gabrielsson, A. (1985). Interplay between analysis and synthesis in studies of music performance and music experience. *Music Perception* 3, 59–86.

Gabrielsson, A. (1986). Rhythm in music. In *Rhythm in psychological, linguistic and musical processes* (ed. J. R. Evans and M. Clynes). Charles C. Thomas, Springfield, Ill.

Gabrielsson, A. and Johnson, A. (1985). Melodic motion in different vocal styles.

In *Analytica, studies in the description and analysis of music in honour of Ingmar Bengtsson*, Publications issued by the Royal Swedish Academy of Music, No. 47. Stockholm.

Gabrielsson, A., Bengtsson, I., and Gabrielsson, B. (1983). Performance of musical rhythm in 3/4 and 6/8 meter. *Scandinavian Journal of Psychology* **24**, 193–213.

Hartmann, A. (1932). Untersuchungen über metrisches Verhalten in musikalischen Interpretationsvarianten. *Archiv für die gesamte Psychologie* **84**, 103–92.

Henderson, M. T. (1937). Rhythmic organization in artistic piano performance. In *Objective analysis of musical performance: University of Iowa studies in the psychology of music* (ed. C. E. Seashore), Vol. 4, pp. 281–305.

Hevner, K. (1937). The affective value of pitch and tempo in music. *American Journal of Psychology* **49**, 621–30.

Longuet-Higgins, H. C. (1979). The perception of music. *Proceedings of the Royal Society of London* **B205**, 307–22.

Longuet-Higgins, N. C. and Lee, C. S. (1982). The perception of musical rhythms. *Perception* **11**, 115–28.

Madsen, C. K. (1979). Modulated beat discrimination among musicians and nonmusicians. *Journal of Research in Music Education* **27**, 57–67.

Motte-Haber, H. de la (1968). *Ein Beitrag zur Klassifikation musikalischer Rhythmen*. Arno Volk, Köln.

Nielsen, F. V. (1983). *Oplevelse av musikalsk spaending* (The experience of musical tension) (with summary in English). Akademisk Forlag, Copenhagen.

Noorden, L. P. A. S. van (1975). *Temporal coherence in the perception of tone sequences*. Institute for Perception Research, Eindhoven.

Rasch, R. A. (1978). The perception of simultaneous notes such as in polyphonic music. *Acustica* **40**, 21–33.

Rasch. R. A. (1979). Synchronization in performed ensemble music. *Acustica* **43**, 121–31.

Rasch, R. A. (1981). *Aspects of the perception and performance of polyphonic music*. Drukkerij Elinkwijk BV, Utrecht.

Rigg, M. G. (1940). Speed as a determiner of musical mood. *Journal of Experimental Psychology* **27**, 566–71.

Risset, J. C. and Wessel, D. L. (1982). Exploration of timbre by analysis and synthesis. In *The psychology of music* (ed. D. Deutsch). Academic Press, New York.

Scherer, K. R. and Ekman, P. (1982). *Handbook of methods in nonverbal behavior research*. Cambridge University Press, Cambridge.

Sears, C. H. (1902). A contribution to the psychology of rhythm. *American Journal of Psychology* **13**, 28–61.

Seashore, C. E. (1938). *Psychology of music*. McGraw-Hill, New York.

Seashore, H. G. (1937). An objective analysis of artistic singing. In *Objective analysis of musical performance: University of Iowa studies in the psychology of music* (ed. C. E. Seashore), Vol. 4, pp. 12–157.

Shaffer, L. H. (1980). Analysing piano performance: a study of concert pianists. In *Tutorials in motor behavior* (ed. G. E. Stelmach and J. Requin). North-Holland, Amsterdam.

Shaffer, L. H. (1981). Performances of Chopin, Bach and Bartók: studies in motor programming. *Cognitive Psychology* **13**, 326–76.

Skinner, L. and Seashore, C. E. (1937). A musical pattern score of the first movement of the Beethoven sonata, opus 27, no. 2. In *Objective analysis of musical performance: University of Iowa studies in the psychology of music* (ed. C. E. Seashore), Vol. 4, pp. 263–80.

Sloboda, J. A. (1983). The communication of musical metre in piano performance. *Quarterly Journal of Experimental Psychology* **A35**, 377–96.

Small, A. M. (1937). An objective analysis of artistic violin performance. In *Objective analysis of musical performance: University of Iowa studies in the psychology of music* (ed. C. E. Seashore), Vol. 4, pp. 172–231.

Steedman, M. J. (1977). The perception of musical rhythm and metre. *Perception* **6**, 555–69.

Tove, P. A., Norman, B., Isaksson, L., and Czekajewski, J. (1966). Direct-recording frequency and amplitude meter for analysis of musical and other sonic waveforms. *Journal of the Acoustical Society of America* **39**, 362–71.

Truslit, A. (1938). *Gestaltung und Bewegung in der Musik*. Chr. Friedrich Vieweg, Berlin-Lichterfelde.

Vernon, L. N. (1937). Synchronization of chords in artistic piano music. In *Objective analysis of musical performance: University of Iowa studies in the psychology of music* (ed. C. E. Seashore), Vol. 4, pp. 306–45.

Wagner, C. (1971). The influence of the tempo of playing on the rhythmic structure studied at pianist's playing scales. In *Medicine and sport*, Vol. 6, *Biomechanics II*, pp. 129–32. Karger, Basel.

Wagner, C. (1974). Experimentelle Untersuchungen über das Tempo. *Österreichische Musikzeitschrift* **29**, 589–604.

Wapnik, J. (1980). The perception of musical and metronomic tempo change in musicians. *Psychology of Music* **8**, 3–12.

Wedin, L. (1972) A multidimensional study of perceptual-emotional qualities in music. *Scandinavian Journal of Psychology* **13**, 241–57.

3

Computer synthesis of music performance

JOHAN SUNDBERG

Introduction

Background of the project

This chapter presents a research project which was started some years ago. Its goal has been to analyse music performance by synthesizing it using a digital computer.

The origin of this project was apparently chance, as is the case with so many other research projects. Three crucial circumstances appeared in combination at the same time and in the same place.

One circumstance was the construction of the singing synthesizer MUSSE (see Larsson 1977), which offered synthesis of sung vowels. These synthetic vowels sounded very natural, as the interested reader can hear from sound illustrations published in Sundberg (1978). When this synthesizer could be controlled from a computer, it could be programmed with melodies, which were subsequently performed by the synthesizer. Musically experienced listeners typically noted that these performances sounded like a singer who was gifted with a good voice but who unfortunately lacked the desire to communicate anything in particular with his singing. This raised the question as to exactly what it is that the performer adds to the music score.

A second circumstance was the author's contact with Lars Frydén, a musician with an extensive background as a violin soloist and quartet player, as well as an accomplished teacher of violin playing at higher levels. His long-term musical experience had resulted in a number of hypotheses regarding some basic principles for the conversion of note signs into sounding music and also in a desire to test these hypotheses.

A third circumstance was the fact that at the laboratory, two of the author's colleagues, Rolf Carlson and Björn Granström, had devoted much work and ingenuity to the conversion of text to sounding speech (Carlson and Granström 1974). This had resulted in computer facilities offering means to synthesize by rules. These rules could concern not only pronunciation but also pitch contour and timing. It appeared that the task of converting text signs to speech sequences was in important respects similar to the task of converting note signs to tone sequences.

These three circumstances, in no way related to each other, turned out to form a good platform for attempts to improve the musical quality of computer-generated performances of music. Several reports have been published on this project over the years (Sundberg *et al* 1983a, b; Sundberg and Frydén 1985). This chapter aims both at presenting the strategy, including its advantages and limitations, and at mediating some experiences that have been gained in working with the project.

Topic

It is a well-known fact that traditional music sounds musically unacceptable when performed by a digital computer in an exact agreement with what is nominally given in the music score. This implies that the discrepancies between the sound sequences shown in the music score and those really generated in music performance constitute an essential part of music communication.

Evidently, these discrepancies cannot be random; for instance, it takes considerable training to learn playing, and, also, there is mostly a general agreement among competent listeners as to what is an unacceptable performance of a piece of music.

The above suggests that the discrepancies between notation and sound must be in some sense meaningful, that is, they carry information which the listener needs in order to enjoy listening to the performance. From the point of view of scientific research this is an interesting fact. What is this information? How is the acoustic code chosen which is used by the musician for conveying it? Is this code used in music only or is part of it borrowed from extramusical communication? These question touch on basic aspects of music communication. It seems that important contributions to the answers could be found by analysing music performance.

Nevertheless, music performance has attracted comparatively few researchers in the past (see Sloboda 1982). After Seashore's pioneering work in the thirties (see Seashore 1938), the work of Ingmar Bengtsson and co-workers, started more than two decades ago, remained more or less singular for a long time. (A recent account of their work is given in Bengtsson and Gabrielsson 1983). Researchers in the music acoustic area have been no exception in this respect, even though music performance must be regarded as an essential topic in the science of musical instruments; for instance, it would be hard to define 'instrument quality' were there no scientific understanding of exactly what the sound characteristics are which the musicians make use of when they play their instruments. However, during the last few years, the scientific interest in music performance has increased considerably (see for instance Clynes 1983). Perhaps the reason for this is the significance of such research to music which is performed without musicians, such as electro-acoustic music, particularly computer music.

The key questions in scientific research are *how?* and *why?* Applied to music performance they concern *how* the note signs are related to their corresponding acoustic signals in acceptable music performances; and *why* such a performance deviates from the nominal values specified in the music score. The present project attempts to contribute to the answers to these questions by formulating and interpreting rules for the conversion of note signs into sounding music.

Method

Set-up

Music performance can be studied by means of two different strategies, namely (1) measurements (see Bengtsson and Gabrielsson 1980) and (2) analysis-by-synthesis. *Measurements* have revealed a complex reality, to say the least. Seashore (1938) found that tones having the same nominal value in the music score occasionally may differ widely in duration. For instance, in the same piece a crotchet sometimes may be played shorter than a dotted quaver and sometimes longer than a dotted crotchet. Similar observations have been made in subsequent studies of timing in music performance (Bengtsson and Gabrielsson 1977; Sloboda 1983). It seems that the rules relating notation to sounding music are numerous and form a complex system. However, when combined with systematic experiments, measurement of music performance is a useful method.

Analysis-by-synthesis is a well-established method in natural sciences, including speech research, of testing hypotheses. When applied to music performance, hypotheses can be tested regarding rules for the conversion of note signs to tones. Thereby, even aspects of performance for which there is no generally accepted term may be investigated, so that a great variety of effects can be investigated.

The block diagram in Fig. 3.1 describes the procedure used in the present project. The overall aim is to convert a melody into tones according to a set of ordered rules. Using a program written by J. Liljencrants the one-part input melody can be written in ordinary music notation on the computer's graphic terminal. In addition to the information normally included in a music score, special signs were introduced to mark (1) chord changes and (2) boundaries between phrases and subphrases.

The rule system then converts the entire string of signs into a string of tone symbols. The rules are expressed in a special programming language,

ANALYSIS BY SYNTHESIS OF
MUSIC PERFORMANCE

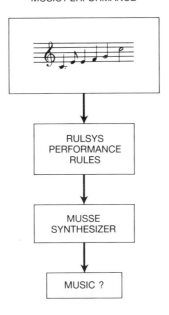

Fig. 3.1. Block diagram of the procedure used in the present project.

'RULSYS', written by Rolf Carlson and Björn Granström (1975) and originally devised for expressing rules regarding pronunciation, etc. in a text-to-speech conversion, as mentioned. The entire melody is processed by each rule in the order given by the rules in the system. The end result is that the tones are represented by vowel symbols which possess a number of different characteristics, such as duration, fundamental frequency, amplitude, vibrato amplitude, and other parameters, which can be manipulated by the rules. Finally, these characteristics are converted into control voltages for the MUSSE synthesizer.

In the present experiment the sound characteristics of the synthesizer were adjusted so as to be similar to the timbre of a double-reed wind instrument with a small vibrato. The fundamental frequencies were in accordance with the equally tempered scale, and could be modified in steps of 7 cents, which is close to the difference limen for frequency in normal subjects (Rakowski 1971). The amplitude was controlled in steps of 1/4 dB. The duration of the tones was computed in ms and then converted into cs. According to measurements by van Noorden (1975) a change in the perceived rhythm of a sequence of tones appeared when the durations were changed by more than 10 ms.

Procedure

As mentioned, the basic idea of the analysis-by-synthesis strategy is that of testing hypotheses. The long-term musical experience of my co-worker Lars Frydén has resulted in a number of hypotheses regarding basic principles for converting note signs into tone sequences.

The hypotheses suggested by Frydén have been expressed in terms of rules which have been implemented in the rule system. Each hypothesis has then been tested informally by listening to several examples which clearly expose the sounding consequences of the rule. Depending on the result, the rule has then been modified. Eventually, formal listening tests were realized in which musically highly competent listeners compared two slightly different versions of the same melody; in one version, all rules were applied in generating the performance, and in the other version all rules except the one tested by that example were applied. In this way each rule can be validated to the extent that it can be decided whether or not it significantly contributes to raising the musical quality of a performance of the melody tested.

Rules

Our present rule system includes about 20 rules. Some of these rules have been presented in detail together with sound examples in some previous reports (Sundberg *et al.* 1983*a*, *b*; Sundberg and Frydén 1985). Even though some rules have been more or less modified since then, only a few examples of the rules will be presented in this section; all of these have been approved of by a listening panel, unless otherwise stated.

The formulation of the rules is quite simple. The basic form of a rule is 'Every note possessing the characteristics A, B, . . . should be assigned the characteristics of D, E, . . . provided that is preceded by F, G, . . . and followed by H, I, . . .'. The context is optional. Also, there are means to fetch values from tones far back and far ahead in the sequence of note symbols.

There are several rules which work within a narrow time window including two or three notes only. In other words, the context is short. Some examples of such rules are the following.

(1) *The higher, the louder.* The amplitude is increased by about 3 dB per octave rise in fundamental frequency.

(2) *Heightening of durational contrasts.* This rule simply states that short note values are shortened. The shortening is very small indeed and, in terms of percentage, it is higher for quavers than for crotchets. No compensaion, such as a pause, is made for the resulting perturbation of the strict regularity of the beats.

(3) *Softening of durational contrasts*. In apparent contradiction to the previous rule this rule states that the durational contrast should be *reduced*. However, there is an important contextual condition for applying the rule, namely that the note is preceded by a note of twice its duration and followed by a tone with longer duration. This rule has not yet been tested in listening experiments.

(4) *Shortening of start tone in rising intervals*. The duration of a note initiating a rising interval is slightly decreased. In sequences of rising intervals the rule has the effect of increasing the tempo somewhat. As before, no compensation is made for the resulting perturbations of the meter.

There are also some rules which work with a wider time window. For these rules the signs representing chords and phrase and subphrase boundaries are decisive. In the input notation the chords are indicated by numbers representing the distance in semitone steps from the root of the chord to the root of the tonic. This number may be complemented by a sign for minor chords. As regards the phrasing we assume that melodies are built up by phrases, which consist of two or more subphrases. The boundaries between such phrases and subphrases are marked in the input notation.

(5) *Marking of harmonic charge*. This rule generates crescendos/decrescendos and ritardandos/accelerandos reflecting the chord progressions. The technicalities are as follows.

The rule assigns to each chord a value reflecting its *harmonic charge*. This harmonic charge is a weighted sum of the chord notes' *tonic charges**. As illustrated in Fig. 3.2, the tonic charge reflects the note's distance from the root of the tonic along the circle of fifths. The harmonic charge value is converted into an amplitude increment, which equals 6 dB for the highest harmonic charge. This amplitude increment is added to the first tone appearing over each chord. Then, the amplitudes of the intermediate tones are linearly interpolated on a dB-scale. Too-slow crescendos are avoided by letting the amplitude remain constant until about 2 s before the new chord appears. The result is crescendos and decrescendos towards harmonic changes which introduce chords having a higher or a lower harmonic charge than the preceding chord, respectively. Figure 3.3 demonstrates how the rule operates. This rule has not yet been verified by a formal listening test.

In addition to this, the tempo is also decreased and increased in synchrony with the crescendos and the diminuendos, respectively. These

---

* In previous reports on this project the terms 'harmonic distance' and 'tonic distance' have been used. However, as pointed out by Drs D. Butler and H. Brown, Music Department, Ohio State University, Columbus (personal communication), the word 'distance' may be misleading. The term 'charge' seems preferable, although a similar term, '*Quintspannung*', was defined slightly differently by Kurth (1917).

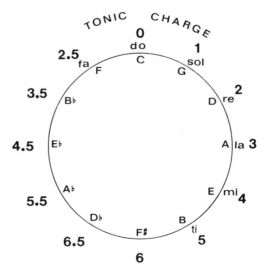

Fig. 3.2. Values of tonic charge for the various tones in the diatonic system. The tonic charge of a tone depends on the tone's distance from the root of the tonic along the circle of fifths. The *harmonic* charge value can be computed for any chord as a weighted sum of the chord notes' *tonic* charge values.

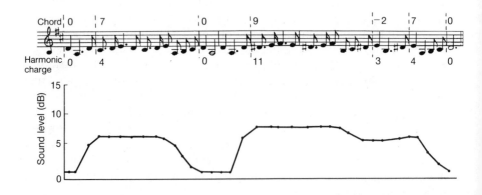

Fig. 3.3. Illustration of the amplitude effects of the rule reflecting changes in the chords' harmonic charge as applied to the second theme from the first movement of Schubert's Symphony No. 8 in B minor, 'Unfinished'. The chords are symbolized by numbers corresponding to the interval (in semitone steps) between the root of the chord and the root of the tonic (top line); the minus sign represents a minor triad. The numbers below the staff represent the chord's harmonic charge value. Crescendos and decrescendos accompany increases and decreases of harmonic charge, respectively.

tempo changes mostly involve note lengthenings of 0 to about 15 per cent.
(6) *Phrase and subphrase marking.* The rule first adds 4 cs to the note
terminating a phrase and 4 additional cs to the final note of the melody. In
addition the final note in each phrase is terminated by a short pause, as the
amplitude falls to zero during the last 20 per cent of the note's duration.
Similarly, in notes terminating subphrases, the amplitude decays to zero
during the last 80 ms of the note.

Discussion

All these rules share an *ad hoc* character, and in some cases they may even
seem mysterious. Therefore, a primary concern is to verify the rules. This
can be realized in various ways. Before this, it is necessary to consider a
more general question, namely the apparent contradiction between two
obvious facts: on the one hand, a melody can be played in many different
ways, all of which are fully acceptable from a musical point of view; on the
other hand, a rule system will predict only one single performance of a
given melody.

First it should be pointed out that identity with respect to the sequence
of notes does not imply that the melodies are the same. This relates to an
experiment recently carried out by Sloboda (1983), who had pianists play a
set of melodies several times. Two melodies in this set were identical
except for the location of the bar lines. The performances of these two
different but 'homonymous' melodies were then analysed. The performances
of the most experienced players differed consistently with respect to both
timing and amplitude in certain places in the melody. The question then is
whether or not different performances will be generated by our rule system
in such a case. The answer is yes; the input notation may differ even in
cases where the note sequence is identical, because in the input, signs are
added for chord changes and phrase and subphrase boundaries, and these
would differ in a case such as the one used in Sloboda's experiment. Thus,
two slightly differing performances will result, if the rule system processes
such 'homonymous' melodies. In many cases it is not even necessary to
move the bar lines or the chord changes for obtaining different interpretations
in terms of phrase and subphrase boundaries. Music is often ambiguous in
this respect, and these ambiguities will cause our rule system to predict
differing performances.

Apart from these cases, where the same sequences of tones represent
different melodies, there is another possibility for our rule system to
predict a variety of performances for the same melody. Even though this
possibility has not yet been explored, it will be mentioned here. In our
present rule system there are about 20 rules, and several of these affect one
parameter, such as the duration of the note. This means that the duration

of one single note in a melody may be lengthened by some rules and shortened by some other rules. Still it is obvious that our system is not yet complete; there must be more rules, which would add to the musical quality of the performance. Introducing them into the rule system may cause problems, though. It seems likely that there is an upper limit on the number of rules which can be used simultaneously to affect one specific sound parameter. Perhaps there are many rules which are alternative, so that the musician may make a new selection of the alternative rules he wants to apply each time he plays the piece. This possibility should be :tested in future research. In any event, it would lead to a rule system that could generate different performances of the same piece.

As suggested before, the above has important implications for the possibilities of verifying the different rules in music practice. Obviously, it is not correct to assume that eventually there will be a perfect match between the performance predicted by a complete rule system and an actual perfect performance, as there are many perfect performances. Still, similarities may occasionally occur in some actual performances, so it is still meaningful to compare generated and observed performances.

In Fig. 3.4 a performance predicted by the rule system is compared with

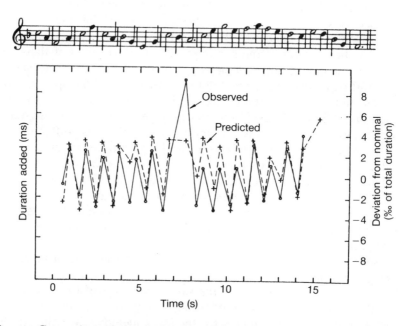

Fig. 3.4. Comparison of observed and predicted durations in a performance of the melody shown. The predicted values are given in cs, and the observed values, quoted from Gabrielsson and Bengtsson (1983), are given in thousandths of the summed duration of the melody.

an actual performance as measured by Gabrielsson and Bengtsson (1983). The figure compares observed average deviations from nominal note values in actual performances with the deviations predicted by the rule system. It appears that rule (3), which reduces durational contrasts in halving of duration, has had a major effect on the end result. Actually, this rule, which was not yet verified in a formal listening test, seems to be efficiently validated by the good agreement between observed and predicted data. Such a high degree of agreement between predicted and observed performances is rare. Particularly in more complex melodic structures, such as the one illustrated in Fig. 3.5, the relationship between observation and prediction is much less clear.

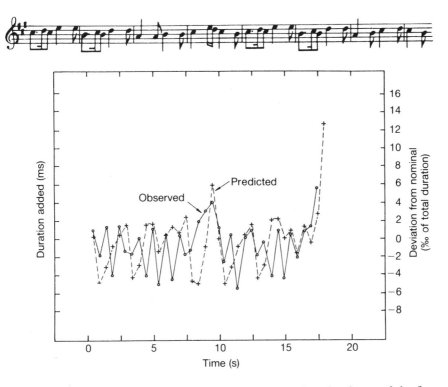

Fig. 3.5. Same type of comparison as in Fig. 3.4 regarding the theme of the first movement in Mozart's Piano Sonata in A (K. 331).

What do such similarities and dissimilarities between predicted and observed performances tell us? Our rule system can be regarded as a predictive model of the reality manifested in music performance. When there is an agreement between observation and prediction, it is safe to conclude that the predicting model represents a fair description of reality.

However, the reverse does not seem to be necessarily true. In other words, a disagreement cannot be used for rejecting the model. The reason for this is the fact that there are many ways of performing the same melody which, although differnt, are all musically perfectly acceptable. Rather, the criterion for an acceptable system of rules is that experienced listeners agree that the performance generated by the rule system sounds musically acceptable. This has been tested in the listening experiments mentioned previously. An evaluation of the complete rule system will be carried out in the future (see Thompson *et al.* 1986).

Let us know turn to a different aspect of the results, namely the quantity of the rules; that is, *how much* amplitude or duration, etc., is added by the various rules. The first question to consider is then to what extent random variation of duration can be tolerated in musically acceptable performances (Gabrielsson and Bengtsson 1983). Our experience is that, mostly, duration changes as small as 10 ms can be noted in motor music (where there is a rapid sequence of beats). This is in accordance with van Noorden's results (1975). It implies that random variations of duration must be smaller than 10 ms, as, obviously, noticeable random variation cannot be accepted in a perfect performance.

As was mentioned, the quantities by which these rules affect the amplitude and duration of the individual note are sometimes exceedingly small. Yet, the effects thus generated as essential to the impression we get of the performance. This is evident when listening to examples where in the input notation the phrase markers have been replaced by subphrase markers and vice versa (the interested reader may experience this by listening to the corresponding sound illustration in Sundberg and Frydén 1985). The typical reaction of music listeners is that this simple substitution results in an unacceptable performance of the melody (Friberg *et al.* 1987). This shows that our sensitivity to these minute perturbations of amplitude and duration is very high indeed. As soon as the microperturbations appear in wrong places, they are easy to hear, but when they appear in correct places, they are hard to notice.

Interference between rules has often forced us to reduce the quantity of one rule when another rule was introduced. For instance, our first crescendo simply implied an increase of the output amplitude. This is an unrealistic crescendo, however, as higher overtones typically gain more than lower overtones when amplitude is increased on traditional musical instruments. When this feature was introduced accompanying the changes in amplitude, it became necessary to reduce the amplitude changes. Similarly, the quantity of other rules has been reduced to a quantity smaller than that which was used when the rule was tested in a listening experiment with experienced musicians. As yet, we have simply added the latest rule to the previous rules which have been adjusted accordingly, if required. This means that the quantity for a rule which is just right with the present combination of rules may turn out to be too large if more rules are added in the future.

A typical observation should be mentioned which we have made several times when trying to adjust the quantity by which a rule affects a note or a series of notes. When the quantity is too small, the effect cannot be heard at all, of course. More interestingly, when the quantity is too great, two phenomena can be noted. One is that it is easy to hear exactly what the rule is doing in a physical sense. The other is that the effect appears musically unacceptable, simply because it sounds exaggerated. The 'correct' or musically useful quantity is in between these two extremes. It is typically characterized by the situation that a listener notices the effect but is unable to analyse it correctly in physical terms; as soon as this is possible, the quantity is too great and the effect sounds exaggerated. Thus, there seems to be a difference between the quantity needed in order to make a correct aural analysis of the physical means used; what is acceptable from a musical point of view seems to be just beyond the border of what is noticeable.

The analysis-by-synthesis method has previously been applied extensively in speech research and there it has been found useful. Still, the method has certain limitations. The most important one is that, being a basically comparative method, it can merely show what is better or worse than something else. For instance, we can find out if a rule improves the musical quality of a performance, but no conclusions can be drawn as to what is the best possible performance. On the other hand, this limitation is no great concern; even with respect to 'real' music it would be wrong to pretend that this or that performance is *the* best possible performance; there are always several ideal performances of a piece.

The analysis-by-synthesis technique as applied to music performance presupposes that musical experts are capable of agreeing on what is more acceptable and what is less acceptable from a musical point of view in a musical performance. We have regarded this ability as a psychological fact, and there seem to be no serious reasons for doubting its existence among music experts. For instance, if it did not exist, it would be hard to explain why music conservatories can exist.

The analysis-by-synthesis procedure shows striking similarities with the procedure used in teaching music playing; in both cases the principle is to give instructions that strive to eliminate some obvious deficiency in the performance. A major difference is that computers always apply all rules, while this would probably be regarded as a sign of little musical talent in a human musician! However, this difference between the computer and the music student is essential for the evaluation of the 'instructions' which we give to the computer.

Summarizing this slightly rhapsodic discussion so far, our examples and listening tests prove that our rules improve the musical acceptability of a performance at least in the piece of music that has been tested. This is an interesting fact that asks for an explanation, regardless of the generality of the rule, and regardless of whether the rule could be formulated in a better or alternative way. Thus, as soon as we have formulated a rule and found that it improves music performance, we have reasons to question why it improves the performance. The answer to this question would be interesting, because the rules must be assumed to represent some sort of reality in music communication. Next we will attempt to analyse this reality.

Purpose of the rules

It seems that each of the rules that we have formulated as yet serves a specific purpose or, rather, it seems to have a function in music communication. There are a number of such purposes, and the rules can be divided into different groups according to their apparent purposes.

One group of rules seems to serve the purpose of emphasizing the contrasts along a commonly used dimension. An example of this in the rules described above is rule (2), which exaggerates durational contrasts.

A second type of rule seems to serve the purpose of eliminating sound characteristics which sound queer because no traditional musical instrument possesses them. An example is rule (1), which increases the loudness as function of pitch; most traditional instruments adhere to this principle. If the synthesis does not adhere to this rule, it sounds unnatural or 'electronic'. This is logical: the listener has never heard this sound characteristic before except from electronic instruments.

A third group of rules seems to take into account the fact that a listener might make associations with previous experiences when listening to music. For instance, (a) a rapid, regular pulse would often lead the listener's thoughts to rapid locomotion such as swift walking or running, and (b) an 'upward motion' on the scale would cause many listeners to imagine something climbing upward in space. Perhaps a combination of these associations constitutes the background of rule (4), increasing the tempo with the upward motion of a melody: the slight increase in tempo can be interpreted as an indication that it is not heavy to walk, even though the road leads upward.

A fourth group of rules seems to serve the purpose of emphasizing more or less unexpected tones. It is as if the musician wanted to say that even though this note sounds a bit peculiar, it is just this note that he intends to play. The occurrence of chords having a high harmonic charge is prepared by loudness increases, while the amplitude is decreased towards chords which have a smaller harmonic charge.

A fifth group of rules apparently serves the function of marking the structure of the melody. One example is the rule lengthening the final element of a phrase. Rule (5), which emphasizes harmonically remote chords by loudness increases, probably serves this purpose too. The background is that in traditional harmony the chord progressions are often used to mark the structure, so that a phrase ending is often marked by a cadenza, that is, a chord preceded by its own dominant—or, in other words, a decrease of the harmonic charge (see Sundberg and Lindblom 1976). For instance, one of the phrases in a melody written in C major might be terminated by the chord progression E major—A minor. Under these circumstances our rules would predict a crescendo towards the E major chord and then a decrescendo towards the A minor chord. This loudness change would then serve a double purpose. One purpose is to inform the listener that the E major is actually intended even though it is rather far from the tonic (no-mistake case), and the other purpose is to inform the listener that this is a termination of a structural unit in the melody (marking-of-structure case).

Apart from the groups of rules exemplified above there is at least one more group. The purpose of the rules in this group is to embed the performance in a sort of emotional atmosphere. Particularly in the synthesis of singing, the need for such rules is experienced as evident; in a melody with a tragic character, it is most disturbing if the performance does not sound tragic. Interesting attempts to investigate how such emotional atmospheres are signalled in music performance are being made by Clynes (see for example Clynes 1983).

If we now survey the groups of rules described above, we find that the rules apparently serve purposes which are not specific to music. The heightening of contrasts in a frequently used dimension seems to be a common psychological phenomenon in communication. Examples of the preference for phenomena that the listener/spectator is already familiar with can probably be found in most fields of human communication. Emphasis is a phenomenon that would appear in all systems of formalized communication. To embed a message in an emotional atmosphere is typical in human behaviour, including speech. Musical communication thus seems to contain several elements that are not specific to music, and many elements seem to be directly imported from speech. This is not surprising: speech and music are the two main forms of systematized interhuman communication by means of sound signals. In future research it would be interesting to see whether great differences in the speech of two cultures correspond to great differences regarding the rules used in music performances.

Code

Above we have considered the question of what *purposes* the various rules in our performance rule system seem to serve. We can now pose another question, namely, what the *means* are that are used to fulfil these different purposes. Thus, we will consider questions such as 'How is emphasis signalled?' and 'How is the structure of the melody marked?' It is by no means obvious how the code is chosen. It is possible that the code is imported from extramusical communication, such as speech, but it is also possible that the code is unique for music.

Before going into these questions it is improtant to point out that the acoustic parameters that we have dealt with in this work are only pitch, amplitude, timing, and vibrato. There is no doubt that these are sufficient for making music; this is evident from the fact that the organ is useful as a musical instrument, because in this instrument it is only timing that can be continuously controlled by the player. Nevertheless, it is important to remember that we can make inferences about the coding in terms of amplitude and timing only.

Much of the code seems to be taken from speech. One example is the phenomenon that a note appears emphasized when it is lengthened; in speech, emphasis can be signalled by means of an increased syllable duration as has been demonstrated by Carlson *et al.* (1974). Another example is the marking of phrase endings by means of lengthening, because many languages use 'final lengthening' for signalling the end of a phrase (Lindblom 1978). By listening to speech, music listeners have been 'programmed' to interpret lengthening as a possible sign of a termination. If so, lengthening would be impossible to use as a sign of continuation. The previously mentioned queer effect obtained when phrase and subphrase markers were switched in a melody supports this hypothesis.

However, it seems doubtful that speech is the ultimate source of the code. For instance, in some languages, such as Danish, lengthening of syllable duration is not the code used in order to flag the end of a phrase. Still, Danish and Swedish musicians can of course make music together. This lends support to the previously mentioned hypothesis that there may be several codes available for expressing the same thing in music performance; the flagging of termination by means of lengthening is perhaps only *one of many* possibilities.

When a player uses lengthening for marking termination, he exploits the fact that the listener is 'programmed' to couple the phenomenon of lengthening with the notion of termination. In the mind of a music listener there would be many other examples of such couplings between sound patterns and various phenomena which allow the listener to interpret the sound sequences. Such couplings are likely to result partly from the listener's extramusical experience, such as his acquaintance with speech, and partly from his previous musical experiences. The typical final retard is a convincing example of a coupling of the first-mentioned type. It is typically used in motor music, where there is a regular, rapid pulse. It is likely that most listeners tend to associate this pattern of pulses with locomotion. One way of stopping locomotion abruptly is by collision, which most listeners would agree is an unpleasant experience. It may be for that reason that the final retard is often used in performance of motor music. (Kronman and Sundberg 1987).

The main point, we believe, is that the player always applies rules in his playing, because it is only by means of following rules that the player enables the listener to interpret the performance. Thus, we would speculate that all details in a music performance are interpretable as long as these details were derived from performance rules which exploit the listener's previous intra- as well as extramusical experience. We also believe that the basic requirements for musical communication can be studied efficiently by means of formulating these performance rules.

Concluding remarks

Music performance seems to be a scientifically rewarding topic, where analysis-by-synthesis is a useful method. A number of unexpected findings and observations have emerged, and, no doubt, much work remains to be done, such as a thorough testing of all hypotheses generated by the results. Still, even before this has been done some conclusions can be drawn.

By demonstrating how the sound sequences must be modelled in order to increase the musical acceptability of a performance, explicit information is gained on what is demanded from a musically acceptable performance. The analysis-by-synthesis method offers information in terms of a precise description of sound patterns. In many case these patterns can be recognized as allusions to patterns, which must be well known to the listener because of his or her experience of speech and also of motion as manifested by, for example, footsteps. By means of such allusions, emphasis, structure, and emotional atmosphere can be expressed in a way that the listener can understand. In this way music seems to gain meaning.

In summary, it seems that analysis of music performance is beginning to reveal what exactly it is that musicans add to written music, what the code they use is and from where this code is taken. Therefore it appears fair to propose that analysis of music performance can shed light on basic aspects of music communication.

Acknowledgements

This project is supported by the Bank of Sweden Tercentenary Fund.

This is one of many articles about this project written for different readerships during the last years. As the rule system has been continuously modified during this period, some rules can be found in a different formulation in previous articles.

References

Bengtsson, I. and Gabrielsson, A. (1977). Rhythm research in Uppsala. In *Music room acoustics*, Publications issued by the Royal Swedish Academy of Music, No. 17, pp. 19–56, Stockholm.
Bengtsson, I. and Gabrielsson, A. (1980). Methods for analyzing performance of musical rhythm. *Scandinavian Journal of Psychology* **21**, 257–68.
Bengtsson, I. and Gabrielsson, A. (1983). Analysis and synthesis of musical rhythm. In *Studies of music performance* (ed. J. Sundberg), Publications issued by the Royal Swedish Academy of Music, No. 39, pp. 76–181. Stockholm.
Carlson, R. and Granström, B. (1974). A phonetically oriented programming language for rule description of speech. In *Proceedings of the speech communication seminar*, Vol. 2, *Speech production and synthesis by rules*, ed. G. Fant) pp. 245–53. Almqvist and Wicksell, Stockholm.
Carlson, R., Erikson, Y., Granström, B. Lindblom, B., and Rapp, K. (1974). Neutral and emphatic stress patterns in Swedish. In *Proceedings of the speech communication seminar* Vol. 2, *Speech production and synthesis by rules*, (ed. G. Fant), pp. 209–18. Almqvist and Wicksell, Stockholm.
Clynes, M. (1983). Expressive microstructure in music, linked to living qualities. In *Studies of music performance* (ed. J. Sundberg), Publications issued by the Royal Swedish Academy of Music, No. 39, pp. 76–181. Stockholm.
Friberg, A., Sundberg, J., and Frydén, L. (1987). How to terminate a phrase. An analysis-by-synthesis experiment on a perceptual aspect of music performance. In *Action and perception in rhythm and music* (ed. A. Gabrielsson), Publications issued by the Royal Swedish Academy of Music, No.55.
Gabrielsson, A., Bengtsson, I., and Gabrielsson, B. (1983). Performance of musical rhythm in 3/4 and 6/8 meter. *Scandinavian Journal of Psychology* **24**, 193–213.
Kronman, U. and Sundberg, J. (1987). Is the musical ritard an allusion to physical motion? In *Action and perception in rhythm and music* (ed. A. Gabrielsson), Publications issued by the Royal Swedish Academy of Music, No. 55.
Larsson, B. (1977). Music and singing synthesis equipment (MUSSE). Speech Transmission Laboratory Quarterly Progress and Status Report UTH, Stockholm 1977/1, pp. 38–40.
Lindblom, B. (1978). Final lengthening in speech and music. In *Nordic prosody* (eds. E. Gårding, G. Bruce, and R. Barnett), Dept. of Linguistics, Lund University pp. 85–101.
Noorden, L. P. A. S. van (1975). Temporal coherence in the perception of tone sequences. Doctoral thesis. Druk vam Voorschooten.
Rakowski, A. (1971). Pitch discrimination at the threshold of hearing. *Proceedings of the 7th International Congress on Acoustics*, Budapest, Vol. 3, pp. 373–76.
Seashore, C. E. (1938). *Psychology of music.* McGraw-Hill, New York. (Reissued 1967 by Dover, New York).

Sloboda, J. (1982). Music performance. In *The psychology of music* (ed. D. Deutsch), pp. 479–96. Academic Press, New York.

Sloboda, J. (1983). The communication of musical metre in piano performance. *Quarterly Journal of Experimental Psychology* **A35**, 377–96.

Sundberg, J. (1978). Synthesis of singing. *Swedish Journal of Musicology* **60**, (1), 107–12.

Sundberg, J. (1982). In tune or not? A study of fundamental frequency in music practice. In *Tiefenstruktur der Musik, Festschrift für Fritz Winckel* (ed. M. Krause), pp. 69–96. Universität und Akademie der Kunste, Berlin.

Sundberg, J. and Frydén, L. (1985). Teaching a computer to play melodies musically. In *Analytica: studies in the descriptions and analysis of music in honour of Ingmar Bengtsson*, Publications issued by the Royal Swedish Academy of Music, No. 47, pp. 67–76. Stockholm.

Sundberg, J. and Lindblom, B. (1976). Generative theories in language and music descriptions. *Cognition* **4**, 99–122.

Sundberg, J., Frydén L., and Askenfelt, A. (1983a). What tells you the player is musical? An analysis-by-synthesis study of music performance. In *Studies of music performance* (ed. J. Sundberg), Publications issued by the Royal Swedish Academy of Music, No. 39, pp. 61–7. Stockholm.

Sundberg, J. Askenfelt, A., and Frydén, L. (1983b). Music performance: a synthesis-by-rule approach. *Computer Music Journal* **7**, 37–43.

Thompson, W. F., Friberg, A., Frydén, L., and Sundberg, J. (1986). Evaluating rules for the synthetic performance of melodies. Speech Transmission Laboratory Quarterly Progress and Status Report, UTH, Stockholm, 2–3/1986, 27–44.

4

Timing and synchronization in ensemble performance

RUDOLF A. RASCH

Introduction

For the last six centuries Western music has been largely polyphonic. This means that a piece of music consists of two or more simultaneous parts or 'voices' (either vocal or instrumental). In order to make performance possible, the temporal relations between the various voices as well as those within a single voice have to be defined exactly and unambiguously. These relations must be clearly stated in the score of the music and appropriately realized in a performance. In its initial stage polyphonic music was often called 'measured music' (*musica mensurata*) as opposed to 'plain music' (*musica plana*), that is, plainchant in which there was no requirement of strict time structure.

Observations from such widely different fields as timbre experiments, instrumental sounds, and notation lead to the conclusion that the beginning or onset of a tone is the decisive point in time for that tone. Timbre experiments have shown that recognition of musical instrument tones is severely impaired by taking away the starting transient portion (Clark *et al.* 163; Berger 1964; Saldanha and Corso 1964). Widely used instruments such as piano, harpsichord, and guitar (in general, all plucked or struck instruments) produce tones without steady-state parts, which begin to decay immediately after the onset. Traditional music notation puts notes at the onset moment of the horizontal time scale, and places those with simultaneous onsets together irrespective of their lengths. Investigation of the temporal structure of music is therefore predominantly a study of onset moments.

In this chapter we deal with the problem of synchronization in musical performance, that is, how musicians manage to co-ordinate their own temporal (onset) structures with those of the other performers in such a way that the temporal structures actually match each other and fuse into one common temporal structure. This means that the tones which are prescribed in the score as simultaneous must be played at the same moment of time, especially with regard to their onsets. In reality, perfect synchronization is never realized and there will always be some asynchronization. Onsets meant to be simultaneous but in performance not exactly simultaneous will be called quasi-simultaneous onsets.

In the first and second sections of this chapter, we will present a model for the description of synchronization of ensemble performances (Rasch 1979, 1981). It is based on the standard deviations of relative onset times and onset time differences. The third section is devoted to the question of how to define the onset times of musical tones in a synchronization situation (Vos and Rasch 1981). Finally, we will speculate a little about the role of the conductor in the synchronization of musical performances.

The description of synchronization

When musicians play together in an ensemble, they will try to synchronize as much as possible the tones meant to be simultaneous. For a number of reasons, such as the restricted accuracy of human motor performance and time perception, the relative ease of tone production within or between instruments, and the time lag between the production of a player's own tones and the perception of the tones produced by others, a perfect synchronization is not possible in a live performance. There will always be some degree of asynchronization.

Onsets of tones meant to be simultaneous will, in reality, scatter a little in time. Assume an ensemble of n players. Figure 4.1, illustrates some of

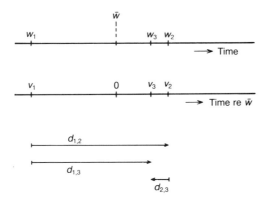

Fig. 4.1. Illustration of the concepts used for synchronization analysis. w_1, w_2 and w_3 are three onsets meant to be simultaneous. $\bar{w}$ is the mean onset time. v_1, v_2, and v_3 are the onset times expressed relative to $\bar{w}$. The onset time differences are denoted by d_{12}, d_{23}, d_{31}.

the concepts used for an ensemble of three performers. The *absolute onset times* of the tones meant to be simultaneous will be denoted by $w_1, w_2, \ldots, w_n$. For each group of such onsets there will be a mean onset time:

$$\bar{w} = \frac{w_1 + w_2 \ldots + w_n}{n}.$$

Now, the absolute onset times can be converted into *relative onset times*:

$$v_1 = w_1 - \bar{w},$$
$$v_2 = w_2 - \bar{w},$$
$$\ldots, \text{ and}$$
$$v_n = w_n - \bar{w}.$$

The relative onset times are relative to the mean onset time, not to other onset times. Below, we will as a rule use the relative onset times. The absolute onset times of the tones in a piece of performed music can be measured and transformed into relative onset times. This will result in a set of n distributions of relative onset times, one per voice. These distributions can be characterized by their means, which will be indicated by $\bar{v}_1, \bar{v}_2, \ldots, \bar{v}_n$, and their variances, which will be denoted by $s_1^2, s_2^2, \ldots, s_n^2$. The means indicate which instruments lead or lag in their onsets relative to the other instruments in a performance.

Time differences between onsets are particularly significant for perception. The *onset time differences* will be denoted by the letter d:

$$d_{12} = v_2 - v_1,$$
$$d_{13} = v_3 - v_1,$$
$$\ldots, \text{ and}$$
$$d_{n-1,n} = v_n - v_{n-1}.$$

The subscripts refer to the respective voices. Onset time difference has been termed *onset asynchrony* in other contexts. For a piece of music with n voices or performers, there will be $n(n-1)/2$ distributions of onset time differences. These distributions can be characterized by their respective means, to be indicated by $\bar{d}_{12}, \bar{d}_{13}, \ldots, \bar{d}_{n-1,n}$, and variances, to be indicated by $s_{12}^2, s_{13}^2, \ldots, s_{n-1,n}^2$.

The distributions of onset time differences are related to those of the relative onset times. The means of the onset time differences can be calculated directly from the means of the relative onset times. The relation between the variances of relative onset times and onset time differences is more complex. It was found empirically that the variances of the several distributions of relative onset times for one specific piece of music do not differ very much from each other. For simplicity we will assume that they are equal, and denote their value by s_v^2. In addition we will assume that the covariances between distributions are equal. Their value will be denoted by c_v. With these assumptions it is possible to derive a simple formula that relates the variances of the relative onset times and the onset time differences.

Each relative onset time can be written as a linear sum of all other relative onset times, for example:

$$v_1 = -(v_2 + v_2 + v_3 + \ldots + v_n).$$

The variances of such a sum equals the sum of the variances of the terms of the sum plus twice the sum of all covariances among the terms:

$$s_v^2 = \sum_{i=2}^{i=N} s_{v_i}^2 + 2 \sum_{i=2}^{i=n} \sum_{j=i+1}^{i=n} c_{v_{ij}} \ (j \neq i)$$

in which $c_{v_{ij}}$ is the covariance of v_i and v_j.

Since, by assumption, $s_{v_1}^2 = s_{v_i}^2 = s_v^2$ and $s_{v_{ij}}^2 = c_v$, the variance of the relative onset times in general can be expressed in the following equation:

$$s_v^2 = (n-1)s_v^2 + (n-1)(n-2)c_v.$$

This leads to:

$$c_v = \frac{s_v^2}{1-n}.$$

Since an onset time difference can be considered to be a linear combination of the form $d_{12} = v_2 - v_1$, its variance is given by:

$$s_d^2 = 2s_v^2 - 2c_v.$$

Substituting the value of c_v in the last equation leads to:

$$s_d^2 = \frac{2n}{n-1} s_v^2.$$

So the relation between the relative onset times and the onset time differences depends on the number of performers in the ensemble. For a duo ($n=2$) the relation is simply $s_d^2 = 4s_v^2$. For a large ensemble, the relation converges to the limit $s_d^2 = 2s_v^2$.

In actual practice, onset time difference is a variable with a mean not very different from zero (mostly within the range of -5 to $+5$ ms) and a standard deviation that is much greater (mostly within the range of 30 to 50 ms). For this reason the standard deviation of the onset time differences is a better measure for the amount of asynchronization in performed music than the mean onset time differences. We will define the *asynchronization of a pair of voices* as the standard deviation of the onset time differences of simultaneous tones of those voice parts. In formula, the asynchronization will be denoted by the capital A: $A_{ij} = s_{ij}$.

The standard deviations of the various distributions of onset time differences in one piece of music do not differ very much from each other. We do not lose very much information if the asychronizations of the various voice pairs are averaged, by taking the root-mean-square. This averaging has the advantage that the asynchronization of a piece of music can be expressed as a single value. We will define the *asynchronization of a piece of performed music* as the root-mean-square of the standard deviations of the onset time differences for all pairs of voice parts. The asynchronization of a piece of music will be denoted by the capital A without subscripts.

It should be noted that the asynchronization defined quantitatively in this way indicates ranges in which onset time differences will fall with certain probabilities. The range from $-A$ to $+A$ includes 68 per cent of onset time differences, the range from $-2A$ to $+2A$ 95 per cent. If we discard the sign of the onset time differences, it can be stated that the median unsigned onset time difference is $0.68A$, the lower quartile $0.32A$, and the higher quartile $1.15A$.

The synchronization of simultaneous tones is only one of the temporal tasks of performing musicians. Within one voice, the succession of tones also has to be strictly timed. We will call the timing of tones of equal duration in one voice the *isochronization* of the tones. The isochronization of a voice will be defined as the standard deviation of tone durations meant to be equal. In actual practice, there will be a number of sources that contribute to the variance of equal tone durations, like tempo trends and fluctuations. Also, the asynchronization of simultaneous tones will be mirrored in isochronization. If we exclude all other sources of the variance of 'equal' tone durations, there is a certain relation between asynchronization and isochronization (actually, a-isochronization). We consider two consecutive tones with absolute onset times w_i and w_{i+1} (see Fig. 4.2). The duration of the first tone is

$$h_i = w_{i+1} - w_i.$$

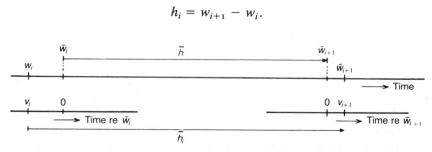

Fig. 4.2. Illustration of the concepts used in determining the relation between asynchronization and the standard deviation of tone durations. $\bar{w}_i$ and $\bar{w}_{i+1}$ are the mean onset times of two successive triplets of tones. w_i and w_{i+1} are the onsets of two successive tones in one voice part; v_i and v_{i+1} are the same onsets but expressed relative to the mean onset times. $\bar{h}$ and h_i are the time intervals between the mean onsets and the onsets in a single voice, respectively.

The absolute onset time is the sum of the mean onset time and the relative onset time. We denote the mean onset time of tones simultaneous to w_i as $\bar{w}_i$, that of tones simultaneous to $\bar{w}_{i+1}$. We assume that the successive mean onset times $(\ldots, \bar{w}_i, \bar{w}_{i+1}, \ldots)$ are perfectly isochronous. Therefore, mean tone duration $\bar{h}$ is

$$\bar{h} = \bar{w}_{i+1} - \bar{w}_i.$$

The relative onset times of the two tones in succession will be denoted by v_i and v_{i+1}. Now we can rewrite the actual tone duration as follows:

$$h_i = \bar{h} + (v_{i+1} - v_i).$$

The variance of this last expression is

$$s_h^2 = 2(1-r)s_x^2.$$

in which r is the correlation between v_i and v_{i+1}, or, the autocorrelation of relative onset times. The above equation can also be written as

$$s_h^2 = \frac{n-1}{n}(1-r)s_d^2.$$

The relation between isochronization and synchronization can be used in the comparison of the results of our measurements with the results of experiments on sequential timing behaviour which exist in the literature.

The measurement of synchronization

The descriptive model given will now be illustrated with a set of measurements of live musical performances specifically recorded for this purpose (Rasch 1979, 1981).

In order to study synchronization in musical performances it is necessary to know the exact temporal structure of each individual part of the composition performed. Attempts have been made to analyse the compound sound of a piece into its individual parts, for instance by Tove *et al.* (1967) at the Royal Institute of Technology in Stockholm, and by Moorer (1975) at the Center for Computer Research in Music and Acoustics of Stanford University. Up to now, these attempts have been only partially successful. Several serious problems prevent application of the methods employed to larger, not specially selected samples of music. The main problem areas in this field are the storage and processing of the prohibitively large amounts of data, and the separation of fused harmonics in the cases of musical intervals with simple frequency ratios.

A more feasible approach is the one in which the acoustics signals from each instrument are picked up and recorded before they are mixed into the ensemble sound. This can be done by using either contact microphones under normal acoustic conditions or directional microphones in an anechoic chamber. The latter method was chosen for our recordings because the recorded sound most resembled the sound in normal listening conditions. The recorded signals passed a logarithmic envelope detector with an output voltage proportional to the sound-pressure level of the temporal envelope of the signals. The sampling rate was 200 Hz, the time interval between two successive samples being 5 ms. The envelopes could be displayed on the graphic terminal of the computer. Peaks in the enveloped were matched with the notes of the score played by the musicians. The onset time of a peak was defined as the moment that the envelope reached or surpassed a certain, previously defined threshold level. This level was taken about 15 or 20 dB below the maximum levels of the signals. Figure 4.3 shows the envelopes of a fragment of 9 s of music, with the peaks numbered according to the computer output and the score of the music inserted for comparison and identification purposes.

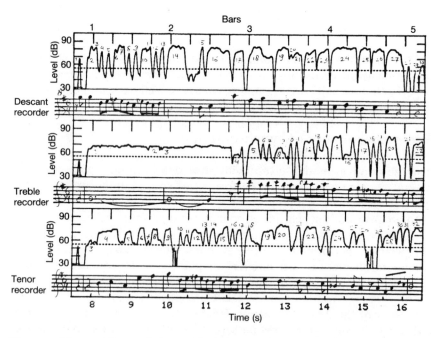

Fig. 4.3. The envelopes of three simultaneous voices of a fragment of 9 s. The peaks have been numbered, and the notes of the score have been inserted.

The following step was to determine which peaks in the three envelopes corresponded to a triplet of simultaneous notes in the musical score. Table 4.1 shows the simultaneous onsets from Fig. 4.3, the relative onset times, and the onset time differences. Note that the temporal resolution of the

Table 4.1 *Peaks corresponding to simultaneous notes from the music fragment of Fig. 4.3, with absolute onset times, relative onset times, and onset time differences.*

Instrument I 2 3			absolute onset time (ms)			relative onset time (ms)			onset time differences (ms)		
Peak no.			w_1	w_2	w_3	v_1	v_2	v_3	d_{12}	d_{23}	d_{31}
18	5	18	11970	11995	11955	−3	21	−18	25	−40	15
19	8	20	12670	12675	12695	−10	−5	15	5	20	−25
22	12	22	13405	13390	13410	3	−12	8	−15	20	−5
24	15	24	14075	14105	14125	−27	3	23	30	20	−50
25	17	26	14795	14800	14795	−2	2	−2	5	−5	0
27	20	18	15500	15510	15470	7	17	−23	10	−40	30

processing system was 5 ms. As a matter of fact, not all the triplets of simultaneous notes found in the score had a corresponding triplet of peaks in the envelopes. If the initial part of a tone did not correspond to a peak in the envelope, no corresponding onset time was available for the calculations.

The statistical computations were mostly done per composition, sometimes per movement of a composition. First, means, standard deviations, and root-mean-squares of standard deviations of relative onset times and onset time differences were calculated. These figures make up the basic data set of our analysis. Further computations included the autocorrelations of relative onset times, correlations with tempo measures, and conversion of synchronization into isochronization values.

Recordings were made of music played by three professional trio ensembles: a recorder trio, a reed trio (oboe, clarinet, bassoon), and a string trio. Each ensemble played two compositions that were typical for the repertoire.

Means and standard deviations of relative onset times were calculated for each recorded composition. The mean relative onset times are graphically presented in Fig. 4(a). They indicate to what extent certain instruments tend to lead or lag in simultaneous onsets relative to the other instruments. Certain tendencies can be discerned. In the string and wind trios the main melody instruments (violin, oboe) tend to lead relative to the others, with the bass instruments (cello, bassoon) in the second place, and the middle voice (viola, clarinet) in the third place. This corresponds to our intuitive notion that in most of the music for these ensembles the melody part is the leading, 'first' voice. Recorder ensemble music is more polyphonic as a rule, and the bass is the most fundamental voice. This is confirmed by the observation that the tenor recorder—the lowest voice—is the leading voice, on the average.

There are three distributions of onset time differences for each

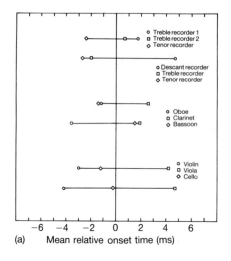

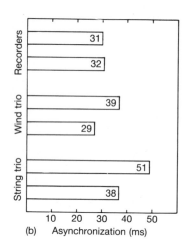

Fig. 4.4(a). Mean relative onset times of the instruments per composition.

Fig. 4.4(b). Mean asynchronization per composition, averaged over the instruments.

composition. The root-mean-squares of the standard deviations are used as measures for asynchronization. Asynchronization per composition is graphically illustrated in Fig. 4(b). Asycnchronization values fall largely within the range of 30 to 50 ms. Mean asynchronization of this set of data is 36 ms. There are some systematic differences between the ensembles. The recorder ensemble shows a relatively small asynchronization of about 30 ms. The two examples of the wind trio have different amounts of asynchronization: 27 and 37 ms respectively. The largest asynchronizations are found in the string trio examples: 37 and 49 ms. These differences may be related to the rise times of the tones of the instruments in question. Recorders have short rise times, so that the beginnings of the tones are clearly marked. These short rise times make good synchronization both possible and necessary. The conventional woodwinds of the wind trio also have relatively short rise times. The onset of string tones is a more gradual process resulting in long rise times (30 to 100 ms). These longer rise times permit a greater leniency as to synchronization.

The relation between asynchronizatoin and tempo was also investigated (see Fig. 4.5). All data in this table concern single movements of the compositions. As tempo measure we used the time between two successive counting beats, the 'inter-beat time', determined as 60 divided by the metronome value (the number of counting beats per minute). This measure includes a subjective element in the choice of the counting unit. The correlation between the asynchronization of the movements and the tempo measure of 0.80. Evidently, the conclusion is justified that faster

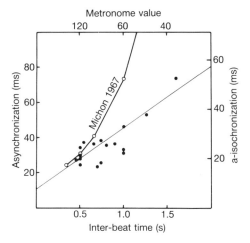

Fig. 4.5. Relation between tempo and asynchronization. Inter-beat time is used as a measure of tempo. The vertical scales indicate asynchronization, defined on the left as the standard deviation of onset time differences, averaged over instruments. On the right, a-isochronization is indicated. The dots are data points for movements. The regression line of tempo on asychronization is based on the correlation between inter-beat time and asynchronization. The results of Michon's experiments (1967, p. 31) are inserted for comparison.

tempo goes with more synchronization, and slower tempo goes with less synchronization.

As already noted, asynchronization of simultaneous onsets can be the cause of a-isochronization, that is, the existence of deviations from equal durations of successive tones within single voices. It is possible to make an estimate of this a-isochronization from asynchronization. For this estimate the correlation between subsequent relative onset times must be known. This correlation is the autocorrelation of a series of relative onset times. The autocorrelations were first calculated per composition and then algebraically averaged over voices and compositions. The resulting value proved to be 0.21. This indicates that there is a slight tendency of relative onset times to be preserved in the subsequent onsets. With $r = 0.21$, we find a ratio of 0.73 between a-isochronization and asynchronization. Apart from the autocorrelation, the asynchronization patterns seem to be more or less random.

Now we can compare our results with those of experiments conducted by Michon (1967). His subjects had to tap synchronously with a pulse train presented through headphones. His results (p. 31, Table 2B) are standard deviations of time intervals meant to be equal, and as such indicate a-isochronization. Tapping rates were 60, 90, 120, and 180 beats per minute. Figure 4.5 includes both the results of Michon's experiments and the regression line for asynchronization to tempo. For high tempos the correspondence between Michon's data and ours is quite good. For lower tempos the synchronization found in our recordings is better than would be expected from Michon's data. A likely explanation of this discrepancy is that subdivisions of the beat also can contribute to synchronization.

Perceptual effects of synchronization

In a study by Rasch (1977) the effect of onset difference times on the perception of quasi-simultaneous tones was investigated. Each trial included two stimuli in those experiments. Each stimulus contained two simultaneous tones. The lower tones of the stimuli in a trial had the same fundamental frequency, the upper ones differed in fundamental frequency by an (upward or downward) fifth (or other interval). The threshold for perceiving the upper tone of the stimulus was defined as the level resulting in a 75 per cent correct score in a 2AFC paradigm of the judgement of the direction of the pitch jump. For synchronous notes (onset difference time 0 ms) the threshold was between 0 and −20 dB depending on the frequency ratio and phase relation of the simultaneous tones. The threshold could be decreased drastically, down to about −60 dB, by introducing an onset difference time of, say, 30 ms. In the latter case, the threshold was largely independent of factors other than temporal ones. This condition can be compared directly with asynchronization in performed music. In the experiments there was no sensation of order. In supra-threshold conditions asynchronization contributes to the apparent transparency of the compound sound multi-tone stimuli.

When listening to music, onset differences mostly go unnoticed. Actually, the performances of professional ensembles give the impression of perfect synchronization. In the now classic investigation by Hirsh (1959) it was found that, roughly speaking, a time interval of 20 ms between two sounds (tones, noises, clicks) was sufficient for judging which one came first. Several reasons can be mentioned why onset difference times that are considerably longer are not perceived in a musical listening situation. Firstly, the qualities of the simultaneous tones differ, especially as to pitch and timbre (instrument); this impairs an exact judgement of the temporal structures. Secondly, rise times of musical tones are much longer (for example 20–80 ms) than the stimuli used in psychophysical experiments (often 5 or 10 ms). The smoother rise curves also impair exact judgements. Thirdly, the distribution of onset differences is practically random. Fourthly, attention of the listener is not directed to onset differences between voices ('vertical') but rather to melody lines within one voice ('horizontal'). The musicians themselves are, in general, also unaware of the amount of asynchronization, except when unwanted asynchronization cannot be avoided in very difficult passages or in cases of 'temporal mistakes'.

Among the onset difference times there appeared to be a small number of relatively large ones, that is, from 100 to 200 ms. They were clearly audible during repeated replay. They can be a consequence of mistakes by the performer, but they are also induced by some musical characteristics, such as: the first onsets of a movement, a section with long notes in one voice and short notes in other voices; ritenuto or accelerando sections; onsets of individual part after rests; final notes following a ritardando or separated from the preceding notes by a rest; sections that are complicated with regard to rhythm and/or metre. Underlying factors for these harder-to-synchronize fragments are the absence of directly preceding tones or uncertainty concerning the temporal structure. The threshold for order of auditory stimuli sets a lower limit for synchronization. As yet, there are no experimental data for thresholds of temporal order in musical situations.

As a final remark, mention must be made of Seashore's theory that 'beauty in music largely lies in the artistic deviation from the exact or rigid' (1938, p. 249). This postulate leaves open the question of how to define artistic deviation. However, its negative formulation ('there is no beauty in music if the performers adhere exactly and rigidly to the instructions of the score') is certainly true. In every artistic musical performance there is constant deviation from what is prescribed exactly in the score, as to time, frequency, duration, level, etc. These deviations have strong statistical components without being purely random. They are of primary importance for the 'live' character of music performed by human beings. The asynchronization of simultaneous tones should be regarded as one of the vital deviations in the performance of music.

The moment of synchronization

In the preceding section, the decisive time moment of the tone, used as a basis for the calculation of synchronization, was taken where the temporal envelope of the tones passed a threshold, quasi-arbitrarily defined as the level 15 or 20 dB below the average maximum level of the respective voice part. Since this choice is fairly central in the description of synchronization behaviour, the threshold model concerning the perceptual onset of musical tones will be considered here in some detail. The model assumes that music listeners (including music performers) base their timing on the passing of the temporal envelope through a certain threshold level, which is defined in relation to the average maximum level of the stream of musical tones (Vos and Rasch 1981). The physical temporal envelope of a musical tone can be roughly divided into three successive portions: the rise, the steady-state, and the decay portions (see Fig. 4.6).

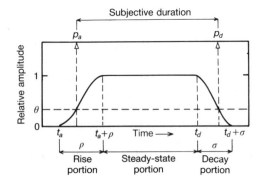

Fig. 4.6. Temporal envelope of a musical tone, divided into three successive portions. The perceptual onset (p_a) and offset (p_d) of the tone are defined as the moment at which the temporal envelope passes the relative threshold amplitude, θ.

If the rise function, which describes the envelope during the rise, is monotonously increasing, then the inverse function is unambiguous. Throughout this chapter, we will regard rise functions as monotonously increasing functions. In our model, the perceptual onset of a tone is the moment at which the temporal envelope during the rise portion passes a certain relative threshold level. If the moment of the perceptual onset is known, the threshold level can be calculated. If the threshold level is known, the perceptual onset can be calculated. The subjective duration of a tone is defined as the time interval between the perceptual onset and offset of a tone. The following paragraphs, describing an extension of our model, will deal only with the perceptual onset.

The model can be extended to groups of tones, either simultaneous or successive ones. Two tones are called *perceptually synchronous* when their perceptual onsets coincide in time (see Fig. 4.7).

Tone sequences are defined as *perceptually isochronous* if the time intervals between successive perceptual onsets are all equal to each other. Figure 4.8(c) shows the temporal envelopes of the tones A, B, and A', which are perceptually isochronous. An experimental paradigm with successive perceptually isochronous tones with different rise functions and/or rise times can be used to determine the threshold amplitude for the perceptual onset (Vos and Rasch 1981). If tones are physically isochronous, that is, when the time intervals between successive physical onsets are all equal to each other but have different rise times and/or functions, the perceptual onsets will not, as a rule, be isochronous.

In the experiments exploring the applicability of the model a paradigm was used in which a sequence of tones had to be isochronized, that is, the tones had to be adjusted in such a way that the onsets were perceived isochronously. Each trial started with a tone sequence that was decidedly nonisochronous. The starting sequence consisted of successive pairs of

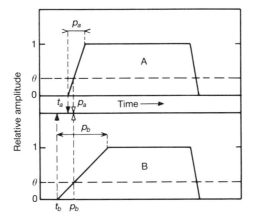

Fig. 4.7. Temporal structure of a perceptually synchronous stimulus, containing tones A and B with physical onsets t_a and t_b, rise times p_a and p_b, and maximum amplitude 1. The perceptual onsets, p_a and p_b, coincide in time and are by definition located at the moment at which the temporal envelopes pass threshold amplitude, θ.

tones, A and B, with a different interval between the physical onsets of A and the following B and between B and the following A (see Fig. 4.8(a)). The onset times of tones B, relative to those of A, could be adjusted by the subjects, by turning a knob. The experimental task was to adjust the onset times of tones B in such a way that the sequence ABABAB . . . was perceptually isochronous, that is, that the perceived onsets of the tones followed each other after strictly the same time interval. This is illustrated in Fig. 4.8(b). Because the tones A were repeated every 800 ms, the subjective repetition time t of the tones in the entirely isochronized sequence is 400 ms. Rise times were varied independently. The time between the successive physical onsets was derived from the position of the turning knob at which the subject judged the tone sequence to be isochronous. Now all variables that are necessary for computing the threshold amplitude for the perceptual onset were known.

Relative threshold amplitudes were computed for a number of combinations of unequal rise times. Mean threshold level was −15.4 dB, and the standard deviation equalled 1.6 dB. Considering this consistent result—that is, that about the *same* relative threshold level was found in ten physically different conditions—it is justified, for the time being, to define the perceptual onset moment of a tone as the time at which its envelope passes a certain threshold level. Moreover, from these experimental data, this threshold level can be estimated as −15 dB, relative to the maximum level of the tones.

The perceptual onset threshold has up to now been given relative to the

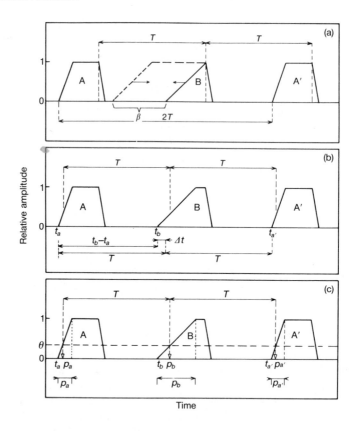

Fig 4.8. (a) Illustration of a perceptually nonisochronous starting sequence. The physical onsets of tones B could be adjusted by the subject within time interval β. At the start of a trial, the physical onset of tone B was either at the beginning or at the end of β. The physical offset of tones A and B, were fixed. (b) Temporal structure of a perceptually isochronous tone sequence in which the time intervals between successive perceptual onsets are all equal to each other. The physical onsets of tones A and B are t_a and t_b, respectively. The repetition time of tone A equals $2T$, so that T is the perceptual repetition time. The dependent variable is denoted by the time interval $\Delta t = T - (t_b - t_a)$. (c) Temporal structure of tones A, B, and A', which are perceptually isochronous. The time interval between successive perceptual onsets is denoted by T. The perceptual onsets p_a, p_b, and p_a' are defined as the moment at which the temporal envelopes pass relative threshold amplitude, θ.

maximum level of the tones. But it is evident that the threshold can also be defined as a level above background noise or hearing threshold. In short, the following question can be asked: Is the threshold fixed, with respect to maximum level, to background, or to some other criterion? Our first experiments were designed to test the threshold hypothesis in general, not to discriminate between these alternatives. Further experiments were carried out to determine the reference relative to which the threshold had to be defined. This was done by varying the maximum levels of the tones. The stimuli were the same as those in the earlier experiments. The sound-pressure level of the tones, however, was 77 dB(A) in the highest level condition; in the other conditions it was 57 and 37 dB(A). Again, relative threshold amplitudes were computed. In the 37-dB condition, the mean relative threshold was −8.0 dB and the standard deviation equalled 0.9 dB. In the 57- and 77-dB conditions, the mean thresholds were −11.7 and −13.0 dB, and the standard deviations were 0.7 and 1.6 dB, respectively.

The results of these experiments show that the time difference between physical and perceptual onsets increases with decreasing tone intensity, that this increase can be described as an upward shift in the relative threshold by which the perceptual onset is determined, and that the shift in threshold is small relative to the shift in stimulus level. Therefore, the threshold can be most conveniently described relative to the maximum level of the stimulus.

From the experiments, it may be concluded that the perceptual onsets of musical tones can be defined as the times at which the envelopes pass a *relative* threshold of about 6 to 15 dB below the maximum level of the tones. In a number of experiments, we have shown that the level of the relative threshold depends on the tone level above masked or absolute threshold. The data from the present experiments seem to suggest adaptation to a certain constant stimulus level. At the time the adaptation threshold is passed by the stimulus level presented, the onset of the stimulus is perceived.

In studies on the temporal structure of performed music, our threshold model can be applied to determine the perceptual onsets of musical tones. When music is performed on instruments with very short rise times, like the piano, harpsichord, and drums (Gabrielsson 1974; Povel 1977; Sundberg and Verrillo 1980), the difference between the physical onset and the perceptual onset is very small. In these cases, level above threshold, too, does not have a great impact on this difference. However, when ensemble music is performed on instruments producing tones with relatively long rise times, such as bowed string instruments, the perceptual onset heavily depends on the relative threshold.

In such musical practice in which dynamic differences are not very large, perceptual onset is clearly affected only by the rise times and rise functions of the different instruments. This, however, is a variable with which the respective musicians can cope by adjusting their physical onset times in order to establish the appropriate timing of the perceptual onsets of their tones.

Future research should be focused on the perceptual onset of musical tones in synchronously perceived tone pairs. The sensation levels of simultaneously presented tones, especially, are dependent on the amount of auditory masking (Zwislocki 1978). To apply our model to simultaneously produced tones, experimental results of binaural masking experiments with complex tones are needed. In addition, it would be interesting to see if our model also works in cases of complex tones consisting of partials with unequal rise times and unequal physical onsets (Freedman 1967; Grey and Moorer 1977) and of tones with substantially differing amplitude envelopes (Strong and Clark 1967).

Synchronization and the conductor

Small ensembles usually perform without a conductor, while larger ensembles and orchestras are guided by the gestures of a conductor. Since one of the tasks of the conductor is to keep the performing musicians synchronized, it is interesting to comment upon the present or absence of a conductor in terms of our descriptive model of synchronization.

When there is no conductor, the musicians will have to synchronize upon each others' sound outputs. For this condition, we consider the standard deviation of the onset time differences as being of some fixed, constant magnitude. In that case, the standard deviation of the relative onset times varies as a function of the number of performers in such a way that it becomes larger when that number is increasing (since $s_v^2 = (\frac{1}{2}(n-1)/n)s_d^2$). If we use our mean value of the standard deviation of onset time differences (36 ms), then the standard deviation of relative onset times is 18 ms for an ensemble of two players, 20.8 ms for three players, 22 for four, 22.8 for five, 23.2 for six, 24 for nine. For ensembles with more than nine players it converges to its maximum value of $36/2\frac{1}{2}$ or 25.5 ms. Evidently, synchronization quality is less in larger ensembles.

When a conductor is leading an ensemble or an orchestra, it may be supposed that the performers will try to synchronize not with each other, but with the movements of the conductor. For that condition, it may be supposed that the standard deviation of the relative onset times will be of some fixed, constant magnitude, since all musicians have the same task in this respect. We cannot extract an estimate for this quantity from our experiments, but via a detour a guess can be made. When the standard deviation of relative onset times is a constant quantity, the standard deviation of onset time differences is diminishing when a number of performers is increasing (since $s_d^2 = (2n/(n-1))s_v^2$), or, put the other way around, the standard deviation of onset time differences is increasing when the number of performers is increasing. With this relationship in mind, it is easy to understand that a large orchestra will always need a conductor, or, at least, will do better with a conductor. If the ensemble shrinks, however, synchronization quality is diminishing when the conductor stays in charge of the synchronization.

A survey of recorded chamber music with five to 15 performances showed that ensembles with up to and including nine performers did, more often than not, without a conductor, while ensembles with 10 or more players almost always had a conductor (see Fig. 4.9). This must mean that the standard deviation of relative onset times of an imaginary ensemble of 9.5 players marks, on the average, the maximum allowable value of that standard deviation (in our average case 24.1 ms). It may be assumed that in this imaginary situation synchronization is as good with conductor as without, which gives us at the same time the assumed constant value of the standard devation of relative onset times in a situation with conductor. When there are those 9.5 performers, the standard deviation of onset time differences (or the asynchronization) is just 36 ms. But when there were only two performers, asynchronization would have been 48 ms; with three, 42 ms; with four, 39 ms; etc. When the number of performers gets substantially larger than 10, asynchronization converges to its limit of 34.1 ms.

Our line of reasoning concerning the usefulness of a conductor when it comes to synchronization is summarized in Fig. 4.10. It amounts to the

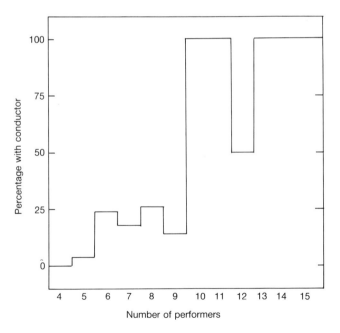

Fig. 4.9. Percentage of performances with a conductor, taken from a representative set of recorded quartets, quintets, sextets, etc. Only two compositions for 12 players could be located, of which one was with, one without conductor.

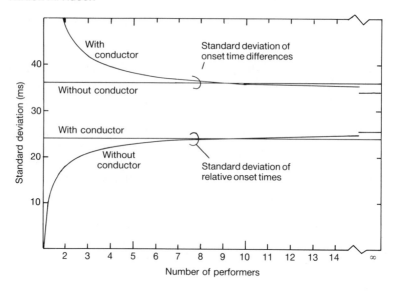

Fig. 4.10. Idealized standard deviations of relative onset times and onset times differences of performances with and without conductor, as a function of the number of performers. Numerical values are anchored to a mean asynchronization of 36 ms.

conclusion that below a certain cut-off value of the number of performers synchronization among performers is better without a conductor, while above that value it is better with a conductor. A caveat must be added, however. The lines marked 'with' and 'without' (conductor) cross at rather small angles, so that the crossing points are relatively strongly influenced by small up or down movements of the lines, which makes the choice of the crossing open to serious discussion. We found differences in synchronization related to the instruments of the ensemble and related to the tempo of the movement performed. The kind of music performed may also be expected to affect the value of a conductor. All these effects may cause upward or downward shifts of the lines inserted in Fig. 4.10. Indeed, the cut-off between the numbers of performers that need and that do not need a conductor is not sharply defined. Our cut-off value of 9.5 performers represents only an average value, although it is much sharper than was to be expected from the shallow curve of the standard deviation of the relative onset times as a function of the number of performers.

Conclusion

In this chapter, we have presented some thoughts and data about timing and synchronization in ensemble performance. The position taken in this chapter has to do with model making and acoustical measurement rather than with processes of the psychology of music. However, before any such psychological interpretation comes into play, a sound and reliable way of measuring the relevant characteristics of musical behaviour should exist, and that is what this chapter aims to provide.

Measures of musical behaviour, including musical performance, are essentially statistical measures. For this reason we developed our statistical model of synchronization, based on relations between variances of relative time moments. We showed that with this framework it is possible to describe in a sensible way synchronization in ensemble performance. The research we have done was not initiated by the wish to uncover the psychological processes that are behind synchronization behaviour. Eventually, however, the descriptive part should be supplemented by a psychological, interpretative part.

References

Berger, K. (1964). Some factors in the recognition of timbre. *Journal of the Acoustical Society of America* **36**, 1888.

Clark, M., et al. (1963). Preliminary experiments on the aural significance of parts on tones of orchestral instruments and on choral tones. *Journal of the Audio Engineering Society* **11**, 45.

Freedman, M. D. (1967). Analysis of musical instrument tones. *Journal of the Acoustical Society of America* **41**, 793–806.

Gabrielsson, A. (1974). Performance of rhythm patterns. *Scandinavian Journal of Psychology* **15**, 63–72.

Grey, J. M. and Moorer, J. A. (1977). Perceptual evaluations of synthesized musical instrument tones. *Journal of the Acoustical Society of America* **62**, 454–62.

Hirsh, I. J. (1959). Auditory perception of order. *Journal of the Acoustical Society of America* **31**, 759.

Michon, J. A. (1967). *Timing in temporal tracking*. Institute for Perception TNO, Soesterberg.

Moorer, J. A. (1975). On the segmentation and analysis of continuous musical sound by digital computer. Report STAN-M-3, Center for Computer Research in Music and Acoustics, Stanford University, Stanford, Calif.

Povel, D. (1977). Temporal structure of performed music, some preliminary observations. *Acta Psychologica* **41**, 309–20.

Rasch, R. A. (1978). The perception of simultaneous notes such as in polyphonic music. *Acustica* **40**, 21.

Rasch, R. A. (1979). Synchronization in performed ensemble music. *Acustica* **43**, 121–31.

Rasch, R. A. (1981). Aspects of the perception and performance of polyphonic music. Unpublished thesis. Groningen.

Saldanha, E. and Corso, J. (1964). Timbre cues and the identification of musical instruments. *Journal of the Acoustical Society of America* **36**, 2021.

Seashore, C. E. (1938). *Psychology of music.* McGraw-Hill, New York. (Reissued in 1967 by Dover, New York).

Strong, W. and Clark, M. (1967). Synthesis of wind-instrument tones. *Journal of the Acoustical Society of America* **41**, 39–52.

Sundberg, J. and Verrillo, V. (1980). On the anatomy of the retard: a study of timing in music. *Journal of the Acoustical Society of America 68*, 772–9.

Tove, P. A., Ejdesjö, L., and Svärdström, A. (1967). Frequency and time analysis of polyphonic music. *Journal of the Acoustical Society of America* **41**, 1265.

Vos, J. and Rasch, R. (1981). The perceptual onset of musical tones. *Perception and Psychophysics* **29**, 323–35.

Zwislocki, J. J. (1978). Masking: experimental and theoretical aspects of simultaneous, forward, backward and central masking. In *Handbook of perception* (ed. E. Carterette and M. Friedman), Vol. 4. Academic Press, New York.

5

Rehearsal skill and musical competence: does practice make perfect?*

LINDA M. GRUSON

In recent years, research on the acquisition of skills has focused upon the study of a variety of complex skills including, for example, competence in games such as chess (de Groot 1965; Chase and Simon 1973; Simon and Chase 1973), bridge (Charness 1979) and the board game, Go (Reitman 1976); in the academic domain, acquisition of skills in such subjects as mathematics (Krutetskii 1976), physics (Simon and Simon 1978; 1980; Chi *et al.* 1980; Larkin *et al.* in press), compositional writing (Flower and Hayes 1979), and engineering thermodynamics (Bhaskar and Simon 1977); and a number of cognitive-motor skills such as typewriting (Thomas and Jones 1970; Shaffer 1975, 1978) and, most pertinent to the present study, musical skills (Bean 1938; Weaver 1943; Wolf 1976; Shaffer 1980, 1981; Sloboda 1974, 1977; MacKenzie *et al.* 1983).

While the research paradigms and target behaviours studied have been quite diverse, one of the most consistent findings that emerges from the research on skills is that as an individual learns a skill, he or she acquires the ability to process increasingly larger and more complex units of meaningful, skill-related information. Chase and Simon's (1973) work with chess players illustrates this process of 'chunking'. They have demonstrated that with increasing mastery, chess players are able to reconstruct significantly more pieces of meaningful chess positions exposed briefly to them. The reconstruction of randomly placed pieces did not improve with increased mastery. Chase and Simon hypothesized that chess masters' superiority over less expert players was due to their ability to encode

* This study was carried out in partial fulfilment of the Ph.D. degree. An earlier version of this paper was presented at the eighty-ninth Annual Convention of the American Psychological Association, Los Angeles, California, August 1981

meaningful chess information more efficiently into 'chunks' in short-term memory.

The research on musical sight-reading lends support to the 'chunking' notion. Bean (1938) found that professional musicians could play almost five notes of a musical segment presented to them tachistoscopically while non-professional musicians could recall between two and three notes, and beginners, only one to two notes. He discovered that differences in perceptual span could be accounted for by differences in perceptual style; the majority of his professional pianists approached the task by reading musical patterns while most of the non-professinals read the music analytically, note-by-note. Weaver's (1943) finding that professional musicians could perceive between three and five notes at a single glance provided further evidence that proficient sight-readers can, in fact, process groups of notes as a single perceptual unit. Lannert and Ullman (1945) found that sight-reading skill was positively correlated with span of reproduction and ability to read ahead in the score, and Sloboda (1974) reported a correlation of 0.86 between sight-reading ability and the eye-hand span (the number of notes correctly played after the unexpected removal of the stimulus). In an interview study, Wolf (1976) discovered that good sight-readers report that they rely upon their recognition of familiar patterns and on their ability to organize the music into a few familiar patterns and dependable pattern cues. He also found that sight-reading appeared to be a very specific skill depending upon such a pattern-recognition style of information processing. The professional musicians who reported using an analytic strategy (note-by-note) as opposed to a pattern-recognition strategy were poor sight-readers although their ability to memorize was superior to that of expert sight-readers.

Chase and Simon (1973) attribute the skilled experts' superiority to their extensive information bank in long-term memory, developed through experience with the skill domain, which enables them to rapidly perceive and recognize familiar patterns. Thus, long-term memory is hypothesized to contain an internal representation of such familiar patterns together with information concerning appropriate associated actions. Furthermore, Chase and Chi (1980) propose that the information is organized hierarchically. A number of patterns may, therefore, be represented in a single familiar configuration in long-term memory. Experience is proposed as the process through which one's knowledge base and cognitive structure are built up. The importance of skill-related experience or practice in the acquisition of a skill was illustrated in a study by Chi (1978) who compared experienced and inexperienced chess players. In her study, there was an interesting twist; the expert players were children (mean age, 10.5 years) and the novice players were adults. As in the Chase and Simon study, players were required to reconstruct meaningful chess positions presented briefly to them. They were also tested on a digit span task. Although adults were found to have superior recall for digits, the child experts' memory for chess positions was significantly superior. These results indicate that it is specifically skill-related practice that underlies expert performance rather than maturational factors or general, non-specific experience. It would not come as a surprise to music teachers to assert that 'practice is the major independent variable in the acquisition of skill' (Chase and Simon 1973). However, although practice is undoubtedly a crucial aspect of musical skills acquisition, the behaviour of music students as they practise remains an unexplored area.

In the domain of music, research has focused on sight-reading to investigate the acquisition of skills. While Shaffer (1981) has examined motor programming by investigating musical performance of professional pianists, little work has been directed to the acquisition process itself. The present study was designed to investigate the process of musical acquisition through an examination of the rehearsal behaviour of piano students varying in musical competence. The specific focus of the study was on practising strategies and how they change with increasing musical knowledge and expertise. In the first part of the study, the behaviour of 43 subjects from all music levels from Grade I to the Artist (Diploma) level, including three concert pianists, was compared as they practised three musical selections during a single practice session. In addition, the effect of increased familiarity with particular musical scores on practising behaviour was investigated in an attempt to discern the relative contributions to changes in rehearsal behaviour of musical competence acquired through long-term study and through short-term practice of specific materials. In the second part of the study, a subset of the players representing novice (Grade II students), intermediate (Grade VI students), and advanced (Artist; ARCT) levels of skill continued to practise their pieces for nine additional sessions (10 sessions in all). The pattern of practising behaviour across sessions was investigated in this part of the study. The study therefore used a cross-sectional approach, investigating performance across multiple trials. The behavioural domain under investigation was the subjects' natural practising of musical segments selected for their level of skill. Assessment consisted of two components, behavioural observations coded according to an observational rating scale, the Observational Scale for Piano Practising (OSPP), and self-report, tapped by means of a structured interview format. Of interest in the study were changes in the form and content of both behaviour and cognitive strategy as practising behaviour changed with increasing experience in music. Attention was specifically focused on how students chunked the music and how their chunking changed with musical experience, together with other changes that occurred concomitantly.

Method

Subjects

Subjects were 40 piano students taking individual instruction in piano, and three professional concert pianists. The students were graded according to the requirements of the University of Toronto's Royal Conservatory of Music, which provides grading standards for the region of South-Western Ontario. Subjects were defined as belonging to a particular level if they passed the Conservatory examinations for the previous level and were working on pieces for the designated grade. The subjects were selected so that three or four students from each musical level from Grade 1 to Grade X, and from the artist (ARCT) and professional levels, were included in the study. There were 33 females and 10 males ranging in age from six to 46 years and in experience from six months to 34 years, receiving instruction from one of 17 piano teachers. Details of the subjects' characteristics are presented in Table 5.1.

Table 5.1   *Subject characteristics*

Grade Level	*n*	Sex M	F	Age (*m̄* years)	Experience (*m̄* years)
I	3	2	1	10.00	2.53
II	4	1	3	9.75	2.15
III	3	1	2	10.30	2.40
IV	4	1	3	10.50	3.25
V	3	0	4	12.33	6.00
VI	4	1	3	13.75	4.87
VII	4	1	3	14.50	7.65
VIII	4	0	4	15.25	8.20
IX	3	0	3	20.33	10.17
X	4	0	4	17.50	10.87
ARCT	4	1	3	23.75	17.00
PROF	3	2	1	39.33	30.67

Materials

In order to present the subjects with music representing a variety of styles and challenges, music pieces were selected for each music level from three musical forms: a Baroque piece, a contemporary piece, and a sonatina. The selections were limited to approximately one page in length in order to maintain the practising demand for the students at a reasonable level.

Accurate grading of the music was important to ensure comparable levels of difficulty for the pieces across grade levels. In order to control for famliarity, pieces were selected that would have been unlikely to have been played previously. The Conservatory syllabus and the ratings of experienced music teachers were used to select pieces appropriate to the players' grade level that were unlikely to have been practised before.

All subjects were queried concerning whether they had actually played the pieces before; this revealed that the pieces were unknown to all but three subjects. When students had played a piece before, it was excluded from the study for those subjects.

Procedure

Part I

All 43 players were instructed to practise the three experimental scores as they would usually practise new pieces, and the practice sessions were recorded on cassette audio tape and later recorded according to the Observational Scale for Piano Practising described below. The very high reliability (Pearson $r = 0.97$) between *in vivo* observations and observations taken from audio tapes obtained in a previous study (Gruson 1978) confirmed the validity of the audio-taping procedure.

Part II

A subgroup of the players, four students in each of Grade II, Grade VI, and the Artist (ARCT) levels, were selected to represent novice, intermediate, and advanced levels of music proficiency. This subgroup of students was instructed to tape-record nine additional practice sessions (10 sessions in all). To represent a number of points in the acquisition process, the first, fourth, seventh, and tenth practice sessions were coded and analysed.

Observational Scale for Piano Practising (OSPP)

The Observational Scale for Piano Practising (OSPP) consists of the 20 categories defined in Table 5.2. The scale tapped length of uninterrupted playing, errors, repetitions of various unit lengths (notes, measures, larger sections), tempo changes, self-guiding speech, breaking down the piece into separate hands, giving up, playing music other than the designated piece, intervention of another person (for instance, parent), and a number of measures of practice time.

The format for recording required the rater to note, in its natural sequence, each incidence of a behavioural category as it occurred. To aid in this task, a recording sheet was constructed which divided the practice sessions into 5-s intervals. A stopwatch was used to mark the beginning of each 5-s interval. Frequency measures were employed for the majority of behaviours recorded since they tended to be discrete, momentary events. For measures that were more continuous (for example count aloud, hands separately, and uninterrupted playing), the behaviour was scored for each 5-s interval in which it occurred.

To assess inter-rater reliability, a randomly selected sample from 17 practice sessions recorded from 15 subjects was chosen. The 15 subjects represented in the sample were randomly selected with respect to experience level, age, and sex. In addition, a random selection was made from all practice sessions using the experimental stimulus pieces, from the first to the tenth session. A sample of 3174 behavioural codes recorded over a period of 185.8 min was rated by two experienced observers from audio-tapes using the OSPP. The Kappa coefficients (K) for each behavioural category ranged from 0.96 to 1.00, all of which were highly significant and confirm that the OSPP may be considered to have a high level of inter-observer reliability.

Table 5.2   *Observational Scale for Piano Practising (OSPP)*

Symbol	Name	Definition
Unint	Playing without interruption	S plays the piece for 5-s interval during which no other behavioural categories occur. Score for each 5-s interval S plays uninterrupted.
Error	Error	S plays incorrect note.
Repetition		
RNote	Repeat Note	S repeats a note on which an error may or may not have occurred with or without correction.
RMeasure	Repeat Measure	S repeats a measure, or a part of a measure, in which an error may or may not have occurred with or without correction.
RSection	Repeat Section	S repeats a section of the piece longer than a measure in which an error may or may not have occurred with or without correction.
RPiece	Repeat Piece	S repeats whole piece from the beginning after completing previous practice of entire piece. If S goes to the beginning of piece after playing only part of the piece, score as RSection.
Tempo changes		
Slow	Slow down	S slows the musical tempo beyond the range permitted by the music.

Pause	Pause	S stops playing for at least 2 s in a 5-s interval. Score for each 5-s interval.
Fast	Speed up	S increases the musical tempo from the normal tempo for a part of the piece. Score for each 5-s interval.
Verbalizations		
Guide Sp	Self-guiding statements	S directs his/her playing verbally, e.g. 'Slow down', 'I made a mistake, I'd better try again'.
Read	Read Aloud	S reads notes aloud before playing them.
Count	Count Aloud	S counts aloud to aid timing. Scored for each 5-s interval.
Frust	Frustration	S verbalizes or emits signs of frustration, e.g. sighs, grimaces, groans, frowns, complaints, negative self-statements.
Hands Sep	Hands Separately	S plays a piece or a section of a piece with one hand only. The onset only is scored by H. The offset is marked by TOG (indicating coordinated hands) or by the end of the piece (/).
Give Up	Gives up	S fails to complete the piece. This behaviour is followed by a new piece or the end of the session. This category would also be scored if S attempts only a part of the piece and does not play piece through to completion.
Play other	Playing other than the designated piece.	S plays something other than the music in the score.
Person	Intervention by another	Other (usually a parent) intervenes in the practice, offering assistance or direction.
TTime	Total time	The duration of time spent in practising, calculated as the sum of time spent practising each piece.
Time	Mean time/piece	$\dfrac{\text{Total time}}{\text{No. of pieces practised}}$
Tempo	Tempo	No. of notes/s of first practice in each session, averaged over pieces. This value was calculated from the first stretch of *unint* of at least 10-s duration.

Interview

An additional concern of the present study was the subjects' knowledge and understanding of their own practising behaviour. In order to assess the subjects' cognitions concerning their piano practising, all subjects in Part II and the three concert pianists were given an interview concerning their rehearsal behaviour following the tenth or last practice session. The interview included the following six questions:

(1) How did you go about practising the pieces?
(2) What did you pay attention to?
(3) How did your practising change as you learned the pieces?
(4) What did you do when you made an error?
(5) What advice would you have for another student at your level learning these pieces?
(6) Is there anything that you should have done when you practised that you know that you did not do?

Results

Part I

The rate of OSPP behaviours for the Part I data is presented in Fig. 5.1. Across all subjects, the most frequently occurring event was uninterrupted

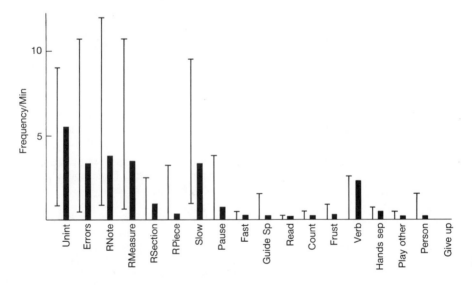

Fig. 5.1. Mean rate and range of practising behaviours per min: Session 1 (n = 43).

playing. The repetition of shorter units was the next most frequent type of event, repeating a single note accounting for 16.9 per cent of behaviours, and repeating measures, 16.7 per cent, while repeating sections accounted for only 2.6 per cent and repeating pieces, only 1.3 per cent. Slowing down was a frequently occurring event (16.0 per cent) while other tempo changes occurred less frequently. Errors also occurred frequently (14.3 per cent). The remaining behaviours occurred rarely, each accounting for less than 1 per cent of the total number of behaviours, although the sum of all self-verbalizations totalled 1.6 per cent of the total behaviours. In sum, students generally spend a quarter of their initial practice sessions in uninterrupted playing. When the flow of playing is broken, it is usually interrupted by errors, repetition (usually of short units), tempo reductions, pauses, and self-verbalizations.

But do all students practise alike? In order to investigate differences that may occur with increasing musical experience, the correlations between practising behaviours and skill level may be examined in Table 5.4. While it is a relatively infrequent event, repeating sections was the variable most significantly correlated with music level. Indeed, music level accounted for over 50 per cent of the variance in repeating sections. Music level

Table 5.3 *Correlations of OSPP categories with music level:* * *Study 1*

Category	r
Unint	0.22
Error	−0.31†
RNote	−0.31†
RMeasure	0.17
RSection	0.72††
RPiece	−0.21
Slow	−0.21
Fast	0.23
Pause	−0.31††
Guide Sp	0.39†
Read	−0.05†
Count	0.20
Frust	0.14
Hands Sep	0.49††
Play Other	0.07
Person	−0.26
Give Up	—
Verb	0.37†
Time	0.40†
Tempo	0.28

* Pearson product-moment correlation coefficient (r)
† $p < 0.05$
†† $p < 0.001$

accounted for 24 per cent of the variance in playing hands separately and between 10 and 16 per cent for each of errors, repeating notes, pauses, verbalizations, and, specifically, self-guiding speech, playing hands separately, and time. Higher music levels were also associated with reduced frequency of errors, repeating notes, and pauses.

Another way of looking at the relationship between competence and practising behaviour is to use the practising behaviour itself to discriminate between students of varying levels of competence. A discriminant functions analysis was carried out in order to determine which combination of practising behaviours could most parsimoniously and accurately discriminate students of differing skill levels. An examination of the 43 subjects suggested three groups in terms of the way music educators conceptualize music study. The three groups were divided by points that reflect certain watersheds in the career of a music student. Basic music training takes place in the first eight grades and students successfully completing Grade VIII receive a high-school credit for music. Senior music study begins in Grade IX, and the more difficult study of harmony is included in the programme at this level. Thus, the first cutpoint for the discriminant analysis was set between Grades VIII and IX. The second cutpoint was placed between the ARCT level and the concert pianist level, therefore distinguishing senior students from professional musicians. The three groups were, therefore, Grades I to VIII, Grade IX to ARCT, and professional concert pianists.

In order to arrive at the most parsimonious combination of variables that would successfully discriminate the three groups, a series of discriminant analyses was carried out, successively reducing the number of variables until the shortest, most discriminating series of variables was derived.

The analysis yielded 16 variables which in combination accurately classified all the 43 students into the three groups. A jack-knifed classification (which indicates the classification of a particular case into a group according to a function computed from all the data excluding that particular case) yielded an 88.4 per cent accuracy rate. The discriminant analysis indicated that the number of variables that emerged from the correlational analysis as relating to music level, such as repeating sections, pauses, playing hands separately, and time, were in fact important in discriminating the practising behaviour of students varying in level of skill. Repeating sections, particularly, emerged as an important discriminating variable and in order investigate the proportion of subjects that could be classified using only this single variable as discriminator, a discriminant function was computed including only repeating sections. The function yielded a 79.1 per cent success rate indicating that almost four-fifths of the subjects could be classified according to their use of this single behaviour.

In *summary*, the analysis of the data from the initial session revealed that a number of changes in practising behaviour occurred as students gained musical skill. Errors, repeated notes, and pauses tended to decrease with competence while self-guiding speech, total verbalizations, playing hands separately, time spent on each piece, and, particularly, repeating sections (0.18 per min for Grades I to VIII, 0.75 per min for Grades IX to ARCT, and 2.40 per min for professionals) increased as music level increased.

Part II

Let us now take a closer look at the subset of Grade II, Grade VI, and ARCT students, how their practising differed and how it changed across practice sessions. Sessions 1, 4, 7, and 10 were selected as samples of the practising process. The descriptive data are presented in Fig. 5.2.

A correlational analysis was first carried out between practising behaviour and music level for each of the four sessions sampled. The results are presented in Table 5.6. In the initial session of Study 2, grade level accounted for the most significant proportion of variance in repeating sections (77 per cent). Repeating sections continued to increase with skill level across all sessions (0.39 per min in Session 1 to 0.62 per min in Session 4). While playing hands separately and time also increased significantly as music level increased in the first session, these variables were not significantly correlated with skill in the later sessions. A number of other behaviours were related to experience at various points in the practising process. Specifically, uninterrupted play in Sessions 4 and 10 increased as music level increased; slowing down and repeating notes in Session 4, and tempo in Session 10, decreased as skill increased.

Another way of assessing changes in the relationship between practising behaviour and music level across practice sessions is by means of discriminant analyses repeated for the data from each of the four sessions examined. The discriminant analyses were used to investigate the stability of the variables discriminating between the three levels (Grade II, Grade VI, and ARCT) across sessions.

The three groups of subjects were successfully discriminated by three variables. For sessions 1, 4, and 7, the discriminating variables were identical: repeating sections, playing hands separately and pausing. In the final (tenth) session, playing hands separately was no longer found to be discriminating and uninterrupted play entered the function as the third discriminator. In all sessions, repeating sections was the most discriminating variable. Indeed, as the sole variable in the discriminant function, repeating sections was able to correctly classify 81.8 per cent of subjects in Session 1 and 72.7 per cent in each of Sessions 4, 7, and 10.

In order to investigate more directly the relationship between practising behaviour and sessions, a correlational analysis was carried out on all

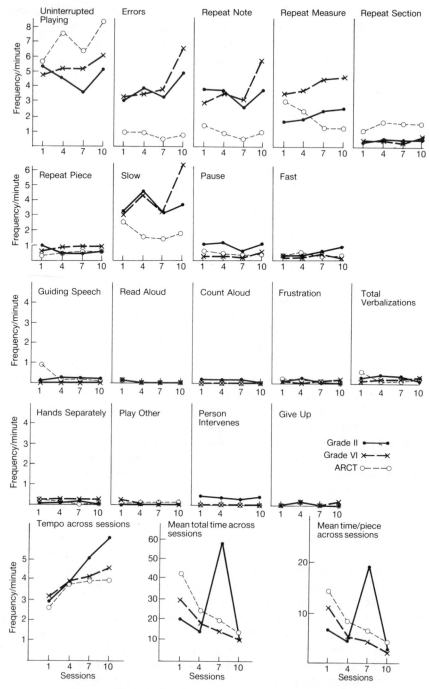

Fig. 5.2. Descriptive data for each level across sessions.

Table 5.4 *Correlations of OSPP categories with music level:* Study 2, Sessions 1, 4, 7, and 10.*

Category	Session 1	Session 4	Session 7	Session 10
Unint	0.00	0.63†	0.36	0.69†
Error	−0.54	−0.72	−0.53	−0.35
RNote	−0.44	−0.61†	−0.41	0.25
RMeasure	0.54	0.10	−0.16	0.14
RSection	0.88††	0.72†	0.72†	0.79†
RPiece	−0.36	−0.02	0.13	0.03
Slow	−0.21	−0.68†	−0.48	−0.16
Fast	0.50	0.30	−0.30	−0.34
Pause	−0.30	−0.55	−0.47	−0.50
Guidesp	0.43	−0.44	−0.35	−0.51
Read	−0.35	—	−0.35	—
Count	−0.25	−0.35	−0.26	0.35
Frust	0.28	−0.32	0.01	0.12
Hands Sep	0.62†	0.09	−0.05	0.15
Play Other	0.01	0.45	—	0.45
Person	−0.35	−0.35	0.35	−0.35
Give Up	—	−0.35	—	0.01
Verb	0.37	−0.23	−0.31	0.04
Time	0.71†	0.48	−0.27	0.25
Tempo	−0.19	−0.13	−0.55	−0.67†

* Pearson product-moment correlation coefficient (r)
† $p < 0.05$
†† $p < 0.001$

variables for each group and a one-way repeated measures analysis of variance was performed.

A number of significant correlations emerged although they were not found consistently for all three groups. Across sessions, repeating measures increased for Grade II (1.62 per min in Session 1 to 2.50 in Session 10) and Grade VI (3.55 per min in Session 1 to 4.69 in Session 10) students, repeating pieces increased for ARCT students (0.20 to 0.38), and speeding up increased only for the Grade II group (0.03 to 0.45). Repeating sections increased across sessions for all groups but not to a significant degree.

Analyses of variance were carried out involving a one-way repeated measures design for each behavioural category with music level as the independent variable and session number as the repeated variable. Significant main effects of music level were found for repeating sections, pausing, and verbalizations. These results support the findings of the correlational analyses that as music level increased, repeating sections increased. The correlational analysis for pauses and verbalizations produced no significant correlations although the discriminant functions analysis indicated that pauses could be helpful in discriminating between groups.

The descriptive data indicated a decrease in pauses with increasing skill. Looking at the data for repeated sessions, only tempo yielded a significant main effect across sessions and this variable also produced a significant interaction between music level and session number. The ANOVA and descriptive data indicate that while there were no large, consistent differences in tempo across the three subject groups, the Grade II students increased their tempo considerably more rapidly over sessions than did the more experienced groups. In addition, while the tempo maintained by the Grade II and Grade VI students increased steadily as session number increased, the tempo of the ARCT students had reached an asymptotic level before the seventh session. Thus, the less experienced students spent all 10 sessions increasing their tempo while the most experienced students mastered the pieces' tempo early in practising and were free to focus on other aspects. Self-reports indicated that the ARCT students knew the pieces fairly well after a few sessions and spent the later sessions experimenting with the pieces or memorizing them.

The impact of increased competence and practise experience may also be investigated on a more microscopic level by analysing the sequences of behaviours within practice sessions. In addition to the above analyses, a sequence analysis was carried out in which the behaviours following errors were examined. The analysis indicated that a repeated note was the most common event following an error, although for the more senior artist (ARCT) group, repeated measures increased in frequency across sessions. The category Repeating sections occurred rarely. The subjects' self-reports indicated that repeating sections was an event that would occur later in the response chain, following the repetition of shorter units.

In *summary* then, the results of Part II did not support the hypothesis that consistent changes in practising behaviours occurred with increasing practise of particular music pieces. The most salient finding was the impressive consistency across sessions of the importance of a number of variables, particularly repeating sections, as discriminators of students of different musical levels. Thus it appears to be many hours of practising a wide variety of music pieces that influences practising behaviours.

Interview

The interview was carried out as a means of tapping students' knowledge concerning their practising and investigating differences between subjects differing in musical experience. The Grade II, Grade VI, ARCT students and concert pianists (professionals) were included in this part of the study. Their responses to the six questions were given a quantitative and qualitative score, the quantitative score being the number of strategies described in the response and the qualitative score representing the degree of cognitive complexity and abstraction reflected in the response. The latter measure involved the rating of each response according to a four-point scale, each point representing the following types of practising strategy:

(1) *Simple undifferentiated.* This category refers to responses that do not specify behavioural strategies nor differentiate between types of music pieces played. The response is excessively general and gives no indication of any particular knowledge of specific strategies, for example, 'I try to do my best'; 'I try to work hard on the piece'.

(2) *Concrete behavioural.* This category includes responses that articulate specific behavioural responses that remain the same regardless of the piece played. The strategies are mechanically employed for all pieces and do not take into consideration the kind of material being practised nor the individual's experience with that kind of piece, for example, 'I go over the piece three times'; 'I play each piece hands separately first', 'I go over each error five times'.

(3) *General strategies.* This category includes responses that indicate the use of generalized strategies for dealing with the practising task. The strategy allows for specific behavioural elaborations that can be flexibly modified for the demands of the particular musical piece, for example, 'I divide the piece into chunks'; 'I correct the error and fit it into its phrase context'; 'I work on the fingering' (or timing, or phrasing' etc.).

(4) *Higher-order strategies.* This category refers to responses that involve higher-order chunking of the task. The strategies specify the general strategies that are carried out. They are abstract and general rather than behaviourally oriented, for example, 'I try to get a feel for the piece'; 'I work on technical problems'; 'I work on interpretation'.

The mean qualitative and quantitative scores for each music level are presented in Fig. 5.3. The graphs indicate that both the qualitative and quantitative scores increased with increasing musical skill. Analyses of variance revealed highly significant main effects for musical level for both qualitative scores ($F=8.72$; df=3,11; $p<0.005$) and quantitative scores ($F=32.19$; df=3.11; $p<0.001$). Thus, more experienced musicians report using more complex practising strategies and these strategies are more complex and abstract than those of less experienced students. One difficulty with the present results is the possible confounding of linguistic and cognitive complexity associated with age. In the present sample, age was highly correlated with music level ($r=0.75$) and the number of words produced in the subjects' interview protocols was highly correlated both with the number of strategies enumerated ($r=0.78$) and with their cognitive complexity ($r=0.73$). The effects of age on music students' self-reports merits further investigation in future research. For example, with a study following the methodology of Chi (1978) comparing the interview data of older, inexperienced players and younger, experienced musicians,

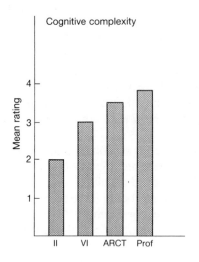 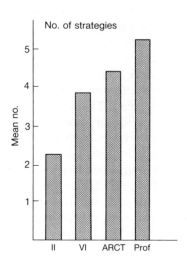

Fig. 5.3. Interview: descriptive statistics and ANOVA.

the confounding of age and cognitive and linguistic complexity could be evaluated.

The behavioural analyses pointed to the importance of repetition in the practising of music students. A specific analysis of Question (4) of the interview (What did you do when you made an error?) was carried out in order to investigate subjects' knowledge concerning the units of music they repeated. Fig. 5.4 presents the percentage of responses represented by each of the units of repetition examined for each group, confirmed by the performers as following errors in the interview protocols. Examination of the figure reveals that repeating notes occurred less frequently and repeating sections more frequently as music level increased. Thus the interview data corroborates the findings from the behavioural data.

Discussion

The results of the study indicate that significant changes in practising behaviour take place as individuals acquire competence as musicians. As music level increased, there was an increase in repeating sections, verbalizing, playing hands separately, and practice time, while errors, repeating notes, and pauses decreased. There were fewer behavioural changes across sessions. Tempo increased across practising sessions for all music levels but reached an asymptote in the early sessions for the more advanced pianists. The most consistent and significant finding was the change in the units of music repeated during practising as musical experience increased. The behavioural analyses indicated that as musical skill increased, students repeated sections of music more frequently and there was a tendency to reduce the number of notes repeated. Subjects' self-reports also indicated that the size of the unit of repetition increased with music level, corroborating the behavioural data. The interview data also revealed that more experienced students were able to conceptualize their practising behaviour in a more differentiated and abstract manner. They described more practising strategies and these strategies were found to be more cognitively complex. The changes in practising behaviour were far more significant between music levels than between practice sessions of individual pieces. Thus it appears to be the many, many hours of practising involved in mastering a new music level rather than the relatively few sessions it takes to learn an individual piece that bring about consistent and enduring changes in information processing.

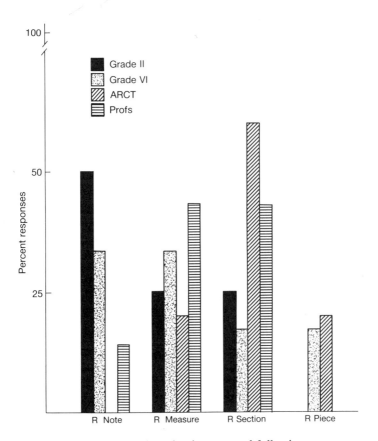

Fig. 5.4 Interview: size of units repeated following error.

In order to understand how changes are brought about through rehearsal, that is, how chunking takes place, two models may be helpful, that of automatization (Shiffrin and Schneider 1977) and that of motor programming (Shaffer 1980).The notion of automatization as articulated by Shiffrin and Schneider proposed that learning a skill requires a shift between information processing modes from controlled to automatic processing. Controlled processing was described as a slow and effortful mode under attentional control which is subject to the limitations of short-term memory and is serial in nature. Controlled processes tend to be accurate and can be flexibly applied to unfamiliar or changing situational demands. Extended and consistent repetition, such as occurs in practising, permits the establishment of associations in the long-term memory store which, with continued practice, may be triggered by familiar stimulus configurations appearing in short-term memory. Thus, an overlearned, routinized stimulus pattern comes to trigger the performance of a highly stereotyped inflexible behavioural sequence which runs to completion automatically, without the involvement of conscious control. Automatically learned sequences may be combined to form more complex units through a process labelled 'composition' by Neves and Anderson (1981). The composition process enables the more rapid execution of the combined routine.

Musical practising may be viewed as a sequence of transitions from controlled to automatic processing in which larger and larger chunks of musical information are built up from more basic subcomponents. The novice student might be expected to focus upon associating individual notes in the printed score with the corresponding positions on the musical instrument by means of controlled processing. With practice, the associations between printed notes and manual positions become automatized and attention may be focused upon more complex musical patterns such as chords, measures, and ultimately phrases and larger units which may, in turn, come to be executed automatically from a single glance at the score. With repeated practising, the unique sequence and integration of musical patterns in the piece may be executed automatically and the practiser finds himself or herself able to play the piece from memory.

Students' repetition patterns following errors can provide us with clues regarding how they process musical information. With musical expertise, a process of structural differentiation takes place. The beginning student tends to perceive a piece as an amorphous whole consisting of a series of independent notes which, with practising, he or she is able to execute in a more automated fashion. Thus, when a mistake is made, the novice will be likely to repeat the erroneous note or measure. The acquisition process for the beginner involves construction with musical building blocks to erect an integrated whole. The expert musician, however, tends to approach a piece from the top down. He or she is more likely to break the piece down into hierarchically organized patterns, differentiating it, for example, into a number of independent but linked sections. To correct an error, the skilled player is more likely to repeat the entire structural unit, the section, rather than a component note.

The results of the present research indicated that with increasing skill, on a cognitive level, pianists are able to describe a wider variety of practising strategies and these strategies are more complex, more abstract, and more flexible. Together with the notion of structural differentiation, the notion of motor programming may be added to the formulation to explain these changes. A motor programme, according to Shaffer (1980), may be viewed as a hierarchically organized series of plans. The acquisition of skill involves the development of higher-order plans that are more abstract and incorporate a number of simple components of the skill into more complex, superordinate units. Shaffer defines a plan as:

an abstract homomorphism of the performance, representing its essential structure. It does not represent all the details of the performance but allows these to be generated or accessed as they are needed in the execution.

In the performance of a skill, the motor programme calls into action an intention that provides a goal and the overall structure for the performance. This intention then calls into play increasingly more specific plans that may be executed automatically and in parallel. Thus this model incorporates the notion of the hierarchical organization of cognitive structures proposed by Chase and Chi (1980). In music, such hierarchical processing is found to take place both at a behavioural and a cognitive level. The inclusion of plans in the formulation takes into account not only the execution of automatized sequences of behaviour, but also the flexibility required in the performance of a complex skill.

In the study discussed here, the articulation of higher-order, more flexible plans was found in the self-reports of the more advanced musicians. On a behavioural level, the increase in the size of the units of repetition associated with increasing expertise reflects the hierarchical nature of motor programming in music performance.

Directions for future research

The research decribed in this paper was exploratory. There are a number of limitations and opportunities for future research efforts.

One of the major difficulties in the study was the small number of students investigated at each musical level. The reliability and generalizability of the findings need to be assessed by means of a replication incorporating a larger sample. In addition, a problem in the sample selection was the high correlation between age and music level, which made it difficult to ascertain whether differences in practising behaviour were related to increasing musical experience, increasing age, or a combination of both. While research in other areas, such as chess (for example Chi 1978), indicates that skill depends upon domain-specific experience rather than age, a similar finding needs to be demonstrated in the musical domain by comparing older beginners to more advanced younger students and including such individuals in the general sample. In addition to age, a number of other variables such as differences in teachers' style, students' motivation, and musical aptitude could also be investigated.

While the present study focused on differences in behaviour among music levels, it would be interesting to examine whether differences in practising behaviours exist between subjects of the same level. A larger subject sample would make such an analysis feasible and would provide important information concerning whether some subjects are able to use comparable musical experience to develop more mature patterns of practising than other students. Such data could be used to predict which students might become virtuosi in the future. In addressing the issue of prediction, a longitudinal investigation would be valuable in examining more directly the development of practising technique with experience. One could compare the earlier practising behaviour of students who are later musically successful to that of those who are less successful (for example, those who fail examinations) and those who drop out of music study. It would be particularly interesting to identify those behaviours which best predict future musical involvement and expertise; aspects of the performance, knowledge assessed by the interview, or both. If it is indeed possible to isolate more mature or effective practising strategies, it would be interesting to investigate by means of a specific training programme whether practising is modifiable or whether it is purely a function of experience.

In terms of the analyses, further modification of the OSPP would be useful. While the results underscored the importance of repetition of sections in the development of musical competence, this category could vary widely in size from a few notes to several lines of music. For future work, it would be important to examine sections of varying length separately. The research of Sloboda (1974, 1977) and the self-reports of students in the present study suggest that the phrase is a fundamental musical unit and it could be investigated singly, in addition to larger units such as a thematic line, a physical line, a page, a movement, and so forth. Hence, a more discriminating investigation of the units of information processing could be carried out.

Also of interest is what happens when information processing breaks down and errors occur. Subjects' interview data indicated that they differentiate between different types of errors and respond differently depending upon the kind of error made. In order to obtain a taxonomy of errors for use in future research, a microscopic analysis of errors derived from videotaped practice sessions could be performed.

A number of problems emerged in the interview study. First, there existed a possibility of confounding linguistic fluency and complexity, since verbal productivity was found to be highly correlated with both the qualitative and quantitative scores. To control for this variable, one could compose one's sample of subjects whose age and music level are not as highly correlated, and include age-matched control subjects with no musical experience. Another direction for future research would be a more formal analysis of the content of the protocols of subjects of varying levels.

In the present study, the interview was carried out following the tenth and last practice session. In order to gain an understanding of changes in students' knowledge and affective experience regarding their practising as it progresses, their self-reports may be obtained at a number of points in the practising process. Such a procedure would also permit an assessment of the impact of subjects' cognitions and affects on their practising behaviour. In addition, one could investigate alternate ways of assessing cognitions and affects by changing the format of the interview. For example, one might investigate differences in the data derived from a structured interview such as the one used in the present study, an endorsement (forced choice) procedure, and a coaching procedure (in which a student is required to teach another student at his or her level to play the same piece).

Finally, the generalizability of the findings may be assessed through the application of the methodology to a variety of complex skill domains. Indeed, the methodology employed in this research may be seen as a model which may be applied more generally to the investigation of the development of any skill.

Acknowledgement

The author wishes to thank Dr Donald Meichenbaum for his advice in designing the study and his helpful comments on an earlier version of this paper.

References

Bean, K. L. (1937). An approach to the reading of music. *Psychological Monograph,* **226**, 1–80.

Bhaskar, R. and Simon, H. A. (1977). Problem solving in semantically rich domains: an example from engineering thermodynamics. *Cognitive Science* **1**, 193–215.

Charness, N. (1979). Components of skill in bridge. *Canadian Journal of Psychology* **33** (1), 1–16.

Chase, W. G. and Chi, M. T. H. (1980). Cognitivie skill: implications for spatial skill in large scale environments. In *Cognition, social behaviour and the environment* (ed. T. Harvey). Lawrence Erlbaum Associates, Pontiac, Md.

Chase, W. G. and Simon, H. A. (1973). The mind's eye in chess. In *Visual Information Processing* (ed. W. G. Chase), Academic Press, New York.

Chi, M. T. H. (1978). Knowledge structures and memory development. In *Children's thinking: what develops?* (ed. R. Sieder). Thirteenth annual Carnegie Symposium on cognition, Lawrence Erlbaum Associates, Hillsdale, NJ.

Chi, M. T. H., Feltovich, P. J., and Glaser, R. (1980). Representation of physics knowledge by experts and novices. Technical Report No. 2. Learning Research and Development Center, University of Pittsburgh.

de Groot, A. D. (1965). *Thought and choice in chess*. Basic Books, New York.

Flower, L. S. and Hayes, L. R. (1979). *A process model of composition*. Technical Report No. 1. Carnegie-Mellon University, Pittsburgh.

Gruson, L. M. (1978). An observational study of the acquisition of musical skills. Unpublished M.A. thesis. University of Waterloo.

Krutetskii, V. A. (1976). *The Psychology of mathematical abilities in school children*. University of Chicago Press, Chicago.

Lannert, V. and Ullman, M. (1945). Factors in the reading of piano music. *American Journal of Psychology*, **58**, 91–9.

Larkin, J., McDermott, J., Simon, D. P., and Simon, H. A. (in press). Expert and novice performance in solving physics problems. *Science*.

Neves, D. M. and Anderson, J. R. (1981). Knowledge complication: mechanisms for the automatization of cognitive skills. In *Cognitive skills and their acquisition* (ed. J. R. Anderson). Lawrence Erlbaum, Hillsdale, NJ.

Reitman, J. S. (1976). Skilled perception in Go: deducing memory structures from inter-response times. *Cognitive Psychology* **8**, 336–56.

Shaffer, L. H. (1980). Analysing piano performance: a study of concert pianists. In *Tutorials in Motor Behaviour* (ed. G. E. Stelmach and T. Requin). North-Holland Publishing, New York.

Shaffer, L. H. (1981). Performances of Chopin, Bach and Bartok: studies in motor programming. *Cognitive Psychology* **13**, 326–76.

Shiffrin, R. M. and Schneider, W. (1977). Controlled and automatic human information processing 11: Perceptual learning, automatic attending and a general theory. *Psychological Review* **84**, (2), 127–90.

Simon, D. P. and Simon, H. A. (1978). individual differences in solving physics problems. In *Children's thinking: What develops?* (ed. R. S. Siegler). Lawrence Erlbaum, Hillsdale, NJ.

Simon, H. A. and Chase, W. G. (1973). Skill in chess. *American Scientist* **61**, 394–403.

Sloboda, J. A. (1974). The eye-hand span—an approach to the study of sight-reading. *Psychology of Music* **2**, (2), 4–10.

Sloboda, J. A. (1977). Phrase units as determinants of visual processing in music reading. *British Journal of Psychology* **68**, 117–24.

Thomas, E. H. C. and Jones, R. G. (1970). A model for subjective grouping in typewriting. *Quarterly Journal of Experimental Psychology* **22**, 353–67.

Weaver, H. E. (1943). Studies of ocular behaviour in music reading. *Psychological Monographs* **55**, (1), 1–29.

Wolf, T. (1976). A cognitive model of musical sight-reading. *Journal of Psycholinguistic Research* **5**, (1), 143–72.

6

Tonal structure and children's early learning of music

W. JAY DOWLING

When we listen to speech in our own language we hear words and sentences, and not mere sounds. Just so, when we listen to the music of our culture we hear melodies composed of meaningful pitches, and not uninterpreted sound. As Pick (1979) has pointed out, to hear a melody is to perceive a meaningful event extended in time—an event with structure, with constraints on its pattern organization, and in which still briefer events are embedded. Even the simplest of melodies presents a complex rhythmic organization of pitches in time. This structure is expressed in pitch and time relationships that link the notes of a melody and that remain largely invariant over the course of the event; melodies tend to move at a regular tempo and draw their pitches from a limited set of the infinite range of possibilities. Furthermore, some event patterns found within a given melody remain invariant across other melodies within the style and culture. For example, in Western music melodies usually end and often begin on the tonic (the focal pitch of a key or tonality) and share patterns of phrase repetition (such as the AABA pattern common to many popular songs and hymns). As Pick and Gibson (1969; Gibson and Levin 1975) have suggested, the perceptual learning that provides the listener with the means of understanding meaningful events such as melodies involves learning to extract relevant pattern invariants from the complex of information available.

Invariants of tonal structure

Some invariants of melodic structure are explicitly accessible in conscious experience to the typical adult. For example, most adults know explicitly that 'Three Blind Mice' closes with a copy of its opening phrase, and notice when a child does not end it that way. Other invariants are not explicitly accessible to adults without training, but with training can become so. For example, adults without music lessons are rarely able to describe the pattern of 1- and 2-semitone intervals in the major diatonic scale, while that pattern is one of the fundamentals learned early in formal musical training. Still other invariants remain implicit in the knowledge of even highly trained adults. For example, certain broad aspects of pattern organization described by Lerdahl and Jackendoff (1983) are unlikely to occur to musicians before reading their book (otherwise the book would not be so interesting). And the regularities of melodic structure pointed out by Rosner and Meyer (1982) had probably not occurred to the reader beforehand. Yet presumably such pattern invariants formed an implicit part of musicians' knowledge of the style described.

Even invariants that can on occasion be explicitly accessible usually remain implicit in their usual functioning in the cognition of music. In fact, effective, enjoyable listening normally relies on their remaining so, since, as Meyer (1956) has noted, focusing attention on formal properties while listening can easily interfere with meaningful experience of the music. That our knowledge of pattern invariants shapes our cognition of music can be illustrated by numerous examples. Shepard and Jordan (1984) showed that listeners' judgements of a scale formed of actually equal logarithmic intervals were distorted in ways predicted by their reliance on knowledge of the irregular diatonic pattern. As Francès (1958) noted, our implicit knowledge of the diatonic scale allows us to hear a performer's minor intonation errors as instances of scale categories. Greater departures from the pattern invariant such as out-of-key notes are glaringly noticeable, as Cuddy *et al.* (1979) showed. Furthermore, listeners often confuse exact transpositions of a melody with imitations in which the same diatonic interval pattern has been shifted along the scale they have just been hearing (Dowling 1978), and this confusion diminishes with increasing alterations in the scale; that is, with shifts in the underlying pattern invariants (Bartlett and Dowling 1980).

Expectancy and encoding

The listener's largely implicit knowledge of invariants of musical patterns serves both to guide expectancies (or 'set') for new events and to provide ready encoding schemes for the events that actually occur. These two processes typically work hand in hand in the cognition of pieces of music. The expectancies created by initial events in a piece probably facilitate efficient encoding of ensuing events, as Haber (1966) suggests. And the ways in which those events are encoded in turn determines the expectancies that are generated for subsequent events. The readying of knowledge-based encoding schemes is very useful in the processing of the rapid and complex stimulus sequences found in speech and music. As Haber (1966) noted,

Stimuli for which [a person] has no code for translation into memory are notoriously difficult to remember, even though [an observer] may perform perfectly on . . . discriminations with such stimuli. . . . Most people experience this difficulty in describing colors, tastes, odors, and feelings from recollection. . . . These examples represent instances of excellent matching between the stimulus and prior experience, but very poor encoding of the stimulus into memory.

Fortunately, mere exposure to the music of one's culture induces sufficient perceptual learning to provide a fundamental encoding scheme for pitch. With further training the listener's encoding schemes become more elaborated, leading to changes in performance on memory tasks, and presumably in what is heard when listening to music. This is a process in which listeners become attuned to the perceptual invariants of the music of their culture, and consequently become more efficient perceivers of that music.

This encoding scheme for pitch develops during the first eight years of life, and the pattern of its development is quite regular. New evidence, however, suggests that children's progress in this development may be more rapid than had previously been supposed.

Invariants and development

Infancy

Relatively recent reviews have depicted the development of sensitivity to melodic invariants in broad outline (Dowling 1982a, Dowling and Harwood 1986, Chap. 5). The evidence indicates that melodic contour—the pitch pattern of ups and downs—is an important feature in melody perception from early infancy on. In a noteworthy study Trehub et al. (1984) used conditioning of head turning to show that infants of 8 to 11 months are sensitive to a variety of changes in immediate repetitions of six-note melodies—changes in pitches height of the whole melody (transposition and changes in pitch within a melody (either substitutions at the same general pitch height, or octave alterations of some pitches), as well as changes in melodic contour. However, when Trehub et al. increased the difficulty of the task by adding a 'distractor sequence' interpolated between repetitions of the melodies, the infants responded principally to changes in contour. The infants treated repetitions with altered diatonic pitches and transpositions involving small alterations of pitch height as equivalent to exact repetitions, while noticing gross changes in the pitch height of single notes (octave alterations) and contour changes. Melodic contour is a critically important feature of melodies for infants, and remains so into adulthood (Dowling and Fujitani 1971). Contour is one of the most obvious features of a melody to remain invariant across its instances.

Contour is important to early song production as well as to perception. Around the age of one year children begin to sing spontaneous songs that are clearly differentiated from speech patterns by their rhythmic regularity and their tendency to elongate vowels on discrete pitch levels.* While the child during the first two years uses discrete pitch levels, those pitch patterns do not correspond to adult pitch categories established by the culture. That is, though single notes typically rest on well-defined pitches (as opposed to a siren effect), those pitches do not recur in invariant patterns from song to song, or even within songs. Children when they begin singing do not have pitch scales, though they have a prerequisite component of scales, namely, discrete pitches.

Singing during the early years consists largely of the control of melodic-rhythmic contour patterns.** In an analysis of 579 spontaneous songs produced by two children between the ages of one and six years, Dowling (1984b) found that even at the earliest ages songs consisted of patterns of repetition and alternation of brief melodic-rhythmic kernels. Around the age of two years a typical song consisted of the repetition at different pitch levels of a brief melodic phrase. These phrases remained constant in rhythmic and melodic outline throughout the song, and typically involved the repetition of a verbal phrase (such as 'Come a duck on my house', or 'Hoppy-hoppy run 'round the road'). Time within phrases was organized in a metrical beat structure on which the speech rhythms of the words of the phrase were overlaid, but that structure was often interrupted between phrases by breathing and other discontinuities.

The complexity of spontaneous songs increased over the first four years of life, both in terms of the number of phrases used and the pattern of their use. While songs with more than four distinguishable phrase contours were rare throughout that age range, there was a shift in the frequency of songs with just one repeated phrase. Songs with one phrase contour were fairly common between the ages of one and two years. By the age of three years

* Though I had noted indications in the literature that this spontaneous singing behaviour sometimes began as early as six months (for example, Ostwald 1973), I had been doubtful concerning the clarity of discrete pitch levels and rhythmic organization at such early ages. However, Ann Tubbs, a graduate student at UT/Dallas, has recently collected examples from a six-month-old boy that clearly exhibit rhythmic regularity and discrete pitches. I believe the onset of spontaneous singing can vary widely in the range of six to 18 months.
** We should not allow the emphasis in the adult experimental psychology literature on purely melodic contour (with rhythmic patterns typically held constant) to obscure the fact that in the perception and production of real melodies in the world the critically important component is an abstract contour pattern that captures both rhythmic and pitch-pattern invariants (Monahan 1984). As Dowling and Harwood (1986) pointed out, changing the rhythmic pattern of a tune while retaining the melodic contour will make the tune all but unrecognizable.

those had become rare, and songs in which three phrases occurred in varied patterns of repetition and alternation predominated. For songs where two or three phrases were involved the phrase-structure pattern changed between the ages of one and three years. A pattern that became more and more common with increasing age was one in which two, three, or four phrases would recur in some pattern of repetition, and which ended with yet another 'coda' phrase that had not yet occurred in the song. This last structure occurs in a number of nursery songs such as 'Mary Had a Little Lamb', 'Here We Go 'Round the Mulberry Bush', 'London Bridge', and 'On Top of Old Smokey' (all ABAC); 'D'ye Ken John Peel' (AABC); and 'Good King Wenceslaus' (ABABCBDE). But interestingly, this regular phrase structure pattern was more common in the children's songs that in their nursery song models. The children had latched on to a simple pattern that they used to control their songs, thereby constraining them in this respect more tightly than the song models provided them.

Childhood

Singing during the ages of one to five years is thus largely a matter of controlling the pattern of repetition of rhythmic-melodic phrase contours. On the basis of earlier evidence I had come to believe that until the age of five years or so children remain insensitive to subtler aspects of pitch; that is, they mostly sing 'out of tune' by adult standards. However, during that period they do learn more and more nursery songs that model the adult pitch classes of the *do-re-mi* scale, and they do sing them more and more in tune. And now there is new evidence that such experience leads at least some children by the age of four years to be sensitive to invariants in the details of the pitch pattern of melodies, both in noticing contour-preserving changes in the pitch intervals of familiar melodies, and in distingushing novel tonal melodies (that conform to the scale invariants) from atonal ones (that do not).

Trehub *et al.* (1985) asked four-to-six-year-olds to identify variants of 'Happy Birthday' and 'Twinkle, Twinkle, Little Star' as either normal or 'funny'. Presumably distortions that violated the child's own internal models of the songs, and that could be detected given the precision of the child's processing capabilities, would trigger 'funny' responses. If the child were relying solely on contour in responding to the songs, then alterations that preserved contour should not sound 'funny'. However, 'funny' responses to changes in pitch intervals where contour is preserved can be taken to indicate that the child is relying on more than just contour in judging the melodies. Adults, even with no musical training, are very sensitive to changes of pitch intervals in familiar melodies. Trehub *et al.* found that the children behaved like adults in rejecting versions of both of these tunes in which pitch intervals had been changed, as well as versions that changed contour. For 'Twinkle, Twinkle' rejection on the basis of interval change was as great as for contour change, while for 'Happy Birthday' contour violations caused more rejections than interval violations. Thus for some well-known, familiar melodies four-and five-year-olds are able to notice changes in intervals from the models, as well as changes in contour.

Trehub *et al.* (1985) incidentally tested the notion that kindergarteners are sensitive to changes of key—to shifts in the tonal center and the set of pitches that make up the 'do-re-mi' scale underlying a melody. This tendency had been observed by Bartlett and Dowling (1980) as an increased tendency to reject a comparison melody the further it departed from a standard stimulus in terms of 'key distance' (a measure of shared pitches in the diatonic scale—the greater the number of shared pitches the smaller the distance). Trehub *et al.* observed such an effect as well, obtaining more 'funny' responses to far-key comparisons than to same-key comparisons (with near-but-different-key comparisons intermediate). This adds to our evidence that children in this age range are becoming sensitive to certain invariants of the culturally determined scale patterns.

The foregoing evidence shows that preschoolers are sometimes sensitive to pitch substitutions that alter the intervals of familiar tunes, and to transpositions of familiar tunes that take them into relatively distant keys using different sets of tonal scale pitches. Adults, especially musically trained adults, can also discriminate between melodies that are tonal—that conform to the invariants of a tonal scale pattern—and those that are not (Dowling 1978). I was curious to find out whether preschoolers would display sensitivity to the tonality vs. the atonality of melodies. Sensitivity to altered pitches in familiar melodies might simply reflect specific knowledge of certain well-learned tunes, and not reflect general knowledge of invariants of scale structure. However, sensitivity to 'atonal' alterations of pitch that violate scale invariants, as compared with tonal alterations that remain within the scale structure, can be taken as an indication that the child had some knowledge of the tonal structure of melodies in general—knowledge of the cultural invariants. Therefore, we conducted the following experiment.*

Preschoolers' sensitivity to atonal melodies

Method

The experimenter visited preschools and kindergartens in the Dallas area, and tested the children individually in isolated rooms in the schools. Eight

* I thank James C. Bartlett for helpful suggestions in the design of this experiment, and Melinda Andrews for carrying it out.

three-year-olds (that is subjects between the ages of 3.0 and 4.0 years), 12 four-year-olds, and 12 five- and six-year-olds served in individual sessions. The experiment was replicated with a group session for eight college students at UT/Dallas (mean age = 29.6 years), who divided evenly into those with two or more years of music lessons, and those with no musical training.

The stimuli were 16 brief melodies approximately 8 s long, presented at a rate of two crotchets per s (where a crotchet represents the most common note value of the melody). The melodies were derived from eight familiar tunes in the key of C major: 'Mary Had a Little Lamb', 'Frère Jacques', 'Yankee Doodle', 'Old Macdonald', 'Oh, Susanna', 'Good King Wenceslaus', 'London Bridge', and 'Waltzing Matilda'. From each tune two new melodies were derived: one tonal and the other atonal. The tonal derivatives were created by shifting the melodic pattern along the C major scale so as to preserve the contour and diatonic intervals, but alter the interval sizes among the notes. (All the tonal derivatives still either began or ended—and usually both began and ended—on one of the pitches of the tonic triad: C–E–G.) The atonal derivatives were created by placing the melodic patterns at analogous points on an 'atonal' scale designed to produce interval patterns not contained in either the major or the minor diatonic scales in Western music. This scale consisted of the set of pitches C–D flat–E–F–G flat–A flat–B—an interval set with half-steps between the first and second, third and fourth, fourth and fifth, and seventh and eighth degrees, augmented seconds between the second and third degrees and sixth and seventh degrees, and a whole-step between the fifth and sixth degrees. The purpose of this method of generating stimuli was to preserve the average interval size and the amount of pitch repetition characteristic of melodies familiar to the children. This was especially important in the atonal derivatives, where it would not have been as satisfactory simply to substitute non-scalar pitches for scalar ones in isolated instances. The mean interval sizes were 1.66 and 1.69 semitones/interval for tonal and atonal stimuli respectively, counting unisons (note repetitions) as zero semitones.

All 16 stimuli were presented to each subject. Two different random orders of the stimuli were tape-recorded using the 'clarinet' voice of a Yamaha synthesizer, and each tape was presented to half the subjects in each age group. Thus the two derivatives—tonal and atonal—of each seed melody were presented to each subject.

The experimenter brought a tape-recorder, two stuffed animals (rabbit and bear), and a 'puppet-theatre' screen to the school. At the start of the session the experimenter conversed briefly with the child, and asked the child to sing a song, most often 'Happy Birthday'. (For the younger children the experimenter suggested that it was the bear's birthday.) All the children except for four three-year-olds sang something, which the experimenter recorded. The experimenter sat behind the puppet-theatre screen, and the child sat in front of it. The experimenter explained that the two animals liked different sorts of songs. (The animals' preferences were alternated from subject to subject. For older children who considered them too childish the animals were dispensed with.) One of the animals liked songs that had all normal notes in them. The experimenter played an example of a tonal melody, and displayed the animal that liked that type. The other animal liked 'funny' songs that had notes in them that sounded 'odd' or 'different from the other notes'. The experimenter displayed the other animal and played an example of an atonal melody. Then the experimenter presented the task in which the curtain of the puppet theatre would be drawn and the subject would listen to a melody. Behind the screen was the animal that liked that song, and the subject had to guess which animal it was. After the subject guessed, the curtain was opened to reveal which animal it really was. (This provided feedback for the trial.)

The songs the children taped at the start of the session were rated by 12 independent judges for 'how well in tune' the children sang. The children in each age group were divided at the median for those ratings into higher- and lower-rated singing groups. The four three-year-olds who did not sing at all constituted the lower-rated group for that age.

Results

Table 6.1 shows per cent correct judgements for the subjects with higher- and lower-rated singing in the three children's age groups, and for the adults. A 2-ratings ×3 ages analysis of variance on the children's data showed only a main effect of song rating, F (1,26) = 5.37, $p<.05$. Children's performance in all the age groups was essentially at chance for those whose singing received low ratings, and was significantly better than that for the chidren with higher ratings of singing intonation.

Table 6.1 *Per cent correct responses discriminating tonal from atonal melodies distributed according to song performance (children) or musical experience (adults)*

| | Group | |
Age	Low Song Rating (inexperienced)	High Song Rating (experienced)
3 yr	50	58
4 yr	50	59
5–6 yr	46	61
Mean for children	49	59
adult	70	72

Discussion

The most interesting feature of these results is that children as young as three and four years, provided they were among the more competent singers, displayed the ability to respond to the degree of tonality of the stimuli. Presumably even at such early ages increased facility with simple musical materials—the songs learned at home and at school—goes hand in hand with facility in discriminating melodies on the basis of invariant properties such as conformity to standard scales. It seems plausible that nursery songs that emphasize the pitch content of the basic scales in the culture, without shifts of key or the introduction of altered pitches foreign to the key, would best facilitate perceptual learning involving the scale invariants. The next piece of evidence suggests that nursery songs are simple in just that way.

Tonal structure of nursery tunes

The best materials from which to learn the invariants of the tonal scale patterns are tunes in which those invariants are most clearly present; namely, tunes that introduce few alterations of pitch into the basic pattern. To the extent that nursery songs fill this need for simple learning materials for the scale system, we should expect them to be strongly tonal, and to contain relatively few departures from the key in which they start. Folk-songs from the same culture, but intended for adult singing, could be expected to contain more variant pitches departing from their initial keys. 'Art' songs, intended to be sung by advanced amateurs and professionals, should contain still more variation of pitch material. To test these possibilities I counted songs in those three categories that contained, and that did not contain, alterations of pitch which respect to the starting key of the song.

Method

I assembled a collection of 223 nursery songs from a group of books labelled as such by their editors (Seeger 1948; Moorat 1980; Beall and Nipp 1982). For adult folk-songs I used the 317 songs in Lomax (1975). And for art songs I used the 44 songs in Schubert's (1823, 1827) *Die schöne Müllerin* and *Die Winterreise*. I chose Schubert for this comparison because his songs, especially in these song cycles, have a folk-like, singable character, and are of the same general length and form as the songs in the other categories. That is, these songs of Schubert are as close as any in the Classical–Romantic tradition of European music to the European folk-song tradition.

Results

I categorized each song according to whether it contained alterations of pitch that departed from its initial key. The results are shown in Table 6.2. Clearly very few nursery tunes contain such departures, while the adult folk-songs contained more. All but two of the Schubert songs contained alterations. A chi-square on the 2×2 matrix involving nursery and adult folk-songs, altered or not, was signficant, chi-square $(1)=45.38$, $p<.01$.

Table 6.2   *Number of nursery, folk, and Schubert songs with and without pitches altered with respect to the starting key of the song*

	Nursery Songs	Adult Folk-songs	Schubert Songs
No Altered Notes	208	220	2
Altered Notes	15	97	42
Total	223	317	44

Discussion

Nursery tunes clearly differ, not only from Classical–Romantic art songs, but also from adult folk-songs in the culture, with respect to the simplicity of their tonal schemes. Nursery songs emphasize the repetition of strongly tonal patterns, and avoid the introduction of pitches that depart from the key established at the outset. They are thus ideal vehicles for perceptual learning of the invariants of the tonal scale pattern.

In passing, let me add a word about the differences between the adult folk-songs, one-fourth of which include altered pitches, and the Schubert songs. Generally, when a folk-song uses an altered pitch it is either as a chromatic passing tone, interpolated into the passage between two solidly tonal scale steps, or it involves playing with the differences between the major and minor (or other) modes, as with the alterations in the song 'Greensleeves'. Rarely do such alterations involve a change of key—a shift in the tonal centre and in the scale pattern. However, of the 42 songs in the Schubert sample that introduced alterations, 36 involved brief changes of key, typically modulations to the dominant. Thus the Schubert songs, simple and folk-like though they appear, contain not only more instances of altered pitches, but also a preponderance of altered pitches that signal shifts in the tonal structure of the song. Kessen (1981), in emphasizing the child's need for simple learning materials in acquiring basic knowledge of musical structure, points out the inappropriateness of the derivatives of tonally elaborate late-Romanticism for that function. From this comparison it appears that even Schubert songs may be more complicated than is optimal for preschoolers' acquisition of the tonal system.

Musical experience and adult encoding

I wish to turn now to some new evidence bearing on the role of perceptual learning in the development of encoding schemes that reflect invariant patterns in musical structure. I will present evidence that even musically untrained listeners will, under certain circumstances, encode pitches in terms of the culturally defined pitch categories of the equal-tempered scale, as well as evidence that listeners with more training utilize more elaborate encoding strategies that involve diatonic pitch categories, defined within key structures.

Assimilation of quarter-steps

Even without specialized training in music, listeners use an encoding scheme for pitch arising from perceptual learning through exposure to their culture's 'tonal material'—the invariant describing the set of all possible pitch relationships in the culture (in Western music the 'chromatic' scale of all the semitones on the piano—Dowling 1978, 1982b, 1984a). This categorical encoding is apparent in the judgements of both musically trained and untrained listeners when judging pitches embedded in melodic contexts. In order to disclose this effect listeners must be put in a situation requiring rapid processing of tones, presumably via encoding guided by expectancies. As the quotation cited above from Haber (1966) suggests, listeners tend to be quite accurate when they can simply make direct comparisons between stimuli without using memory. However, following a familiar melody temporally interleaved with distractor tones presents them with a much more complicated problem. Previous results had shown that listeners can detect a familiar melody when its notes are temporally interleaved with the notes of a distractor pattern (at a rate of 8 or 10 notes/s in the same pitch range and of the same timbre and loudness, Dowling 1973). Recent results show that when listeners follow the pitch of a wandering tone in such a melody, and then compare its pitch with that of a subsequent probe tone, they make systematic errors (Dowling 1985). Those errors generally consist of judging half-step probes equal in pitch to actually presented quarter-steps, while making accurate responses to actually present half-steps. Thus quarter-steps appear to be encoded as neighbouring half-steps, while the half-steps appear to be encoded accurately.

Since listeners with no formal musical training show this assimilation effect of encoding quarter-steps as neighbouring semitones of the tonal material, that encoding scheme would seem to be due to the extraction of the tonal-material invariant as a result of listening to a considerable quantity of the music that invariant describes. This result provides counter-evidence to the view of those who, with Serafine (1983), consider results establishing the psychological reality of formal properties of music to be artifacts arising from the formal training of the subjects. In that sense it converges with results noted above concerning untrained listeners' confusions in immediate memory of similar melodies displaced along the diatonic scale (Dowling 1978, Bartlett and Dowling 1980).

Effects of tonal context

With increasing experience from non-musician through professional, listeners become more and more proficient in tasks involving memory for music (Francès 1958). In some cases increased experience brings about qualitative changes in *what* information is encoded into memory. For example, it has been shown that both experienced and untrained listeners distinguish alterations to melodies stored in long-term memory (Dowling and Bartlett 1981; Dewitt and Crowder 1986). Qualitative differences in memory performance were disclosed by a task in which a to-be-remembered melody was introduced with chords that specified the melody's location on the major diatonic scale (Dowling 1986). Listeners were told when tested to respond positively to transpositions and to reject test items with alterations. Chordal context either remained constant or shifted at test (for example, a melody beginning 'do-re-mi' introduced after a tonic chord could remain the same, or become a melody beginning 'sol-la-ti' introduced after a dominant chord). Untrained listeners performed better than chance and were unaffected by context shifts, presumably basing their judgements upon the interval patterns of the transpositions, perhaps encoding them as semitone intervals, as in the study described above. Adults with moderate amounts of musical training (average age 30 years, with about five years of music lessons) performed better than the untrained adults as long as context remained constant at test; when context shifted, however, their performance fell to chance. This suggests that a moderate amount of training leads listeners to use an implicit coding scheme based on the familiar major diatonic scale, analogous to a movable-'do' system, in which melodies are remembered as sequences of diatonic scale steps. Professional musicians faced with the same task performed equally well with changed as with constant context. Presumably the professionals have the diatonic encoding scheme at their disposal, but also have other resources with which to avoid errors when that scheme would lead them into trouble.

The performance of the moderately experienced listeners in the foregoing study illustrates an important point about the nature of perceptual learning and the schemes it produces. Those listeners' knowledge of the diatonic scale pattern, which they used in the melody-recognition task, was based on their experience as school-age youngsters with hearing and (especially) producing music. That knowledge remained, however, inaccessible to their conscious experience. Making this kowledge of scale-step values of pitches explicitly accessible is difficult, as witnessed by the fact that first-year conservatory students (with about twice the amount of training) nevertheless typically need to take courses in *solfège* and ear-training, in which they learn explicit labels (such as 'do, re, mi') for the scale steps.The moderately experienced listeners would be bewildered if asked to assign *solfège* labels to the notes of melodies. But though their knowledge of the scale patterns was implicit, it remained effective in governing their memory for novel melodies, even after more than 10 years had elapsed since their last music lesson. An encoding scheme can be learned implicitly through exposure to and practice with structured events. And once learned, such a scheme continues in use even though the behaviours that led to its acquisition have largely faded into the past.

Octave-scrambled melodies

A third type of experiment that disclosed differences in encoding strategy resulting from musical training is one in which listeners are asked to identify octave-scrambled melodies—patterns in which successive notes of a melody are randomly assigned to different octaves while retaining their 'chromas', their positions in the tonal scale. As with the rapid interleaved melodies, listeners are unable to identify an octave-scrambled melody when they hear it without any context to suggest its identity (Deutsch 1972). However, if some cue precedes the octave-scrambled test melody, listeners perform better than chance in evaluating it as either matching or not matching that cue. I believe the cue melody provides a set of expected pitches against which the listener can try to match the pitches of the octave-scrambled test pattern. Differences attributable to experience are most clearly shown when atonal melodies are contrasted with tonal ones in this task (Dowling 1984c). On each trial a seven-note cue was presented, all in one octave. Then 3 s later the listener heard an octave-scrambled pattern that either matched, or did not match, the cue melody with respect to where within the octave its pitches fell. In keeping with the supposition that inexperienced listeners principally encode pitches without regard to their place in the tonal structure, inexperienced subjects in this task performed about the same whether the target melodies were tonal or atonal, achieving about 60 per cent correct responses in both cases. The experienced listeners, however, found tonal targets easier to evaluate, identifying about 70 per cent correctly (vs. about 56 per cent for the atonal targets). Here again, moderately experienced listeners appear to be encoding the pitches of the melodies in terms of tonal scale steps, and in this task (unlike the context-shift task described above) that strategy pays off in better performance. And again, this strategy was not explicitly adopted by these moderately experienced subjects, but rather had been implicitly built into their auditory processing systems through years of perceptual learning.

Summary

I began this review by considering the process of listening to music as one of perceiving pattern invariants in musical events, as suggested by Pick (1979). Those invariants hold over various ranges of events. Some, such as melodic contour, hold for particular melodies and phrases; while others, such as the structure of a diatonic scale, hold for large sets of melodies including novel ones not yet heard. In some cases listeners have explicit, verbal knowledge of musical pattern invariants, but for the most part that knowledge remains implicit, appearing only when disclosed by especially contrived tasks.

Knowledge of pattern structure develops through perceptual learning. As Shepard (1984, pp. 431–2) has pointed out,

Perception cannot adequately be described simply as an individual act of picking up an invariant that is presented in that particular stimulus. What is perceived is determined as well by much more general and abstract invariants that have instead been picked up genetically over an enormous history of evolutionary internalization [as well as those] acquired through past experience by each individual.

I reviewed evidence concerning the perceptual learning that goes on throughout childhood, and described an experiment showing that individual differences in the perception of broad-scale structure invariants begins to emerge as early as the age of three years. Further individaul differences arise later in life, depending on perceptual learning experiences with music. Differences in experience lead to differences in implicit encoding strategies for pitch between listeners with little musical training and those with moderate amounts. Differences in prior perceptual experience lead to differences in what is perceived in the present.

References

Bartlett, J. C. and Dowling, W. J. (1980). The recognition of transposed melodies: a key-distance effect in developmental perspective. *Journal of Experimental Psychology: Human Perception and Performance* **6**, 501–15.

Beall, P. C. and Nipp, S. H. (1982). *Wee sing: around the campfire.* Price/Stern/Sloan, Los Angeles.

Beall, P. C. and Nipp, S. H. (1983). *Wee sing: silly songs*. Price/Stern/Sloan, Los Angeles.

Cuddy, L., Cohen, A. J., and Miller, J. (1979). Melody recognition: the experimental application of musical rules. *Canadian Journal of Psychology* **33**, 148–57.

Deutsch, D. D. (1972). Octave generalization and tune recognition. *Perception and Psychophysics* **23**, 411–12.

Dewitt, L. A. and Crowder, R. G. (1986). Recognition of novel melodies after brief delays. *Music Perception* **3**, 259–74.

Dowling, W. J. (1973). The perception of interleaved melodies. *Cognitive Psychology* **5**, 322–37.

Dowling, W. J. (1978). Scale and contour: two components of a theory of memory for melodies. *Psychological Review* **85**, 341–54.

Dowling, W. J. (1982a). Melodic information processing and its development. In *The psychology of music* (ed. D. Deutsch), pp. 413–29. Academic Press, New York.

Dowling, W. J. (1982b). Musical scales and psychophysical scales: their psychological reality. In *Crosscultural perspectives on music* (ed. T. Rice and R. Falck), pp. 20–8. University of Toronto Press, Toronto.

Dowling, W. J. (1984a). Assimilation and tonal structure: comment on Castellano, Bharucha & Krumhansl. *Journal of Experimental Psychology: General* **113**, 417–20.

Dowling, W. J. (1984b). Development of musical schemata in children's spontaneous singing. In *Cognitive processes in the perception of art* (ed. W. R. Crozier and A. J. Chapman), pp. 145–63. North-Holland, Amsterdam.

Dowling, W. J. (1984c). Musical experience and tonal scales in the recognition of octave-scrambled melodies. *Psychomusicology* **4**, 13–32.

Dowling, W. J. (1985). Assimilation of quarter-steps to half-steps by musically untrained listeners. Paper presented to the Psychonomic Society, Boston.

Dowling, W. J. (1986). Context effects on melody recognition: scale-step versus interval representations. *Music Perception* **3**, 281–96.

Dowling, W. J. and Bartlett, J. C. (1981). The importance of interval information in long-term memory for melodies. *Psychomusicology*, **1**, 30–49.

Dowling, W. J. and Fujitani, D. S. (1971). Contour, interval, and pitch recognition in memory for melodies. *Journal of the Acoustical Society of America* **49**, 524–31.

Dowling, W. J. and Harwood, D. L. (1986). *Music cognition*. Academic Press, New York.

Francès, R. (1958). *La perception de la musique*. Vrin, Paris.

Gibson, E. J. (1969). *Principles of perceptual learning and development*. Appleton-Century-Crofts, New York.

Gibson, E. J. and Levin, H. (1975). *The psychology of reading*. MIT Press, Cambridge, Mass.

Haber, R. N. (1966). Nature of the effect of set on perception. *Psychological Review* **85**, 335–51.

Kessen, W. (1981). Encounters: the American child's meeting with music. In *Documentary report of the Ann Arbor symposium*, pp. 353–61. Muic Educators National Conference, Reston, Va.

Lerdahl, F. and Jackendoff, R. (1983). *A generative theory of tonal music.* MIT Press, Cambridge, Mass.

Lomax, A. (1975). *The folk songs of North America.* Doubleday, Garden City, NY.

Meyer, L. B. (1956). *Emotion and meaning in music.* University of Chicago Press, Chicago.

Monahan, C. B. (1984). Parallels between pitch and time: the determinants of musical space. Unpublished Ph. D. thesis. University of California, Los Angeles.

Moorat, J. (ed.) (1980). *Thirty old-time nursery songs.* Metropolitan Museum of Art, New York.

Ostwald, P. F. (1973). Musical behaviour in early childhood. *Developmental Medicine and Child Neurology* **15**, 367–75.

Pick, A. D. (1979). Listening to melodies: perceiving events. In *Perception and its development* (ed. A. D. Pick), pp. 145–65. Erlbaum, Hillsdale, NJ.

Rosner, B. S. and Meyer, L. B. (1982). Melodic processes and the perception of music. In *The psychology of music* (ed. D. Deutsch), pp. 317–41. Academic Press, New York.

Schubert, F. (1823). *Die schöne Müllerin*, Op. 25. Kalmus, New York.

Schubert, F. (1827). *Die Winterreise*, Op. 89. Kalmus, New York.

Seeger, R. C. (1948). *American folk songs for children.* Doubleday, Garden City, NY.

Serafine, M. L. (1983). Cognition in music. *Cognition* **14**, 119–83.

Shepard, R. N. (1984). Ecological constraints on internal representation: resonant kinematics of perceiving, imagining, thinking, and dreaming. *Psychological Review* **91**, 417–47.

Shepard, R. N. and Jordan, D. S. (1984). Auditory illusions demonstrating that tones are assimilated to an internalized musical scale. *Science* **226**, 1333–4.

Trehub, S. E., Bull, D., and Thorpe, L. A. (1984). Infants' perception of melodies: the role of melodic contour. *Child Development* **55**, 821–30.

Trehub, S. E., Morongiello, B. A., and Thorpe, L. A. (1985). Children's perception of familiar melodies: the role of intervals, contour, and key. *Psychomusicology* **5**, 39–48.

7

Improvisation: methods and models

JEFF PRESSING

Introduction

How do people improvise? How is improvisational skill learned and taught? These questions are the subject of this chapter. They are difficult questions, for behind them are long-standing philosophical quandaries such as the origins of novelty and the nature of expertise, which trouble psychologists and artificial intelligence workers today almost as much as they did Plato and Socrates in the fourth and fifth centuries BC.

In a previous article (Pressing 1984*a*) I summarized a number of general properties of the improvisation process on the basis of the diverse historical writings of artists, teachers, and musicologists. This material was integrated with precepts from cognitive psychology to sketch out the beginnings of a general theory of improvisation.

In this article a much more explicit cognitive formulation is presented, the first proper (though by no means necessarily correct) theory of improvised behaviour in music. The building of this theory has required input from many disparate fields with which the general musical reader may not be familiar. For this reason I begin with the survey of appropriate background research and its relation to improvisation. Some of these areas may initially seem distant from the topic at hand.

A survey of pertinent research

Some physiology and neuropsychology

Although our state of knowledge in these areas is far too meagre to have any definite repercussions for improvisation, there are a few facts which are at least strongly suggestive.

To begin with, improvisation (or any type of music performance) includes the following components, roughly in the following order:

(1) Complex electrochemical signals are passed between parts of the nervous system and on to endocrine and muscle systems;
(2) muscles, bones, and connective tissues execute a complex sequence of actions;
(3) rapid visual, tactile, and proprioceptive monitoring of actions takes place;
(4) music is produced by the instrument or voice;
(5) self-produced sounds, and other auditory input, are sensed;
(6) sensed sounds are set into cognitive representations and evaluated as music;
(7) further cognitive processing in the central nervous system generates the design of the next action sequence and triggers it.

– return to step (1) and repeat –

It seems apparent that the most starkly drawn distinctions between improvisation and fixed performance lie in steps (6) and (7), with possibly important differences in step (3). This chapter therefore inevitably focuses on these aspects.

The given steps are often collapsed into a three-component information-processing model of human behaviour which has ready physiological analogies: input (sense organs), processing and decision-making (central nervous system, abbreviated CNS), and motor output (muscle systems and glands).

Control of movement by the CNS is complex: the cerebral cortex sends signals to both the cerebellum and the basal ganglia, which process the information and send a new set of signals back to the motor cortex. The brainstem nuclei are also involved in details of motor co-ordination. It has been suggested that the basal ganglia and cerebellum have complementary roles, with the basal ganglia initiating and controlling slow movements while the cerebellum is active in the co-ordination of fast, ballistic movements (Sage 1977).

Motor signals from the cortex pass to the spinal cord and motor nuclei of the cranial nerves via two separate channels: the pyramidal and extra-pyramidal systems. These two nerve tracts illustrate the simultaneously hierarchical and parallel-processing aspects of CNS control, for they run in parallel but interconnect at all main levels: cortex, brainstem, and spinal cord. Hence while each tract has some separate functions there is a redundancy that can be used to facilitate error correction and motor refinement. Similar redundancy and parallel processing is found at lower levels of motor control. Alpha-gamma coactivation, for example, describes the partial redundancy of neural information sent to two distinct types of motoneurons, alpha and gamma, whose axons and collaterals terminate on the main skeletal muscles and the intrafusal muscle fibres, respectively.

The organization of behaviour has often been linked with the existence of motor action units (or equivalent concepts), and their aggregation into long chains to develop more complex movements. The validity of the concept of motor action units can be seen mirrored physiologically in the existence of command neurons, single nerve cells in invertebrates whose activation alone suffices to elicit a recognizable fragment of behaviour. The effect is achieved by excitation and/or inhibition of a constellation of motoneurons (Bentley and Konishi 1978; Shepherd 1983). While there are no known single cells that fully trigger complex behaviour in mammals, populations of neurons in the brains of higher animals are strongly suspected of serving a similar function (Beatty 1975). It is therefore possible to speculate that skilled improvisers would, through practice, develop general patterns of neural connections specific to improvisational motor control.

Finally, it is of interest that neurological correlates have recently been discovered for a division of knowledge and memory into two separate categories: declarative and procedural. A degree of independence of these two types of memory (for facts or procedures) has been reported among amnesic and post-encephalitic patients for some time (for example Milner 1962; Brooks and Baddeley 1976). Typically, patients can not remember new facts, but are able to learn new motor skills over a period of time, yet without any awareness on successive days of having performed the tasks before. In recent studies, Cohen (1981) and Cohen and Squire (1981) have shown that declarative learning is linked to specific diencephalic and bitemporal brain structures. Unaware of this work, I drew a related distinction in a recent paper (Pressing 1984a) between *object* and *process* memory, based on the rehearsal strategies of improvising musicians. As Squire (1982) has pointed out, there are parallel distinctions in earlier writings: artificial intelligence (Winograd 1975), knowing how and knowing that (Ryle 1949), habit memory and pure memory (Bergson 1910), and memory with or without record (Bruner 1969). What is suggestive about these correlations is that physiological locations for some specific cognitive skills used in improvisation might very well exist.

Motor control and skilled performance

This area traditionally has centered around industrial skills, sport, typing, handwriting, specially designed laboratory tasks like tracking, and to a lesser degree music. It is a complex field of considerable relevance to improvisation, even though improvisation *per se* is scarcely mentioned. Therefore I first review general theories of motor control, and then delve into a number of special issues in skilled performance and skill development that are relevant here.

Theories of motor control and skill

The starting point for nearly all the existing theories is the three-stage information-processing model mentioned earlier, based on sensory input, cognitive processing, and motor output. To this must be added the notion of feedback (auditory, visual, tactile, or proprioceptive). Traditional 'open-loop' theories include no feedback, and hence no mechanisms for error correction. In its starkest form this theory is clearly inappropriate for improvisation; however, there is persistent evidence, dating back to the medical work of Lashley (1917), and including studies of insect behaviour and de-afferentiation techniques in monkeys that points to the existence of motor programmes that can run off actions in open-loop fashion.

In contrast stand 'closed-loop' theories, which contain feedback, and hence allow for the intuitively natural possibilities of error detection and correction. The closed-loop negative feedback (CLNF) model is one of the oldest. In this model the feedback (primarily auditory in the case of musical improvisation) is sent back to an earlier stage in the control system which compares actual output with intended output, producing a correction based on the difference between the two (see for example Bernstein 1967). Such closed-loop models have their historical roots in engineering models of servomechanisms, control theory, and cybernetics.

A wide variety of closed-loop formulations has been given. Gel'fand and Tsetlin (1962, 1971) used a mathematical minimization procedure to model the cognitive search for appropriate motor behaviour. Pew and Baron (1978) sketched out a theory of skilled performance based on optimum control (see also Kleinman *et al.* 1971). Powers (1973) proposed a hierarchy of motor control systems whereby the correction procedures of higher-order control systems constitute reference signals for lower-order systems. Another hierarchical model was given by Pew (1974), in which specific single movements are combined into sequences, and ultimately into various subroutines that make up goal-directed action. Actions are then organized and initiated by an executive programme (Fitts 1964). As is apparent, many such hierarchy theories are based on the application of computer programming principles (see Miller *et al.* 1960).

These ideas offer a more sophisticated understanding of motor behaviour, but they have serious limitations. They model motor learning either poorly or not at all, and are not based on empirical findings about human actions (Adams 1961). A closed-loop theory of motor *learning* was proposed by Adams (1971, 1976) in an attempt to rectify some of these problems. In this theory there are 'memory traces' which select and initiate movements and 'perceptual traces' which are representations of the intended movements, and are used as templates for error correction. A perceptual trace is gradually built up by repeated practice from feedback, knowledge of results (often abbreviated KR), and error correction. Eventually the perceptual trace can function as an internalized goal, diminishing dependence on the externally based knowledge of results (Namikas 1983). Hence open-loop control characteristics are not completely excluded.

By the late 1970s the consensus was that both open- and closed-loop control must occur in skilled performance (Keele and Summers 1976; Delcomyn 1980; Paillard 1980; see Summers 1981 for a review). That is, movements are both centrally stored as motor programmes, and susceptible to tuning (adjustment) on the basis of feedback. Coupled with the well-established concept of *flexibility* characteristic of skilled (but not rote) performance (Welford 1976), this promoted approaches based on more abstract programming notions that brought the field closer to artificial intelligence (and made it more germane to improvisation).

In this spirit Schmidt (1975, 1976) proposed a theory of motor schemata that models both recall and recognition. The schema is considered to contain the general characteristics of a movement which must be organized in any given situation to satisfy environmental requirements and the goals of the performer. Context then guides the production of a series of motor commands that ultimately generate a spatiotemporal pattern of muscle actions. Feedback is based on a template-comparison idea.

Because schemata are not specific movement instructions but are 'generalized' motor programmes, this theory is capable of modelling novelty (at least in a very general way), which the others above could not (except Pew 1974, which also uses a schema notion). The possibility of novelty is also catered to by Schmidt's inclusion of degree of variability of practice conditions as one determiner of schema 'strength'. At its core, the 'novelty problem' is very close to that of improvisation.

Similar to schemata is the notion of action plan. Miller *et al* (1960) gave a general description of plans, while Clark and Clark (1977) described plans for language discourse, and Sloboda (1982) and Shaffer (1980, 1981, 1984) specified plans for playing music. As discussed by Shaffer (1980), a plan is an abstract homomorphism representing the essential structure of the performance and allowing finer details to be generated or located as they are needed during execution.

Other related theories include Allport's proposal of a system of condition-action units which are links between sensory calling patterns and categories of action (Allport 1980). Also related are adjustable control or description structures for artificial intelligence such as *frames* and *scripts* (see below).

This convergence of theory is useful in constructing a model of improvisation (see below). However, it remains rather unspecific, and has run far ahead of experiment. But as of this writing there seems only one alternative in the area of motor behaviour. This is the organizational invariant approach of Turvey, Kugler, Kelso, and others (Turvey 1977;

Kugler *et al.* 1980; see Kelso 1982 for further references). This approach draws on two sources: the ecological perspective of Gibson (1966, 1979) and the dissipative structure model of non-equilibrium thermodynamics (Prigogine 1967; Prigogine and Nicolis 1971). Essentially the theory de-emphasizes notions of cognitive process and control, replacing them with, in so far as is possible, 'organization invariants'. These organization invariants are characteristic constraint structures that allow the emergence of specific spatial relationships and dynamic processes in the behaviour of non-linear systems when the parameters controlling these systems fall in certain critical ranges. Thus if the human motor action apparatus is considered to be (as it certainly is) a non-linear system, characteristic properties of muscle groups and patterns of human limb co-ordination will naturally emerge from the constraints imposed by a given task situation (Kelso *et al.* 1981; Saltzman and Kelso 1983). The proposals are exciting, but their ultimate fate remains unclear. The theory is still being formulated, and comparable ideas from non-linear mathematics have infiltrated many fields in the last 10 years, with uneven results.

Organizational invariant theory seems also likely to apply primarily to the dynamics of motor programme execution, and not to the formulation of intentions and high-level decision-making (Wilberg 1983). Since these functions are vital elements in improvisation in any but an extreme mechanistic approach, the theory as it stands is not particularly suitable for improvisation modelling. Nevertheless, these ideas may be used in an understanding of the sources of behavioural novelty, and are discussed further below.

Some special issues relevant to improvisation

Skill classification   Various dimensions of skill classification have been proposed and improvisation can be placed within these. Two possible categories are 'open' skills, which require extensive interaction with external stimuli, and 'closed' skills, which may be run off without reference to the environment (Poulton 1957). Solo improvisation is basically a closed skill, as it relies only on self-produced stimuli, whereas ensemble improvisation is more open. Other dimensions of skill classification are gross-fine, discrete-serial-continuous, complex-simple, and perceptual-motor (Holding 1981). Improvisation is a fine, complex skill, with both perceptual and motor components; continuous actions predominate, although there are also discrete and serial motor aspects. This last point varies somewhat with the nature of the instrument played.

It is important to also emphasize the contrast between unskilled and highly skilled performance. A vast majority of reported skill studies treat simple motor tasks like tracking, under an implicity reductionistic scientific methodology. It is increasingly acknowledged, however, that highly developed skills have distinctive emergent properties missed in these earlier short-term studies, properties such as adaptability, efficiency, fluency, flexibility, and expressiveness (Welford 1976; Shaffer 1980; Sparrow 1983). These are vital components of improvisatory skill.

Feedback and error correction   Feedback is a vital component in improvisation for it enables error correction and adaptation—a narrowing of the gap between intended and actual motor and musical effects. But feedback is also important for its motivational (Gibbs and Brown 1956) and attention-focusing effects (Pressing 1984a).

Feedback redundancy is an important concept for music. Aural, visual, proprioceptive, and touch feedback reinforce each other for the instrumental improviser, whereas the vocalist has only hearing and proprioception available (Pressing 1984a). Likewise the design of some instruments allows more precise visual feedback and more categorical kinaesthetic feedback than others. This is almost certainly why sophisticated improvisation using advanced pitch materials is more difficult on the violin than the piano, and extremely challenging for the vocalist. For every first-rate scat-singer in the world there must be 500 talented jazz saxophonists.

Feedback can also be considered to operate over different time scales. Thus short-term feedback guides ongoing movements, while longer term feedback is used in decision-making and response selection. Still longer term feedback exists in the form of knowledge of results (KR) for skills where external evaluation is present or result perception is not sufficiently precise or immediate. The importance of this for improvisation has been demonstrated by Partchey (1974), who compared the effects of feedback, models, and repetition on students' ability to improvise melodies. Feedback, in the form of playbacks of recordings of the students' own improvisations, was clearly superior to listening to pre-composed model melodies, or repetition, as an improvisation learning technique. In group improvisation, feedback loops would also operate between performers (Pressing 1980).

In view of the interconnectedness of the parts of the central nervous system, it is also clear that there exist internal feedback (and feedforward) loops not based on sensory processing (Brooks 1978). That is, if higher cognitive levels set the design of motor programmes while movement fine structure is specified in closed-loop fashion by lower levels of the CNS, notably the spinal cord, then copies of these lower level motor instructions are almost certainly sent directly back up to higher centres. In other words, there is some kind of central monitoring of efference. This would serve to increase overall processing speed and accuracy.

The role of errors in improvisation has been discussed previously (Pressing 1984a). It will simply be pointed out here that errors may accrue at all stages of the human information processing system: perception, movement/musical gesture selection and design, and execution. Minor errors typically demand no compensation in following actions, whereas major errors typically do.

Anticipation, preselection, and feedforward   These three concepts have to do with preparation for acton. Physiological recording of the Bereitschaft potential (BP) and contingent negative variation (CNV) (see Brunia 1980) now provides explicit support for the long-standing idea that higher cognitive control centres bias lower ones towards anticipated movements. This is therefore a type of feedforward, and has been described from various perspectives: spinal 'tuning' (Turvey 1977; Easton 1978), corollary discharge or efference copy (von Holst 1954), and preselection (see Kelso and Wallace 1978 for discussion).

The idea of preparation is very important for improvisation, where real-time cognitive processing is often pushed up near its attentional limits. It can be formally proved, for example, that only a control system with a model of disturbances and predictive power can become error free (Kickert *et al.* 1978). For improvised performance that aims at artistic presentation, where discrepancies between intention and result must be kept within strict bounds, practice must attempt to explore the full range of possible motor actions and musical effects, to enable both finer control and the internal modelling of discrepancies and correction procedures, including feedforward.

Hierarchy vs. heterarchy   Because of influences of the physical sciences and control theory, an overwhelming majority of models for motor behaviour have used a hierarchical control system. However, the inter-connectedness between difference locations in the CNS and the many documented types of feedack and feedforward processes mentioned above argue that this perspective is probably too narrow. Furthermore, explicit parallel-processing possibilities exist due to the separate pyramidal and extrapyramidal neural tracts, alpha-gamma coactivation, etc., as mentioned above. Hence other types of organization, referred to as heterarchical or coalition, have been proposed (McCulloch 1945; von Foerster 1960; Greene 1972; Turvey 1977). In this perspective, executive control of the system may be transferred between different 'levels' depending on the needs of the situation (Miller *et al.* 1960).

Time scales for the control of movement   This is a subject with an enormous and complex literature. For background purposes in modelling improvisation a few points only seem sufficient.

Actual neural transmission times are on the order of tens of milliseconds. According to Davis (1957; see also Sage 1977), auditory stimulus activity reaches the cerebral cortex 8–9 ms after stimulation while visual stimulation involves a longer latency of 20–40 ms. Since the two neural pathways are of comparable length, this difference points to a greater transmission speed for audition than vision. It should, however, be noted that the auditory system contains both ipsilateral and contralateral pathways, while the pathways of the visual system are exclusively crossed. The cortical response time for a movement stimulus appears to be on the order of 10–20 ms (Adams 1976).

Reaction time is the time taken for a sense stimulus to travel to the CNS and return to initiate and execute a largely pre-programmed motor response. Simple reaction time (RT) with only one chosen motor response typically fall in the range 100–250 ms, depending on conditions and sensory modality (Summers 1981). Auditory, kinaesthetic, and tactile reaction times have typically been found to fall in the range 100–160 ms (Chernikoff and Taylor 1952; Higgins and Angel 1970; Glencross 1977; Sage 1977), while visual reaction times have been considered longer, typically reported as at least 190 ms (Keele and Posner 1968). Reaction times for other sensory modalities seem to be in the range above 200 ms, while RTs involving choice of response are in general longer and are reasonably modelled by Hick's Law (Hick 1952). Kinaesthetic and tactile choice reactions seem also to be faster than visual (Leonard 1959; Glencross and Koreman 1979). Data on auditory choice RTs do not seem to be readily available.

Error correction (EC) times vary with sensory modality and context. EC times are important for improvisation because it may reasonably be argued that they reflect minimum times for decision-making that is expressive or compositional. Visual error correction is usually reported to be about 200 ms, whereas kinaesthetic EC can occur over intervals as short as 50–60 ms (Kerr 1982), as seen in reports on tracking tasks (Gibbs 1965; Higgins and Angel 1970). However, other recent work in the case of vision has found some instances of visual EC times down in the range near 100 ms as well (Smith and Brown 1980; Zelaznik et al. 1983). It seems likely that the time taken for error correction would be a function of the degree of invoked processing involvement; that is, motor programme construction would take more time than selection, while exacting criteria of discrimination or motor accuracy or a wide range of response choice would naturally increase EC time. Rabbitt and Vyas (1970) and Welford (1974) have enunciated this view, one which is well supported by the introspective reports of improvisers going back for many centuries (Ferand 1961).

Explicit information on auditory error correction times does not seem to be available, but it is possible to point out a general tendency in the above data. Namely, processing speed seems to be greatest for audition and touch/kinaesthesia, of all the possible sensory systems. These are precisely the elements involved in musical improvisation and provide a vivid psychological interpretation for the historical fact that music, of all art and sport forms, has developed improvisation to by far the greatest degree. Under this interpretation, human beings, as creative agents, have as a matter of course drawn on the sensory systems most adapted to quick decision-making: in other words, a predilection for improvised sound manipulation might be genetically programmed. Of course, such an interpretation remains highly speculative.

Finally it should be noted that unexpected sensory changes requiring significant voluntary compensations require a minimum time of about 400–500 ms (Welford 1976). This is therefore the time scale over which improvising players in ensembles can react to each others' introduced novelties (about twice a second). Nuances in continuous improvised performance based on self-monitoring are probably limited by error correction times of about 100 ms (Welford 1976), so that speeds of approximately 10 actions per second and higher involve virtually exclusively pre-programmed actions (Pressing 1984a). An informal analysis of jazz solos over a variety of tempos supports this ball-park estimate of the time limits for improvisational novelty.

Timing and movement invariants   Up to this point very little has been said about the timing of skilled performance, yet it is obviously a vital point. Considerable experimental work in the domains of fluent speech (Huggins 1978), typing (Shaffer 1978; Terzuolo and Viviani 1979), handwriting (Denier van der Gon and Thuring 1965; Viviani and Terzuolo 1980; Hollerbach 1981), generalized arm trajectories (Morasso 1983), and piano performance (Shaffer 1980, 1984) has established that invariant timing and spatial sequences, strongly suggestive of schemata, underlie skilled actions. Such performance rhythms, or 'hometetic' behaviour, as some have termed it, shows great tuneability: over wide variations in distance and overall time constraints, invariance of phasing and accelerations (equivalently, forces) can be observed (Schmidt 1983). By phasing is meant the relative timings of component parts of the entire movement sequence.

But it is also true that the relative timings of movement components can be changed intentionally, at least to a considerable degree. Hence the improviser has access to generalized action programmes (in both motor and music representation), which allow overall parametric control (time, space, force) *and* subprogram tuneability. This may well be responsible for the flexibility of conception characteristic of experienced improvisation.

Motor memory   It has often been suggested that a distinct form of memory for action, called motor memory, exists. The subjective impression of improvisers (and other performers) is certainly that potentially separate yet often interconnected motor, symbolic, and aural forms of memory do exist. For a review of this extensive topic and its relationship to verbal memory the reader may wish to consult Laabs and Simmons (1981).

Skill development

All skill learning seems to share certain common features. In the early stages, a basic movement vocabulary is being assembled and fundamental perceptual distinctions needed for the use of feedback are drawn. In intermediate stages, larger action units are assembled, based on stringing together the existing movement vocabulary in accordance with the developing cognitive framework. These action units begin to enable predictive open-loop response. The ability to perceive distinctions is refined considerably, and internal models of action and error correction are developed. Expressive fluency begins to appear, characterized by a feeling of mindful 'letting go' (Schneider and Fisk 1983; Pressing 1984*a*). By the time advanced or expert stages have been reached, the performer has become highly attuned to subtle perceptual information and has available a vast array of finely timed and tuneable motor programmes. This results in the qualities of efficiency, fluency, flexibility, and expressiveness. All motor organization functions can be handled automatically (without conscious attention) and the performer attends almost exclusively to a higher level of emergent expressive control parameters.

In the case of improvised music these emergent control parameters are notions such as form, timbre, texture, articulation, gesture, activity level, pitch relationships, motoric 'feel', expressive design, emotion, note placement, and dynamics. There must also be a developed priority given to auditory monitoring over kinaesthetic and especially visual monitoring. This idea is supported by research on typists (West 1967), which showed that the dominant visual control used for optimal results in early stages of learning to type gave way later to reliance on tactile and kinaesthetic cues. It also seems likely that sensory discrimination and motor control functions make increasing use of higher order space–time relationships (velocity, acceleration) as skill learning progresses (Marteniuk and Romanow 1983).

The change from *controlled* processing to *automatic* motor processing as a result of extensive skill rehearsal is an idea of long standing (James 1890; Shiffrin and Schneider 1977), and it undoubtedly improves movement quality and integration (Eccles 1972). The accompanying feeling of automaticity, about which much metaphysical speculation exists in the improvisation literature, can be simply viewed as a natural result of considerable practice, a stage at which it has become possible to completely dispense with conscious monitoring of motor programmes, so that the hands appear to have a life of their own, driven by the musical constraints of the situation (Bartlett 1947; Welford 1976; Pressing 1984*a*). In a sense, the performer is played by the music. The same thing happens with common actions like walking and eating. As Welford (1976) has cogently pointed out, automaticity is therefore especially likely when the actions involved are always, or virtually always, accurate to within the requirements of the task. Hence automaticity in improvisation can be frequent in both free and highly structured contexts, since task requirements are often self-chosen, but is more likely to be successful in musical terms for the less experienced player towards the free end of the specturm.

Schneider and Fisk (1983) have proposed an interesting corollary to the above, based upon a classification of tasks into those requiring *consistent* or *varied* processing: 'Practice leads to apparently resource free automatic productions for consistent processing but does not reduce (attentional) resources needed for a varied processing task.' (p. 129) This idea is appealing and perhaps widely valid, but is too simple to encompass the full complexity of improvisation. For part of the result of extensive practice of improvisation is an abstraction to greater and greater generality of motor and musical controls to the point where highly variable, often novel, *specific* results can be produced based on the automatic use of *general*, highly flexible and tuneable motor programmes. More irrevocable constraints causing attentional loading seem to be timing and interhand co-ordination (Pressing 1984*a*).

Another relevant area is the optimum distribution and nature of practice. Generalizations here are particularly hazardous (Newell 1981) and I will confine my comments specifically to improvisation.

The extremes of massed and distributed practice typically have complementary functions for the improviser. Distributed practice develops immediacy, and consistency of results under variable conditions, whereas massed rehearsal, by perhaps bringing to the player's awareness otherwise unperceived repetitive aspects of his or her music, enables the transcendence or improvement of stale musical design. One is reminded of the opinion of master trumpeter Miles Davis that his sidemen only really got loose in the last set of the night, after they had used up all their well-learned tricks (Carr 1982).

Variability of practice conditions is vital for improvisation, for obvious reasons, and this seems to be true of nearly all skilled behaviour (Schmidt 1983). Mental practice away from the instrument can be important for performers of fixed music, based on internal hearing of scores, but there seems very little record of its use in improvisation. This is presumably due to the intrinsically vital motoric link between performer and instrument for improvisation.

Techniques used by musicians to teach improvisation will be described below. However, some general principles of skill teaching are pertinent here. The successful yet contrasting approaches of the 'discovery' method and structural prescription (the use of instructions or demonstrations) may be mentioned. The basic trial-and-error idea of the discovery method probably requires little explanation; it has often been used as an industrial training procedure, where learning sessions are arranged so that trainees must make active choices which are normally correct, and which therefore do not lead to ingrained errors (Welford 1976). Less formalized self-discovery techniques are certainly characteristic of much learning in the arts. But structural prescription is also a vital part of skill learning. For all but very simple skills, instructions seem particularly effective when kept simple, and when focusing on goals and general action principles rather than kinematic details (Hendrickson and Schroeder 1941; Holding 1965; Newell 1981). This certainly holds for improvisation. Probably too much intellectual detail both interferes with the fluid organization of action sequences, as mentioned earlier, and strains attentional resources.

Studies and theories of musical improvisation

A cognitive overview of much of this literature has been given earlier (Pressing 1984a, which includes references to dance and theatre), and will not be repeated here. Historical surveys of improvisation in Western music may be found in Ferand (1938, 1961), *The new Grove dictionary of music* (1983), and Pressing (1984b,c). These deal primarily with the period to 1900. Discussion of avant-garde improvisation since 1950 is included in Cope (1984). Non-Western musical improvisation is described by Reck (1983), Datta and Lath (1967), Wade (1973), Jairazbhoy (1971), and Lipiczky (1985) for Indian music; by Nettl and Riddle (1974), Nettl and Foltin (1972), Zonis (1973), Signell (1974, 1977), and Touma (1971) for various Middle Eastern traditions; by Béhague (1980) for Latin American musics; by Hood (1971, 1975), Sumarsam (1981) for gamelans and other stratified ensembles in Southeast Asia, and by Jones (1959) and Locke (1979) for Ewe music of Ghana. Park (1985) has described the improvisation techniques of Korean shamans, Avery (1984) structure and strategy in Azorean–Canadian folkloric song duelling, and Erlmann (1985) variational procedures in Ful'be praise song. Nettl (1974) has provided thoughtful general insights from the perspective of the ethnomusicologist.

In the twentieth century, prescriptive teaching texts on Western music improvisation are legion. Few, however, have the sorts of cognitive insights useful in model building, and almost all are concerned with the specifics of jazz (a small related number with blues and rock) or keyboard (particularly French-tradition organ) improvisation. The jazz texts are too numerous to survey fully here and are in any case mostly quite repetitious. Important perspectives are however given by Coker (1964, 1975), Schuller (1968), Baker (1969), Owens (1974), Liebman *et al.* (1978), Dobbins (1978), Howard (1978), Murphy (1982), and Radano (1985). Among the better organ and piano texts may be mentioned the works of Dupré (1925/37), Schouten (no date given), Gehring (1963), Berkowitz (1975) and Weidner (1984). Analytical and prescriptive texts which stand apart from the typical stylistic conventions above are the works of Bailey (1980),

Bresgen (1960), Sperber (1974), Stumme (1972), and Whitmer (1934). Except for Bailey, all of these take tonal music as their primary area of discourse. Discussions which emphasize free improvisation often take a more cognitive approach, but their usefulness is sometimes compromised by vagueness or subjectivity. Valuable readings in this area include Silverman (1962), Jost (1974), Parsons (1978), Bailey (1980), and special issues of *Perspectives of new music* (Fall–Winter 1982/Spring–Summer 1983, 26–111), the *Music educator's journal* (1980, **66**, (5), 36–147), *Keyboard* (1984, **10**(10)), and *The British Journal of Music Education* (1985, **2**(2)). Other works of interest are those on choir improvisation (Ehmann 1950, Ueltzen 1986), silent-film accompaniment (Hanlon 1975), dulcimer improvisation (Schickhaus 1978), and percussion gestures (Goldstein 1983).

Musical improvisation has also been considered as a vehicle for consciousness expansion and the tapping of deep intuitions. A full history of this 'transpersonal' approach would go back thousands of years to the sacred texts of many religions. Here I only survey recent Western opinion. Hamel (1979) has intelligently chronicled music of the avant-garde (for example Riley, Stockhausen) from this perspective. Laneri (1975) has developed a philosophy of improvisation based on different states of consciousness, featuring the concepts of synchronicity and introversion. The resultant music is primarily vocal, since the voice is considered the primal instrument. A powerful system of sonic meditation most applicable to local improvisation groups has been developed by Oliveros (1971). 'Sensing' compositions have been published by Gaburo (1968). An attempt to connect music, altered states of consciousness, and research in parapsychology has been given by Pressing (1980), while Galás (1981/82) has created a primal vocal music based on obsession, excessive behaviour, and trance states of severe concentration.

The approaches in the literature to the teaching of improvisation may be broadly grouped as follows. First, there is the perspective overwhelmingly found in historical Western texts, that improvisation is real-time composition and that no fundamental distinction need be drawn between the two. This philosophy was dominant in pre-Baroque times but had become rare by the eighteenth century. In practice this results in a nuts-and-bolts approach with few implications for the modelling of improvisation beyond basic ideas of variation, embellishment, and other traditional processes of musical development. A second approach, which historically took over as the first one waned, sets out patterns, models, and procedures specific to the improvisational situation, which, if followed by those possessing a solid enough level of musicianship, will produce stylistically appropriate music. In this category fall the many figured bass and melodic embellishment texts of the seventeenth and eighteenth centuries (for example Mersenne 1635; Quantz 1752/1966; Bach 1778/1949; Arnold 1965), as well as the riff compendia and how-to-do-it books in the field of jazz (such as Coker, *et al.* 1970; Slonimsky 1975; Nelson 1966).

A third technique is the setting of a spectrum of improvisational problems or constraints. The philosophy behind this technique shows a clear contrast with the second approach above, as described by Doerschuk (1984), referring to the Dalcroze system.

The art of improvisation rests on . . . a developed awareness of one's expressive individuality. This knowledge grows through interactive exercises with a teacher, whose function is not to present models for imitation, but to pose problems intended to provoke personal responses. (p. 52)

Jaques-Dalcroze (1921) seems to have pioneered this approach in our century with a revealing series of improvisation exercises for piano. These include composition-like problems in rhythm, melody, expressive nuance, and harmony; muscular exercises; imitation of a teacher; exercises in hand independence; the notation of improvisation just after performing it; and what may be termed an 'interrupt' technique. In this last technique the word 'hopp' is recited by the teacher, as a cue for the student to perform pre-set operations such as transposition or change of tempo during the performance. This technique is reminiscent of a much later suggestion by Roads (1979) that musical grammars used in improvisation might be 'interrupt-driven'. This idea is developed in the model below.

Parsons (1978) has made effective use of this third technique in a collection of short pieces by many different composers defined largely by improvisational instruction sets; he also presents a taxonomy of psycho-improvisational faults and recommended exercises for correcting them. A shorter multi-author collection of improvisational exercises is found in Armbruster (1984). Jazz fake books like the *Real book* (no listed authors or dates) or *The world's greatest fake book* (Sher 1983) may also be considered to act along the lines of this technique.

A fourth approach is the presentation of multiple versions of important musical entities (most commonly motives) by the teacher, leaving the student to infer completely on his or her own the ways in which improvisation or variation may occur by an appreciation of the intrinsic 'fuzziness' of the musical concept. This imitative self-discovery approach is found in the Persian *radif*, which is a repository of musical material learned in a series of increasingly complex versions by the aspiring performer (Nettl and Foltin 1972), and in Ghanaian traditions (K. Ladzekpo, personal communication), for example. A related procedure made possible by the use of recording technology in the twentieth century is for the student to directly copy a number of improvised solos by repeated listening to recordings, and from this extract common elements and variation procedures. Song-form based improvisations, in which solos consist of a number of choruses which repeat the same underlying chord progression, are particularly suitable. This method has been widely used in jazz and blues since the end of the First World War.

A fifth approach is allied to the self-realization ideas of humanistic psychology. It is based on concepts of creativity and expressive individuality which go back in music explicitly at least to Coleman (1922), implicitly certainly to Czerny (1829/1983), and probably in a general sense at least to the Enlightenment. Important educational applications of this idea are found in the works of Carl Orff, Zoltán Kodály, Suzuki (see Mills and Murthy 1973), and particularly Jaques-Dalcroze (1976, 1930) and Shafer (1969). In the words of Jaques-Dalcroze,

> Improvisation is the study of direct relations between cerebral commands and muscular interpretations in order to express one's own musical feelings . . . Performance is propelled by developing the students' powers of sensation, imagination, and memory.
>
> (In Abramson 1980, p. 64.)

Little actual research on optimal techniques for teaching improvisation has been carried out. The important study by Partchey (1973) which showed the value of models and particularly of subsequent aural feedback in learning to improvise has already been mentioned above. Work by Hores (1977) has shown that visual and aural approaches to the teaching of jazz improvisation can be equally effective. Burnsed (1978) looked at the efficacy of design of an introductory jazz improvisation sequence for band students. Seuhs (1979) developed and assessed (by adjudication) a course of study in Baroque improvisation techniques. Bash (1983) compared the effectiveness of three different instructional methods in learning to improvise jazz. Method I was a standard technical procedure based on scales and chords. Method II supplemented this technical dimension with aural perception techniques which included rote vocal responses to blues patterns, blues vocalizations, and instrumental echo response patterns based on rote or procedures of generalization. Method III supplemented the same technical procedures of Method I with a historical–analytical treatment. All three methods gave improved results over that of a control group, and methods II and III, though no significant difference was found between them, were both superior to method I. The results show the value of specific theoretical and technical instruction, and also of its supplement-ation by relevant aural training or analyses of performance strategies used by virtuoso improvisers.

One final comment on improvisation teaching seems apposite. This is the fact that the optimally effective teacher is able to direct evaluative comments on several different levels. One is the technical—'Your notes don't fit the chord', 'The piano is lagging behind the bass', etc. Another is the compositional—'Try to develop that motive more before discarding it', 'Use more rhythmic variety in pacing your solo', 'Musical quotations seem inappropriate in this free a context', etc. Yet another level is the use of organizing metaphor, a vital part of the tradition of jazz teaching—'Use more space', 'Dig in', 'Go for it', 'Play more laid-back', 'Don't force it— follow the flow', etc. Simple comments of this kind can be remarkably effective at removing improvisational blocks, when delivered at a proper time.

Pike (1974) has presented a brief but insightful phenomenology of jazz. His approach considers the projection of 'tonal imagery' to be the fundamental process in jazz improvisation. Tonal imagery is either 'reproductive' (memory-based) or 'productive' (creative). The improviser operates in a 'perceptual field' which acts as a framework in which the improviser's imagery appears and originates. This field includes not only the perception of external tonal events, but the perception of internal images, as well as the states of consciousness evoked by these images. Images in this field are combined, associated, contrasted, and otherwise organized. The phenomenological operations describing this are processes such as repetition, contrast, continuity, completion, closure, and deviation. Other aspects of improvisation defined by Pike include 'intuitive cognition', an immediate penetration into the singular and expressive nature of an image, and 'prevision', a glimpse into the developmental horizons of an embryonic jazz idea.

Although some of Pike's claims are open to question, for example his uncritical acceptance of concepts like Hodeir's 'vital drive' (Hodeir 1956), his short paper remains an important introspective analysis of the experience of improvisation. The only other extensive phenomenological treatment of improvisation seems to be Mathieu's (1984) study of musician/ dancer duo performances. Other perspectives on the experiences of the improviser have been given by Milano (1984), in an interview with jazz pianist/psychiatrist Denny Zeitlin, and Sudnow (1978), who has produced a basic ethnomethodological description of learning to play jazz on the piano. Related philosophical issues have been raised by Alperson (1984) and Kleeman (1985/86).

Finally it may be proper to note that the computer age has spawned new hybrids of composition and improvisation. Fry (1980, 1982/83) has described music and dance improvisation set-ups using computer sensing and control devices. Chadabe (1984) has described a method of 'interactive composition' whereby movements of the hands in space near two proximity-sensitive antennas trigger and exert partial control over real-time computer sound generation. Interactive computer-based performance systems have also been used by trombonist George Lewis and a host of 'performance artists', including this writer. And recently available commercial software, such as the Macintosh-based *M* and *Jam Factory*, has an interactive improvisational component that seems rich with promise.

Oral traditions and folklore

The idea that traditional folk-tales from many cultures have underlying unities, which may be interpreted as narrative grammars, is a fairly well-established one (Propp 1927; Thompson 1946; Nagler 1974). Explanations of this fact have tended towards one or the other of two viewpoints.

A common (particularly European) perspective in the study of oral tradition and folklore has been a focus on their repetitive and imitative aspects, with the frequent assumption of an *Urtext* which has undergone historical and geographic transformation. A powerful opposing view, and one which seems increasingly relevant as a description of referent-based improvisation, is found in the 'formulaic composition' proposals of Milman Parry and Albert Lord (Parry 1930, 1932; Lord 1964, 1965).

Formulaic composition was derived from Milman's intense study of the Homeric epics, particularly the *Odyssey*, and given further support by research on Yugoslav folk-epic poetry conducted by Milman and Lord. It is also considered to be applicable to other oral epics such as *Beowulf* and the *Chanson de Roland*, and has been used to analyse Latvian folk-song texts (Vīķis-Freibergs 1984). In this view epic oral poetry is created anew at each performance by the singer from a store of formulas, a store of themes, and a technique of composition. There is no 'original' version; instead the tradition is multiform. A 'formula' is a group of words regularly employed under the same metrical conditions to express a given essential idea; it has melodic, metric, syntactic, and acoustic dimensions. By choosing from a repertoire of roughly synonymous formulas of different lengths and expanding or deleting subthemes according to the needs of the performance situation, the experienced performer is able to formulaically compose (in real-time, hence improvise) a detailed and freshly compelling version of a known song epic. As a result of the composition system, instances of pleonasm and parataxis are common.

The formulas considered as a group reveal further patterns. In the words of Lord (1964): 'the really significant element in the process is . . . the setting up of various patterns that make adjustment of phrase and creation of phrases by analogy possible' (p.37). In addition, the permutation of events and formulas may occur, as well as the substitution of one theme for another.

Yet the traditional singer does not seek originality with this technique, but heightened expression. Lord speculates that formulas originally grew out of a need for intensification of meaning or evocation. 'The poet was sorcerer and seer before he became artist' (Lord 1964, p. 67).

The relevance of formulaic composition to specific types of musical improvisation has recently been discussed by several writers. Treitler (1974) has argued that Gregorian chant was composed and transmitted in an analogous process to that used in the oral epics. Smith (1983) has used the process to describe the constraints imposed on the song-based jazz performer, and has gone on to analyse piano improvisations by Bill Evans. Kernfeld (1983) has examined how far formulas may be used to describe the music of saxophonist John Coltrane. Reck (1983) has produced the evocative idea of a musician's 'tool-kit', in a mammoth study of five performances by South Indian musician Thirugokarnam Ramachandra Iyer. The tool-kit is considered to be piece-specific and to contain both individually chosen and culturally determined formulas, musical habits, models of improvisational and compositional forms, aesthetic values, and social attitudes.

The application of Parry–Lord theory to musical improvisation is thus a clear contemporary trend. The limits of its validity and usefulness are still open questions, and are probably linked to whether a satisfactory agreement can be reached on the principles to be used to define musical 'formulas'.

Intuition and creativity

These are two related concepts, each with a vast literature. Their connection with improvisation is undeniable, yet explicit mention of it in either field is rare. On the other hand, 'free' musicians and many music educators commonly use the two terms, but often without a very clear notion of just what is being discussed. This section attempts to bridge that gap.

The concept of intuition is much older than creativity, and it has separate philosophical and psychological traditions. Westcott (1968) has provided an excellent general survey, enumerating three historical approaches to philosophies of intuition. First comes Classical Intuition (for example Spinoza, Croce, Bergson), which views intuition as a special kind of contact with a prime reality, a glimpse of ultimate truth unclouded by the machinations of reason or the compulsions of instinct. Knowledge gained through this kind of intuition is unique, immediate, personal, unverifiable. The second approach, called by Westcott Contemporary Intuitionism (for example Stocks 1939; Ewing 1941; Bahm 1960), takes the more restricted view that intuition is the immediate apprehension of certain basic truths (of deduction, mathematical axioms, causality, etc.). This immediate knowing stands outside logic or reason and yet is the only foundation upon which they can be built. Knowledge gained through intuition constitutes a set of 'justifiable beliefs', which are nevertheless subject to the possibility of error. A third approach is positivistic (for example Bunge 1962) in that it rejects as illusory both the notions of immediacy and ultimate truth found in some earlier views. Rather, an intuition is simply a rapid inference which produces a hypothesis.

Of all these views, it is perhaps that of French philosopher Henri

Bergson (1859–1941) which shows the greatest affinities with the common metaphors of improvisation. Bergson saw intuition as a way to attain direct contact with a prime reality ordinarily masked from human knowledge. This prime reality is an ongoing movement, an evolving dynamic flux which proceeds along a definite but unpredictable course.

The prime reality is referred to as 'the perpetual happening' or 'duration'. The mind of man, according to Bergson, is shielded from the perpetual happening by the intellect, which imposes 'patterned immobility' on prime reality, distorting, inmobilizing, and separating it into discrete objects, events and processes. In the perpetual happening itself, all events, objects, and processes are unified'

(In Westcott 1968, p. 8).

In Bergson's view, the intellect can freely interact with the fruits of intuition (special knowledge and experience) to develop an enriched personal perspective.

The notion of tapping a prime reality is very similar to the improviser's aesthetic of tapping the flow of the music, as mentioned above. The same apparent process has been eloquently described with regard to the origins of folk-tales from many cultures by English writer Richard Adams:

I have a vision of—the world as the astronauts saw it—a shining globe, poised in space and rotating on its polar axis. Round it, enveloping it entirely, as one Chinese carved ivory ball encloses another within it, is a second . . . gossamer-like sphere . . . rotating freely and independently of the rotation of the earth.

Within this outer web we live. It soaks up, transmutes and is charged with human experience, exuded from the world within like steam or an aroma from cooking food. The story-teller is he who reaches up, grasps that part of the web which happens to be above his head at the moment and draws it down—it is, of course, elastic and unbreakable—to touch the earth. When he has told his story—its story—he releases it and it springs back and continues in rotation. The web moves continually above us, so that in time every point on its interior surface passes directly above every point on the surface of the world. This is why the same stories are found all over the world, among different people who can have had little or no communication with each other.

(Adams 1980, p. 12.)

There is a clear convergence of imagery in this and other descriptions that points to a likely transpersonal component to improvisation.

The psychological perspectives on intuition are many and varied, but only two seem relevant here. The first is the widely occurring idea that intuition is a special case of inference which draws on cues and associations not ordinarily used (Westcott 1968). A similarity with certain theories of skill learning mentioned above is apparent. A second and wide-ranging approach is found in the recent work by Bastick (1982), which includes a search of over 2.5 million sources for common properties underlying intuition. After the identification and detailed analysis of some 20 of these properties, Bastick ends up describing intuition as a combinatorial process operating over pre-existing connections among elements of different 'emotional sets'. These emotional sets apparently contain encodings, often redundant, of many different life events (intellectual activities, movement, emotion, etc.). By giving strong emphasis to the role of dynamics, bodily experience, and the maximizing of redundancy in encoding, and by a series of suggestive diagrams of intuitive processing, Bastick seems to be on an important track parallel to emerging ideas of improvisation.

Research in creativity is probably more extensive than that in intuition, for intuition is most commonly considered a subcategory of creativity. Creativity research in music education has been recently surveyed by Richardson (1983). The only clear relations to improvisation she found were in specialized educational methods and a growing tendency to use improvisation tests in assessing musical creativity. Vaughan (1971), Gorder (1976), and Webster (1977) have designed and implemented such tests, but results show uneven patterns of correlation between general intelligence, creativity, musicality, composition, and improvisation, and seem to have no clear consequences for improvisation modelling.

General studies of creativity abound, and follow many divergent paths. Two alone seem relevant here. Guilford's Structure-of-Intellect (SI) model proposed a taxonomy of factors of intelligence (Guilford and Hoepfner 1971 (and earlier references mentioned therein); Guilford 1977). These intelligence factors, which number 120, are classified along three dimensions:
thought content: visual, auditory figural, semantic, symbolic, and behavioural information;
kinds of operation performed on the content: cognition, memory, convergent production, divergent production, evaluation;
products (the results of applying operations to content): units, classes, relations, systems, transformations, and implications.
These classifications are related to improvisation in a general way, but despite their intuitive appeal, they have so far been fairly resistant to empirical verification.

Guilford further defined a set of six aptitudes for creative thinking: fluency, flexibility, originality, elaboration, redefinition, and sensitivity to problems. Torrance (1966) used this same set in designing a more open-ended approach to the testing and definition of creativity. Some of these six aptitudes are identical to the ones found in skilled performance above; they are considered here to be further guidelines for testing the plausibility of improvisational modelling.

Finally, Guilford and Hoepfner classified techniques of evaluation (in problem-solving), which they held to be due to appeals to logical consistency, past experiences, feeling of rightness, or aesthetic principles. Such a classification also has implications for improvisation (see model below).

Artificial intelligence

This field is concerned with programming computers to be intelligent problem solvers. The framework of action is usually formulated in terms of a problem space which must be searched for correct solutions. Since interesting problem spaces are nearly always too large to be investigated completely, a major focus of the field is the design of better heuristic search techniques. Coupled naturally with this are many methods and frameworks for the representation of knowledge.

There is traditionally no explicit mention of improvisation in the field. In making such a link, it seems clear that the successful application of artificial intelligence concepts to improvisation rests to a large degree on the appropriateness of considering improvisation to be a kind of problem solving. There is little doubt that such an analogy can be fruitful, particularly for referent-guided improvisation. For example, the process of improvisation may be divided up into a number of time points, and viewed as a succession of small problems, each of which is the production of an appropriate chunk of musical action at the current time point, where the constraints on action are the referent, goals, and musical actions at earlier time points. Alternatively, the time-scale may be drawn much coarser, and each complete improvisation may be considered a solution to a much more generally stated problem: for instances, improvise a chorus on 'I Got Rhythm' changes, within the constraints of be-bop style.

Before surveying the fruits of this approach it may be wise to spell out its limitations. Experientially, improvisation can seem to be far removed from problem solving. This is particularly so where the goals of the music making are exploration and process, rather than the presentation of artistic product. It is also very difficult to imagine how one could ever specify the 'problems' in freer types of improvisation with sufficient detail to allow specific artificial intelligence techniques to be used in modelling. Such problem formulations, even if possible, would be very personal, open ended, and sometimes contradictory.

With these provisos, we examine how various artificial intelligence problem-solving techniques might apply to improvisation. Search techniques come in several variants, including depth-first, breadth-first, and best-first. All use a generate-and-test procedure to find solutions to a problem. Clearly there are possible connections with improvisation. Generate-and-test could be applied to learning to improvise, where generation is sound production and testing is listening to generated music; or, it could describe internal cognitive selection processes, where testing is based on internal hearing of generated possibilities, before one is chosen as the actual musical output at a given time. Unfortunately with regard to this second interpretation there is a serious limitation: the inevitable use of back-tracking in the search processes cannot be very significant in improvisation due to the cognitive limitations of real-time processing. The need of the improviser is for a good solution, not the best, for there is probably no single 'best' solution, and even if there were, it would take too long to find it. Therefore, the number of solution paths compared at any one step is probably very strongly limited, perhaps to two or three.

Another problem-solving technique is problem reduction: that is, reducing a problem to a set of subproblems. This is a common way to look at the teaching of improvisation, but seems less likely to apply to doing it, where integration of action is required. Of course there is no proof of this; we know far too little about the workings of the brain. Constraint satisfaction, on the other hand, is a technique whose principles seem to apply to improvisation. The constraints are the referent, goals of the performer, stylistic norms, etc. Finally, means-ends analysis is a technique that is based on comparing current and goal states. Because it involves considerable back-tracking, it is unlikely to apply to the improvisation process. Yet like other methods above, it seems relevant to the process of learning improvisational skill. In general, then, learning to improvise (that is, to structure musical impulses within aesthetic guidelines) is more like problem solving than is improvising itself.

Another main branch of artificial intelligence is knowledge representation. The relevance to improvisation seems clear, for any particular mode of knowledge representation makes it efficient to do certain things and inefficient to do others. And efficiency is what the improviser needs above all.

Knowledge representation in artificial intelligence is based on many ideas, including indexing, conceptual dependency, hierarchies, semantic nets, multiple representation, blackboards (actually a type of interprocess communication), frames, scripts, stereotypes, and rule models (Rich 1983; Lenat 1984). With respect to improvisation, many of these are more suggestive than readily applicable. Indexing, for example, is too artificial, whereas conceptual dependency, in which information is represented by certain conceptual primitives, is too strongly linked with natural language structure. Hierarchies have been discussed previously. Semantic nets are perhaps more promising: information is represented as a network of nodes connected to each other by labelled arcs, each node representing an object, event, or concept, and each arc a relation between nodes. Such a graph could be drawn for musical objects and events, but parametrically tuneable processes are not easy to represent, and this is a serious drawback.

Multiple representation, however, is an important idea, and one which is implicit in parallel-processing ideas mentioned earlier. The increased flexibility and efficiency possible with multiple representation argue very strongly for its inclusion in any model of improvisation. Gelernter (1963) successfully applied the idea to problems in plane geometry by using simultaneous axiomatic and diagrammatic representations. Another interesting application is the notion of the 'blackboard', an organization of the problem space into multiple levels of representation, typically along a dimension indicating level of abstractness. Thus a spoken sentence may be processed at levels of acoustic wave form, phonemes, syllables, words, word sequences, phrases, etc. Each part of the blackboard is triggered automatically as relevant information comes in. Multiple representation also strengthens the possibilities for analogy, and promotes synergy, by which is meant the co-operative action of parts of a complex system (Lenat 1984).

The last four ideas mentioned above, frames, scripts, stereotypes, and rule models, are considered to be various types of schemata (Rich 1983). The use of the word here is slightly different from that in the area of motor behaviour (see Adams 1976 for a survey). Frames are used to describe collections of attributes of an object. A frame consists of slots filled with attributes and associated values. Like most slot-and-filler structures, frames facilitate the drawing of analogies. Ideas equivalent to the frame are found in the improvisation model below. Scripts are simply normative event sequences and in so far as they apply to improvisation have much in common with the generalized motor schemata described above. Stereotypes have their usual meaning and are parts of the norms of musical style, but are often avoided by the best improvisers. Rule models describe the common features shared by a set of rules which form the basis for a 'production system'. If the improvising musician is the production system, the important rules will be largely heuristic and the rules about rules may be termed metaheuristics. Some of these will be culturally and historically based, while others presumably reflect intrinsic properties of the cognitive apparatus. Serafine (1983) has presented an insightful discussion of this distinction from the standpoint of the cognitive psychologist.

In principle it should be possible to integrate appropriate artificial intelligence techniques to construct an expert system which improvises. One of the very few such attempts is the unpublished work of Levitt (1981), which dealt with jazz improvisation. The idea awaits further development.

A model of improvisation

Any theory of improvisation must explain three things: how people improvise; how people learn improvisational skill; and the origin of novel behaviour. It must also be consistent with the numerous recurring themes reviewed above. The model given here seems to satisfy these conditions.

How people improvise

The first part of this model describes the process of improvisation. It begins with the observation that any improvisation may be partitioned into a sequence of non-overlapping sections. By non-overlapping it is simply meant that sounds are assigned to only one section, not that the sounds themselves do not overlap. Let each of these sections contain a number of musical events and be called an event cluster E_i. Then the improvisation I is simply an ordered union of all these event clusters. Formally,

$$I = \{E_1, E_2 \ldots E_n\} \tag{1}$$

From a naïve analytical perspective there is a large number of ways such a partitioning could be made. Our first major assumption is that every improvisation is actually generated by triggers at specific time points t_1, t_2 . . . t_n that instigate the movement patterns appropriate to effect intended musical actions. Each time point is thus the point at which decided action begins to be executed. Note that it is schemata for action that are triggered, not precise movement details, and subsequent motor fine tuning based on feedback processes goes on after each time point. Often time points will have clear musical correlates, with adjacent event clusters being set off from each other by local musical boundary criteria; pauses, phrase junctures, cadences, grouping by sequence etc.; but this need not always be the case.

With this interpretation, equation (1) is a unique specification of the timing of central decision making made by the improviser. The improvisation may then be viewed as a series of 'situations', where the $(i+1)$th situation is confined primarily to the time interval (t_i, t_{i+1}) and entails the generation of the cluster E_{i+1} on the basis of the previous events $\{E_1, E_2, \ldots E_i\} \equiv \{E\}_i$, the referent R (if one exists), a set of current goals $\mathcal{G}$, and long-term memory M. The referent R is an underlying piece-specific guide or scheme used by the musician to facilitate the generation of improvised behaviour (Pressing 1984a). The process of event-cluster generation may then be written

$$(\{E\}, R, \mathcal{G}, M)_i \to E_{i+1}. \tag{2}$$

Decision-making in the $(i+1)$th situation may in principle extend well back before time t_i, depending on the degree of pre-selection used by the performer, and will also extend slightly into the future, in that fine details of motor control will be left to lower control centres and hence may occur after t_{i+1}.

Equation (2) applies strictly only to solo improvisation. The only changes with group improvisation are that, first, all performers will have their own distinct time-point sequences (even though they would often be partially correlated), and, second, players will normally interact. Equation (2) can be readily extended to apply to all K members of an improvisation ensemble by writing

$$(\{E\}, C, R, \mathcal{G}, M)_{i_k} \to E_{i_k+1}, \ k=1, \ldots K, \tag{3}$$

where subscripts refer to the kth performer, and C stands for performer k's cognitive representation of all previous event clusters produced by the other performers and any expectations of their likely future actions. For simplicity, we use the formalism of equation (2) and speak primarily in terms of solo improvisation in what follows, adding in the effects of other performers in a straightforward manner as needed at certain points.

Any given event cluster E has a number of simultaneously valid and partially redundant 'aspects'. Each aspect is a representation of E from a certain perspective. Most important are the acoustic aspect (produced and sensed sound), the musical aspect (cognitive representation of the sounds in terms of music-technical and expressive dimensions), and the movement aspect (including timing of muscular actions, proprioception, touch, spatial perception, and central monitoring of efference). Visual and emotional aspects normally also play a role, and in principle there may be others. Furthermore each aspect exists in two forms, intended and actual. Each intended form is specified at a specific time point: the corresponding actual form is constructed from subsequent sensory feedback. The gap between these two forms is reduced by sound training in musicianship and improvisation practice, but it never dwindles completely to zero. Hence in equation (2) or (3) the variable $\{E\}_i$ represents intended and actual forms of all aspects of event clusters E_1 to E_{i-1}, the intended form of E_i, plus, over the course of the time interval (t_i, t_i+1), increasing feedback on the actual form of E_i. By t_{i+1}, when central commands for E_{i+1} are transmitted, the ongoing nature of improvisation probably demands that integration of the intended and actual forms of E_i be virtually complete.

The details of the proposed model of what occurs in the $(i+1)$th situation, that is, the selection of E_{i+1}, are as follows:

(A) E_i is triggered and executed (it may spill on briefly to times $t>t_{i+1}$).

(B) Each aspect of E_i may be decomposed into three types of analytical representation: objects, features, and processes. An 'object' is a unified cognitive or perceptual entity. It may, for example, correspond to a chord, a sound, or a certain finger motion. 'Features' are parameters that describe shared properties of objects, and 'processes' are descriptions of changes of objects or features over time. At t_i this decomposition is based only on intended information (efference); by t_{i+1} much of the actual form of E_i, received through the senses and internal feedback, has been used to refine the cognitive representation of E_i. This may continue after t_{i+1}. Let this decomposition into objects, features, and processes (for each aspect) be represented by three variable-dimension arrays $\mathbf{O}$, $\mathbf{F}$, and $\mathbf{P}$, and assume that they represent all information about E_i needed by the improviser in decision making.

(C) The structures of the three types of arrays are as follows. The object array is a $2 \times N$ array where row 1 components label the objects present and row 2 gives their associated cognitive strengths s_k (explained below). The feature and process arrays are typically non-rectangular. Their first rows consist of object and process labels respectively, and each column below that row is built up of a number of pairs of elements which give the values v_{jk} of associated features or process parameters and their corresponding cognitive strengths s_{jk}. The arrays are non-rectangular because different objects may possess different numbers of significant features or process parameters. The feature and parameter process values v_{jk} vary over ranges appropriate to their nature, whereas cognitive strengths s_{jk} are normalized to vary between 0 and 1. Cognitive strength is essentially an indicator of attentional loading, that is, the importance that the given factor has in the performer's internal representation. Thus even though certain features may be objectively present, as analysed by others, if the player does not use them in his or her cognitive representation, their s values would be zero. Sample object, feature, and process arrays for the following event cluster (a short trombone motive) are given by way of example (Fig. 7.1), for the musical aspect only. Considerable redundancy of representation has been set out in the process array.

(D) Production of E_{i+1} occurs primarily on the basis of long-term factors (R, $\mathcal{G}$, stylistic norms, and ongoing processes), and by evaluation of the effects and possibilities of E_i. There seem to be only two methods of continuation used: associative or interrupt generation. In associative generation the improviser desires to effect continuity between E_i and E_{i+1} and picks new arrays O_{i+1}, F_{i+1}, P_{i+1} whose set of strong cognitive components includes all or nearly all of the strong cognitive components of O_i, F_i, and P_i, with the parameter values of these shared components being directly related (as described in (E) below). In other words the E_i components with high s values carry their information on in some way to E_{i+1}. These new arrays act as a set of constraints which determine, in conjunction with various generation processes, the musical actions generated for E_{i+1}. The relative importance of different constraints in the generation process is indicated by their respective cognitive strengths s_k and s_{jk}. Note that the E_{i+1} arrays may contain new strong components (constraints) that were previously weak or completely absent. In particular, it is possible to add a new independent musical process to a continuing one to produce an associative continuation which has a clear sense of novelty (e.g. the introduction of a new part in polyphonic music). In the case of interrupt generation the improviser has had enough of the event train ending with E_i (for whatever reasons) and breaks off into a different musical direction by resetting a significant number of strong components of O_{i+1}, F_{i+1}, P_{i+1} without any relations to E_i except possibly those chosen to be normative with regard to style in the piece, or intrinsic to the referent (if present) or goals. Clearly, the more strong components that are reset, the greater the sense of interruption.

Object array **O**

$$\mathbf{O}=\begin{pmatrix} N & G & R & N & S \\ \tfrac{1}{2} & \tfrac{1}{2} & \tfrac{1}{2} & 1 & 1 \end{pmatrix}$$

⟵ Label
⟵ Cognitive strength

N=note
G=glissando
R=rest
S=scale

Feature array **F**

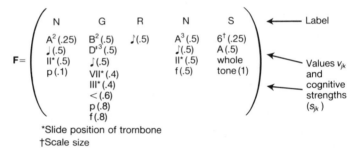

*Slide position of trombone
†Scale size

Process array **P**

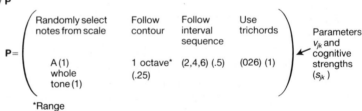

*Range

Fig. 7.1. Possible object, feature, and process arrays corresponding to a short trombone motive.

(E) Associative generation is based on either similarity or contrast. In the case of similarity all or nearly all important (important as determined from the vantage point of the improviser) array components stay approximately the same. In other words, for those components v_{jk} with s_{jk}'s signicantly above zero at time $t=t_i$, $(v_{jk})_{t_i}\approx(v_{jk})t_{i+1}$. Significant object array components behave analogously. In the case of constrast-type associative generation, at least one strong component of either the feature or process arrays must either move from near one end of its possible range of values to near the opposite end, or cross some perceptually significant boundary. Meanwhile, all other strong components change either very little or not at all. Examples are when a group of high notes is followed by a group of low notes, or an accelerando changes of decelerando, or bright timbres are replaced by dull timbres. The idea behind this classification is that the most powerful and general types of improvisational control are those that are cued to features and processes. The objects, though a crucial part of the entire procedure, are at the same time often merely the very familiar musical clothing of cognitive action space.

(F) Interrupt generation is based on the resetting of all or a significant number of the strong array components without regard to their values in the current event cluster E_i. A decision to interrupt brings to an end a sequence of related event clusters, say $K = \{E_{i-r}, E_{i-r+1}, \ldots E_i\}$, where the number of event clusters in this 'event-cluster class' is $r+1$. Hence interrupt decisions partition the entire improvisation into A discontinuous event-cluster classes K_α, so that the formal design of the piece becomes

$$I = \{K_1, K_2 \ldots K_A\}. \tag{4}$$

Each event-cluster class K_α contains at least one event cluster, and may be defined in terms of the strong components of the object, feature, and process arrays shared by all the member event clusters. If these special components are represented as O_s^α, F_s^α, and P_s^α, then K_α is defined by $(O_s, F_s, P_s)^\alpha$. One of the sets F_s^α and P_s^α must be non-empty. If $(O_s, F_s, P_s)^\alpha =$ or $\approx (O_s, F_s, P_s)^\beta$, for some β not immediately following α, we have recursion in formal design of the improvisation. Under these assumptions the process of improvisation may be sketched diagrammatically as in Fig. 7.2.

(G) The choice between association and interrupt generation may be formally modelled by a time-dependent tolerance level for repetition, $L(t)$. An interrupt tester, whose inputs are presumably the time since the onset of the K_α event cluster class, $(t-t_{i-r})$, and the size and nature of K_α, computes the degree of current repetition, $Z(t)$, and if $Z(t) \geqslant L(t)$, institutes an interrupt generation, so that $Z(t)$ jumps to a low value. Otherwise associative generation continues. Diagrammatically this is shown in Fig. 7.3 for the same improvisation as in Fig. 7.2.

(H) Once O_{i+1}, F_{i+1}, and P_{i+1} are selected for all relevant aspects, tuneable cognitive and motor subprogrammes are set in motion that generate, on the basis of these higher constraints and current motor positions, a specific action design. At this point we have reached t_{i+1} and this loop of the process $(E_i \rightarrow E_{i+1})$ is complete. By iteration, then, the entire improvisation is built up. The starting point E_1 may be considered a situation of interrupt generation (where E_0 is silence) and the final event cluster E_n is simply a second case of interrupt generation where $E_{n+1} =$ silence, after which the improvisation process is turned off.

These, then, are the salient features of the model in outline. They are diagramatically displayed in Fig. 7.4.

Next we look more deeply at certain critical stages of the improvisation

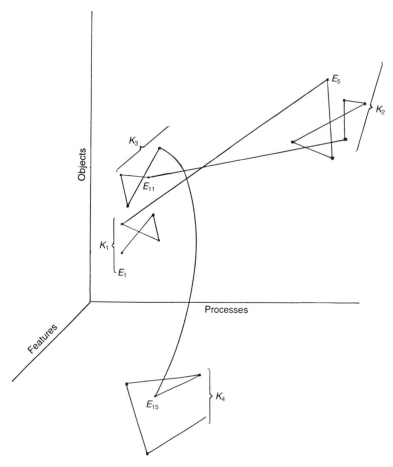

Fig. 7.2. An improvisation in musical action space, showing four event-cluster classes, and form ABA'C.

model. To begin with, it is characterized throughout by extensive redundancy. There is first of all redundancy between the aspects of each event cluster. The performer knows, for example, that certain motor actions involved in striking a kettle drum (motor aspect) will correspond to a particular sound (acoustic aspect), with associated musical implications (musical aspect). Furthermore, each aspect is decomposed into extensive object, feature, and process representations which contain considerable redundancy. For example, the musical motive of Example 7.1 may be pitch encoded as the objects $D^2F^2A^2B^2$, or as the object $B\phi$ diminished 7 chord in first inversion, or as a diatonic sweep to the leading tone in the key of C major, or as a ii ϕ diminished 7 chord in a minor, or as an ascending contour, and so forth. Its features include melodic motion by seconds or

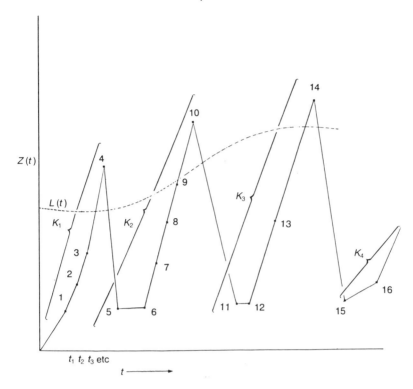

Fig. 7.3. Interrupt generation via the repetition functions L and Z.

thirds, diatonic note choice, the degree and speed of crescendo, rhythmic
regularity of attack, certain values of finger force and velocity used by the
performer, and so forth. Many processes could be implicated to generate
the given motive: arpeggiate a Bϕ diminished 7 chord, pick notes
consistent with a triplet feel in C major, move the fingers 4321 of the left
hand in such a fashion as to depress keys on the piano, and so forth. If the
nature of improvisation entails the seeking out of a satisfactory trajectory
in musical action space, such redundancy of description and generation
allows maximal flexibility of path selection, so that whatever creative
impulse presents itself as an intention, and whatever attentional loadings

Example 7.1

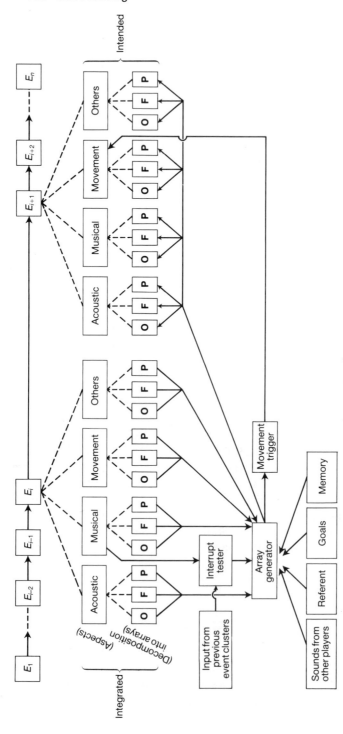

Fig. 7.4 The improvisation model in diagrammatic form. Only the process $E_i \rightarrow E_{i+1}$ (intended) is detailed. Each event cluster E_i is present in a number of partially redundant aspects, and each of these is decomposed into object, feature, and process arrays. Largely on the basis of musical representation a decision about type of continuation is made by an interrupt tester. In accordance with this decision an intended array decomposition is generated, with input from E_i arrays, referent, goals, and memory. This decomposition acts as a set of constraints in the generation of musical action, and production of E_{i+1} is subsequently begun by a movement trigger at t_{i+1}. The diagram detail shows what happens in the time interval (t_i, t_{i+1}), so that the indicated decomposition of E_i is integrated (that is, intended plus actual forms of E_i are combined), whereas the indicated decomposition of E_{i+1} is intended (no feedback has been received yet). Hence **O**, **F**, and **P** at time point t_{i+1} do not have indicated outputs.

may be set up, some means of cognitive organization and corresponding motor realization will be available within the limiting constraints of real-time processing.

Such extensive redundancy I take here to mean that control of event production is heterarchical, and may potentially shift rapidly from one cognitive control area to another. Indeed this must be considered the most effective strategy for improvisation. Experientially it very probably corresponds to 'letting go', or 'going with the flow' as described earlier, whereby central hierarchical control, identified here with conscious monitoring of decision making, yields to heterarchical control (and corresponding unconscious allocation of attention).

Next we look further at the object, feature, and process arrays that are critical in the representation and generation of event clusters. First of all it may well be asked how such arrays are formed. The answer given here is based on an ecological perspective, which considers that the capacity to extract or create such arrays is neurologically innate, but that they are only brought into being by interaction with the environment. More specifically, cognitive objects are inferred to exist on the basis of perceived invariance in sensory input over time, and boundedness in a space (whether physical, musical, or abstract). Features are tuneable parameters and come to be abstracted on the basis of perceived similarity or contrast in sensory input. Processes come about from perceived change in an object or along a feature dimension with time.

Thus over the course of one's life new arrays and array components are constantly being created by new perceptions and new perceptual groupings. During any given improvisation at most very few new features or processes will be created, and only a limited number of new objects. In general, though, this is one source of novel behaviour: the evolution of movement control structures for newly discovered objects, features, and processes. However, there seems to be another, probably more common source of behavioural novelty: the motor enactment of novel combinations of values of array components. This second possibility is shown for example by considering a child musician who has learned motor actions corresponding to the distinctions loud/soft and fast/slow separately, but without encountering soft and fast simultaneously. By combining these two dimensions an action novel to the child's experience can result. Furthermore, the results of such novel parametric combinations need not be so predictable. If we recall that the human performance system is non-linear, then, as mentioned above in the paragraphs on organizational invariant theory, novel, strikingly different behaviour may follow when controlling system parameters assume certain novel combinations of ranges. It can further be shown mathematically that behaviour described as 'chaotic' may occur under such conditions (Li and Yorke 1975; May 1976), even for simple systems. This perspective has led to a biomathematical analysis, for example, of many so-called 'dynamical' diseases, including schizophrenia, AV heart block, epilepsy, and some haematological disorders (see Guevara *et al.* 1983 for a survey). The point with regard to improvisation is that the same sort of smooth parametric tuning can be used to generate abrupt intentional novelties in movement and musical expression. The integration of the results of novel ranges of array components is presumed to be handled by control structures of the CNS responsible for timing and smoothness of action.

During any given improvisation, when possible object, feature, and process array types are basically fixed, novel sensory input will be analysed and assigned to existing categories, or, if the fit is too poor, into existing categories plus deviations. In this model such a description is also considered to apply to the generation of action. That is, novel actions are built primarily by distorting aspects of existing ones. This sheds light on the organizing power of the metaphor, mentioned earlier, since it may be considered to be a global link across categories, one that facilitates movement integration. In other words, the image or metaphor enables the co-ordinated modification and resetting of whole classes of array components in a fashion ensuring spatial and temporal coherence.

The central core of the model is the generation of a new set of array components for E_{i+1} from those preceding it. To make this process clearer, we now look at two examples.

(1) Let E_i be

Example 7.2

played by the right hand at the piano.

Above are a number of possible improvisational continuations, based on attentional emphasis (that is, cognitive strength) given to the mentioned array components (see Fig. 7.5). Emphasis given to a particular component means that it will guide the generation of subsequent events. The type of arrays emphasized are also indicated; note that this is not uniquely determined, since the model makes a feature of redundancy. Continuations 1–8 exemplify associative continuation, with numbers 7 and 8 more abstract than the others, while number 9 is interrupt based.

Continuation	Emphasized components used for continuation	Type of arrays
I	key of A major; quaver durations	**O,F,P**

Fig. 7.5. Examples of continuation of an event cluster under the emphasis of selected array components.

2	perfect fourth interval	**F**
3	notes E, A, D; rhythmic displacement	**O,P**
4	melodic contour	**O,F**
5	motor generation with right-hand fingers 1, 2, and 4	**O,F**

6	gesture (note use of contrast), perfect fourth interval	**F,P**
7	phrase design (antecedent/consequent), interval class 2	**F**
8	notes E, A, D: chromatic decoration	**O,P**
9	interrupt generation: new motive	**O,F,P**

If the same line had been played on flute, the continuations might all have been very similar except for continuation number 5, which has as its constraint focus the actual movement patterns for manipulating the instrument.

(2) Here we consider an event cluster less clearly tied to structural-historical processes. Let E_i be a segment of sounds produced by a single slow tilting and rotation of a tambourine one-quarter filled with a single layer of small lead shot. E_i is a coloured noise sound which subjectively is reminiscent of distant ocean waves or rain. Some possible continuations are then as follows:

Continuation	Description	Type of arrays
I	continue tilt but speed up rotation of tambourine	**F,P**
2	shake tambourine from side to side	**F,P**
3	stop motion of tambourine	**F,P**
4	toss lead shot in air and catch it	**F,P**
5	perform a drum roll on the bottom of the tambourine skin with fingers of the right hand	**O,F,P**

Continuations 1 and 2 are of associative type, whereas 3, 4, and 5 are interrupt type. Notice that here description emphasizes the motor aspect, since there is no extensive tradition of music theory which applies to such a sound source.

If these examples succeed in illustrating how continuations may be constructed, they are mute on the details of how one continuation comes to be chosen over all other possible ones. What has been said so far is only that, in associative generation, a set of constraints is produced associatively, while in interrupt generation the set of strong constraints on action includes uncorrelated resetting. Obviously, event generation is informed by a vast panorama of culturally and cognitively based musical processes and stylistic preferences (motivic development, phrase design, historical forms, transposition, rhythmic design, etc.). But a considerable degree of residual decision-making remains, as for example the choice of array components that will be singled out to act as strong constraints or to be reset. How are such residual decisions made?

It does not seem possible to give a final answer to this question, for it has at its ultimate root the question of volition and hence the mind-body problem, about which there is no general philosophical agreement in our culture or even among scientists. There is also no conclusive empirical evidence to support one view or another, despite the opposing claims of some positivists and phenomenologists. It seems useful therefore to characterize a number of strategies of explanation for the residual decision-making mentioned above, and subsequently explore what possibilities exist for experimentally decided among them.

It is first of all possible to take the intuitive perspective, that the individual acts best when he or she merely taps a certain powerful source that dictates the course of musical action in a naturally correct fashion, one that may not be analysable or predictable in physical or musical terms. Although this perspective is usually transpersonal and may seem romantic to some, this does not imply that it is untestable and therefore unscientific.

A second perspective is to assume that this residual decision making actually reflects the effects of individual free will. In other words, the improviser is a unique conscious entity, and residual decision making rests to some degree on internal variables not predictable even in principle from a fully detailed knowledge of the physical-state variables of the improviser and his or her environment.

A third perspective is the physicalist one. Here complex decision making is seen to be an emergent property of the fantastically complex physical system known as a human being, in interaction with a series of environments. Free will in this perspective is either illusory, or simply a somewhat misleading metaphor for certain complex characteristics of the system. There are a number of models possible within this perspective for residual decision making: interactive control with lower CNS centres, network statistical voting models, distributed memory-type models, decision making based on fuzzy logic, etc.

Fourth and last is the perspective of randomness. Here the unconstrained residual decision making is simply modelled by use of random generators. As the improviser becomes more and more expert through practice and more and more control procedures are built up, random processes need to be invoked less and less frequently and overall error levels decrease, perhaps approaching a minimum threshold.

To experimentally distinguish between these points of view a high resolution improvisation transcription system has been built here at La Trobe University. Co-worker Greg Troup and myself, as well as technical staff of the departments of psychology and music, have designed and set up the apparatus. It is a synthesizer-based system, using modified MIDI format, and enables detailed recording, to millisecond resolution, of musical actions at a keyboard. It is also possible to input sound from other (non-keyboard) instruments. Simultaneously as music is recorded a videotape of the performance can be made. The results of this investigation are not yet complete and will be reported elsewhere, but it seems likely that the limits of validity of intuitionist and random perspectives will be determinable. There seems to be, however, no obvious experimental design that will decide between the physicalist and free-will perspectives. Hence the two may be considered co-existing formulations. The problem in deciding between the two rests with setting up the repeatable conditions which should theoretically lead to the same 'improvised' result in the hard-core physicalist model and to a different improvised result under conditions of free will. But since each event potentially affects all those that follow, all initial conditions are intrinsically unrepeatable.

The development of improvisational skill

The modelling of this process remains in a less developed state and only a brief discussion is included here. Its starting point is the emergent results of practice found in all types of skill, as mentioned earlier: improved efficiency, fluency, flexibility, capacity for error correction, and, less universally, expressiveness. But there are at least two additional components of improvisational skill: inventiveness and the achievement of coherence. In more fixed skills these are less important, since inventiveness provides few tangible advantages, and coherence is built in by the rigidity of the task demands.*

The specific cognitive changes that allow these properties to develop in improvised musical behaviour are considered to be:

(1) an increase in the memory store of objects, features, and processes—in musical, acoustic, motor (and other) aspects;

(2) an increase in accessibility of this memory store due to the build-up of redundant relationships between its constituents and the aggregation of these constituents into larger cognitive assemblies;

(3) an increasingly refined attunement to subtle and contextually relevant perceptual information.

The build-up and improved access to memory of points (1) and (2) is presumably central to any learning process. In the language of the model of this chapter this involves the use of extensive redundancy, and also the aggregation of memory constituents (objects, features, processes) into new cognitive assembles which may be accessed autonomously. Because such a procedure can presumably be nested to arbitrary depth, very complicated interconnected knowledge structures may develop.

This last idea is not new here. It has a considerable history and has been most clearly outlined for the purposes of this paper by Hayes-Roth (1977), who generalized an earlier model of Hebb (1949). The central feature of

---

* It is interesting to note that these two skills push in opposite directions, for inventiveness comes from the commitment to avoid repetition as much as possible, while coherence is only achieved by some degree of structural unity, which is only possible with repetition.

aggregation of memory elements Hayes-Roth termed *unitisation*, and her knowledge-assembly theory was built up around the presence of elemental 'cognitive units'. In the terminology of this chapter these are object, feature, and process array components. In knowledge-assembly theory such cognitive units are associatively activated and may combine to form assemblies, whose 'strengths' are increasing functions of recency and frequency of activation, and decreasing functions of their own complexity. From these strengths are derived probabilities and speeds of activation. There is a level of redundancy appropriate to improvisation in this model, since for example a cognitive unit may be activated individually or as part of a larger assembly of cognitive units. In her paper, Hayes-Roth shows that knowledge-assembly learning theory is consistent with a large body of experimental results. It is also consistent with the introspective reports of improvisers and the review given above of improvisation teaching methods. But a decision on the superior applicability of this theory to improvisation over those of other related formulations must rest upon experimental work as yet undone. For this reason I give no further speculation.

The third point mentioned above may be elaborated as follows. The refinement of improvisational skill must depend partly on increasing the efficiency of perceptual processing to allow the inclusion of more and better-selected information in the improviser's decision-making procedures. The need for this efficiency is imposed by every performer's more or less limited individual capacity, per unit time, to process novel sensory input. It seems likely that practice leads to the increasingly efficient use of information in two ways: by reducing the effective amount of information by the recognition of patterns of redundancy in the sensory input, and by focusing attention increasingly on the information that is most relevant for producing a successful improvisation. The increased use of such subtle and 'higher-order' information leads to the higher-order skill characteristics mentioned earlier. The main differences in this process between fixed and improvised actions may be said to reside in the nature of the attention focus used in the two situations. The fixed-skill situation evolves towards a minimal size attention set, whereas the unpredictability of improvisation demands that the attention focus remain wide. To go beyond such insufficiently specific observations experimental work is clearly required.

Conclusions

This chapter has attempted to illuminate the process of musical improvisation by first examining the modelling tools available from a number of different disciplines. Based on this examination, a cognitive model has then been presented for the process itself, followed by a brief discussion of its relation to improvisational skill acquisition. The central features of the model are as follows. It is reductionist, in that cognitive structures of processing and control are considered to be broken down into aspects (acoustic, musical, movement, etc.), each of these into types of analytical representation (objects, features, processes), and each of these into characterizing elements (array components). At the same time the model is synergistic and capable of behavioural novelty, due to the extensive redundancy of the cognitive representations and the distributed and non-linear character of the outlined control processes. The extensive presence of feedback and feedforward contributes to this. The fundamental nature of the improvisation process is considered to be the stringing together of a series of 'event clusters' during each of which a continuation is chosen, based upon either the continuing of some existing stream of musical development (called here an event-cluster class) by association of array entries, or the interruption of that stream by the choosing of a new set of array entries that act as constraints in the generation of a new stream (new event-cluster class).

The model seems to be specific enough to allow its use as a basis for the design of 'improvising' computer programs. Work in this direction is in progress. At the same time some fundamental philosophical questions remain about the origin of certain kinds of decision making in any such model, and four types of answers to these have been outlined: intuition, free will, physical causation, and randomness. Some of these alternatives should be distinguishable on the basis of experimental work currently in progress at our laboratories, which also has as its aim the testing of the basic assumptions of the model. This will be described in subsequent publications.

Acknowledgement

I am indebted to John Sloboda, Margot Prior, Geoff Cumming, Geoff Webb, Denis Glencross, and Glynda Kinsella for helpful criticism.

References

Abramson, R. M. (1980). Dalcroze-based improvisation. *Music Educator's Journal* **66**, (5), 62–8.
Adams, J. A. (1961). Human tracking behaviour. *Psychological Bulletin* **58**, 55–79.
Adams, J. A. (1971). A closed-loop theory of motor learning. *Journal of Motor Behaviour* **3**, 111–49.
Adams, J. A. (1976). Issues for a closed-loop theory of motor learning. In *Motor control: issues and trends* (ed. G. E. Stelmach). Academic Press, New York.
Adams, R. (1980). *The iron wolf*. Penguin, Reading.

Allport, D. A. (1980). Attention and performance. In *Cognitive psychology: new directions,* (ed. G. Claxton). Routledge and Kegan Paul, London.

Alperson, P. (1984). On musical improvisation. *Journal of Aesthetics and Art Criticism* **43**, 17–29

Armbruster, G. (1984). First steps in improvisation. *Keyboard* **10** (Oct.), 37–44.

Arnold, F. T. (1965). *The art of accompaniment from a thoroughbass as practised in the XVIIth and XVIIIth centuries.* Dover, New York.

Austin, L., Oliveros, P., *et al.* (1982/83). Forum: improvisation. *Perspectives of New Music,* Fall-Winter 1982/Spring-Summer 1983, 26–111.

Avery, T. L. (1984) Structure and strategy in Azorean–Canadian song duels. Unpublished Ph.D. thesis, Indiana University.

Bach, C. P. E. (1778/1949). *Essay on the true art of playing keyboard instruments.* Norton, New York.

Bahm, A. (1960). Types of intuition. *University of New Mexico publications in social sciences and philosophy,* No. 3.

Bailey, D. (1980). *Improvisation: its nature and practice in music.* Moorland, London.

Baker, D. (1969). *Jazz improvisation.* Maher, Chicago.

Bartlett, F. C. (1947). The measurement of human skill. *British Medical Journal* **1**, 835, 877.

Bash, L. (1983). The effectiveness of three instructional methods on the acquisition of jazz improvisation skills. Unpublished Ph.D. thesis. State University of New York at Buffalo.

Bastick, T. (1982). *Intuition: how we think and act.* Wiley, Chichester.

Beatty, J. (1975). *Introduction to physiological psychology.* Brooks/Cole, Monterey, Calif.

Béhague, G. (1980). Improvisation in Latin American musics. *Music Educator's Journal* **66**, (5), 118–25.

Bentley, D. and Konishi, M. (1978). Neural control of behaviour. *Annual Review of Neurosciences* **1**, 35–59.

Bergson, H. L. (1910). *Matter and memory* (authorized trans. N. M. Paul and W. S. Palmer). Allen, London.

Berkowitz, S. (1975). *Improvisation through keyboard harmony.* Prentice-Hall, Englewood Cliffs, NJ.

Bernstein, N. (1967). *The coordination and regulation of movements.* Pergamon, London.

Bresgen, C. (1960). *Die improvisation.* Quelle and Meyer, Heidelberg.

Brooks, D. N. and Baddeley, A. (1976), What can amnesic patients learn? *Neuropsychologia* **14**, 111–22.

Brooks, V. B. (1978). Motor programs revisited. In *Posture and movement: perspectives for integrating sensory and motor research on the mammalian nervous sytem.* Raven, New York.

Bruner, J. S. (1969). Modalities of memory. In *The pathology of memory* (ed. G. A. Tallard, and N. C. Waugh), pp. 253–9. Academic Press, New York.

Brunia, C. H. M. (1980). Motor preparation, recorded on the cortical and spinal level. In *Tutorials in motor behaviour* (ed. G. E. Stelmach and J. Requin). North-Holland, Amsterdam.

Bunge, M. (1962). *Intuition and science.* Prentice-Hall, Englewood Cliffs, NJ.

Burnsed, C. V. (1978). The development and evaluation of an introductory jazz improvisation sequence for intermediate band students. *Dissertation Abstracts International*, **41A**, 1214A.

Carr, I. (1982). *Miles Davis*. Paladin, London.

Chadabe, J. (1984). Interactive composing: an overview. *Computer Music Journal* **8**, (1), 22–7.

Chernikoff, R. and Taylor, F. V. (1952). Reaction time to kinesthetic stimulation resulting from sudden arm displacement. *Journal of Experimental Psychology* **43**, 1–8.

Clark, H. H. and Clark, E. V. (1977). *Psychology and language*. Harcourt Brace Jovanovitch, New York.

Cohen, N. J. (1981). Neuropsychological evidence for a distinction between procedural and declarative knowledge in human memory and amnesia. Unpublished Ph.D. thesis. University of California at San Diego.

Cohen, N. J. and Squire, L. R. (1980). Preserved learning and retention of pattern analysing skill in amnesia: dissociation of knowing how and knowing that. *Science* **210**, 207–9.

Coker, J. (1964). *Improvising jazz*. Prentice-Hall, Englewood Cliffs, NJ.

Coker, J. (1975). *The jazz idiom*. Prentice-Hall, Englewood Cliffs, NJ.

Coker J., Casale, J., Campbell, G., and Greene, J. (1970). *Patterns for jazz*. Studio Productions, Lebanon, Ind.

Coleman, S. N. (1922). *Creative music for children*. G. P. Putnam's Sons, New York.

Cope, D. H. (1984). *New directions in music*. William Brown, Dubuque, Iowa.

Czerny, C. (1829/1983). *Systematic introduction to improvisation on the piano* (Trans. A. L. Mitchell). Longman, New York.

Datta, V. and Lath, M. (1967). Improvisation in Indian music. *World of Music*, **9**, (1), 27–34.

Davis, R. (1957). The human operator as a single channel information system. *Quarterly Journal of Experimental Psychology* **9**, 119–29.

Delcomyn, F. (1980). Neural basis of rhythmic behaviour in animals. *Science* **210**, 492–8.

Denier van der Gon, J. J. and Thuring, J. Ph. (1965). The guiding of human writing movements. *Kybernetik* **2**, 145–8.

Dobbins, B. (1978). *The contemporary jazz pianist*, 4 vols. GAMT Music Press, Jamestown, RI.

Doerschuk, B. (1984). The literature of improvisation. *Keyboard* **10** (Oct.), 48–52.

Dupré, M. (1925/37). *Cours complet d'improvisation a' l'orgue*, 2 vols. A. Leduc, Paris.

Easton, T. A. (1978). Coordinative structure—the basis for a motor program. In *Psychology of motor behaviour and sport* (ed. D. M. Landers and R. W. Christina). Human Kinetics, Champaign, Ill.

Eccles, J. C. (1972). *The understanding of the brain*. McGraw-Hill, New York.

Ehmann, Wilhelm (1950). Chorische Improvisation in der Kantorei. *Kirchenchor* **10** (Sept.–Oct.), 65–71.

Erlmann, V. (1985). Model, variation and performance. Ful'be praise song in Northern Cameroon. *Yearbook for traditional music* **17**, 88–112.

Ewing, A. (1941). Reason and intuition. *Proceedings of the British academy* **27**, 67–107.

Ferand, Ernst (1938). *Die Improvisation in der Musik*. Rhein-Verlag, Zurich.

Ferand, Ernst (1961). *Improvisation in nine centuries of western music*. Arno Volk Verlag, Hans Gerig KG, Cologne.

Fitts, P. M. (1964). Perceptual-motor skill learning. In *Categories of human learning* (ed. A. W. Melton). Academic Press, New York.

Fry, C. (1980). Computer improvisation. *Computer Music Journal* **4** (3), 48 ff.

Fry, C. (1982/83). Dancing musicians. *Perspectivies of New Music*, Fall–Winter 1982/Spring–Summer 1983, 585–9.

Gaburo, K. (1968). *Twenty sensing compositions*. Lingua Press, La Jolla, Calif.

Galás, D. (1981/82). Intravenal song. *Perspectives of New Music*, Fall–Winter 1981/Spring–Summer 1982, 59–62.

Gehring, P. K. (1963). Improvisation in contemporary organ playing. Unpublished Ph.D. thesis Syracuse University.

Gelernter, H. (1963). Realisation of a geometry-theorem-proving machine. In *Computers and thought*. (ed. E. A. Feigenbaum and J. Feldman). McGraw-Hill, New York.

Gel'fand, I. M. and Tsetlin, M.L. (1962). Some methods of control for complex systems. *Russian Mathematical Surveys* **17**, 95–116.

Gel'fand, I. M. and Tsetlin, M. L. (1971). Mathematical modelling of mechanisms of the central nervous system. In *Models of the structural–functional organisation of certain biological systems* (eds. I. M. Gel'fand, V. S. Gurfinkel, S. V. Fomin, and M. T. Tsetlin). MIT Press, Cambridge, Mass.

Gibbs, C. B. (1965). Probability learning in step-input tracking. *British Journal of Psychology* **56**, 233–42.

Gibbs, C. B. and Brown, I. C. (1956). Increased production from information incentives in an uninteresting repetitive task. *Manager* **24**, 374–9.

Gibson, J. J. (1966). *The senses considered as perceptual systems*. Houghton Mifflin, Boston.

Gibson, J. J. (1979). *The ecological approach to visual perception*. Houghton Mifflin, Boston.

Glencross, D. J. (1977). Control of skilled movements. *Psychological Bulletin* **84**, 14–29.

Glencross, D. J. and Koreman, M. M. (1979). The processing of proprioceptive signals. *Neuropsychologia* **17**, 683–7.

Goldstein, M. (1983). The gesture of improvisation: some thoughts, reflections and questions regarding percussion music. *Percussionist* **21**, (3), 18–24.

Gorder, W. D. (1976) An investigation of divergent production abilities as constructs of musical creativity. Unpublished Ed. D. thesis. University of Illinois at Urbana–Champaign.

Greene, P. M. (1972). Problems of organisation of motor systems. In *Progress in theoretical biology*, Vol. 2 (eds. R. Rosen and F. M. Snell). Academic Press, New York.

Guevara, M., Glass, L., Mackey, M., and Shrier, A. (1983). Chaos in neurobiology. *IEEE Transactions on systems, Man, and Cybernetics* **SMC-13**, (5), 790–8.

Guildford, J. P. (1977). *Way beyond the I.Q.* Creative Education Foundation, New York.

Guildford, J. P. and Hoepfner, R. (1971). *The analysis of intelligence.* McGraw-Hill, New York.

Hamel, P. M. (1979). *Through music to the self.* Shambhala, Boulder, Col.

Hanlon, E. S. (1975). Improvisation: theory and application for theatrical music and silent film. Unpublished Ph.D. thesis. University of Cincinnati.

Hayes-Roth, B. (1977). Evolution of cognitive structures and processes. *Psychological Review* **84**, (3), 260–78.

Hebb, D. D. (1949). *Organisation of behaviour.* Wiley, New York.

Hendrickson, G. and Schroeder, W. H. (1941). Transfer of training in learning to hit a submerged target. *Journal of Educational Psychology* **32**, 205–13.

Hick, W. E. (1952). On the rate of gain of information. *Quarterly Journal of Experimental Psychology* **4**, 11–26.

Higgins, J. R. and Angel, R. W. (1970). Correction of tracking errors without sensory feedback. *Journal of Experimental Psychology* **84**, 412–16.

Hodeir, Andre (1956). *Jazz: its evolution and essence* (trans. David Noakes). Grove, New York.

Holding, D. H. (1965). *Principles of training.* Pergamon, London.

Holding, D. (1981). Skills research. In *Human skills* (ed. D. Holding). Wiley, Chichester.

Hollerbach, J. M. (1981). An oscillation theory of handwriting. *Biological Cybernetics* **39**, 139–56.

Hood, M. (1971). Aspects of group improvisation in the Javanese gamelan. In *Musics of Asia* (ed. José Maceda), pp. 17–21. Manila.

Hood, M. (1975). Improvisation in the stratified ensembles of Southeast Asia. *Selected Reports in Ethnomusicology* (UCLA) **2**, (2), 25–33.

Hores, R. G. (1977). A comparative study of visual- and aural-orientated approaches to jazz improvisation with implications for instruction. Unpublished Ed. D. thesis. Indiana University.

Howard, J. (1978). Improvisational techniques of Art Tatum. Unpublished Ph.D. thesis. Case Western Reserve University.

Huggins, A. W. F. (1978). Speech timing and intelligibility. In *Attention and performance VII* (ed. J. Requin). Lawrence Erlbaum, Hillsdale, NJ.

Jairazbhoy, N. A. (1971). *The rags of North Indian music.* Faber and Faber, London.

Jaques-Dalcroze, E. (1921/1976). *Rhythm, music and education.* B. Blom, New York.

Jaques-Dalcroze, E. (1930). *Eurythmics, art, and education.* Ayer, New York.

James, W. (1890). *Principles of psychology*, Vol. 1. Holt, New York.

Jones, A. M. (1959). *Studies in African Music.* Oxford, London.

Jost, E. (1974). *Free jazz.* Universal, Graz.

Keele, S. W. and Posner, M. I. (1968). Processing of feedback in rapid movements. *Journal of Experimental Psychology* **77**, 353–63.

Keele, S. W. and Summers, J. J. (1976). The structure of motor programs. In *Motor control: issues and trends* (ed. G. E. Stelmach). Academic Press, New York.

Kelso, J. A. S. (1982). Two strategies for investigating action. In *Human motor behaviour* (ed. J. A. S. Kelso). Lawrence Erlbaum, Hillsdale, NJ.

Kelso, J. A. S. and Wallace, S. A. (1978). Conscious mechanisms in movement. In *Information processing in motor control and learning* (ed. G. E. Stelmach). Academic Press, New York.

Kelso, J. A., Holt, J. G., Rubin, P., and Kugler, P. N. (1981). Patterns of human interlimb coordination emerge from the properties of non-linear, limit cycle oscillatory processes: theory and data. *Journal of Motor Behaviour* **13**, 226–61.

Kernfeld, B. (1983). Two Coltranes. *Annual Review of Jazz Studies* **2**, 7–66.

Kerr, R. (1982). *Psychomotor learning.* Saunders, Philadelphia.

Kickert, W. G., Bertrand, J. W., and Praagman, J. (1978). Some comments on cybernetics and control. *IEEE transactions on systems, man and cybernetics* **SMC-8**, 805–9.

Kleeman, J. E. (1985/86). The parameters of musical transmission. *The Journal of Musicology* **4**, 1–22.

Kleinman, D. L., Baron, S., and Levison, W. H. (1971). A control theoretic approach to manned-vehicle systems analysis. *IEEE Transactions on Automatic Control* **AC-16**, 824–32.

Kugler, P. N., Kelso, J. A. S., and Turvey, M. T. (1980). On the concept of coordinative structures as dissipative structures: I. theoretical lines of convergence. In *Tutorials in motor behaviour* (ed. G. E. Stelmach and J. Requin). North-Holland, Amsterdam.

Laabs, G. J. and Simmons, R. W. (1981). Motor memory. In *Human skills* (ed. D. Holding). Wiley, New York.

Laneri, Roberto (1975). Prima materia: an opus in progress. The natural dimension of music. Unpublished Ph.D. thesis. University of California at San Diego.

Lenat, D. B. (1984). Computer software for intelligent systems. *Scientific American* **251**, (3), 152–60.

Leonard, J. A. (1959). Tactual choice reactions. *Quarterly Journal of Experimental Psychology* **11**, 76–83.

Levitt, D. A. (1981). A melody description system for jazz improvisation. Unpublished M.S. thesis. MIT.

Li, T. Y. and Yorke, J. (1975). Period three implies chaos. *American Mathematical Monthly* **82**, 985–92.

Liebman, D., Beirach, R., Tusa, F., Williams, J.,. and Roy, B. (1978). *Lookout farm.* Almo Publications, Hollywood.

Lipiczky, T. (1985). Tihai formulas and the 'composition' and improvisation in North Indian music. *The Musical Quarterly* **71**, 157–71.

Locke, D. (1979). The music of atsiabeko. Unpublished Ph.D. thesis. Wesleyan University.

Lord, A. B. (1964). *The singer of tales.* Harvard University Press, Cambridge, Mass.

Lord, A. B. (1965). Yugoslav epic folk poetry. In *The study in folklore* (ed. A. Dundes). Prentice-Hall, Englewood Cliffs, NJ.

McCulloch, W. S. (1945). A heterarchy of values determined by the topology of nervous nets. *Bulletin of Mathematical Biophysics* **7**, 89–93.

Marteniuk, R. G. and Romanow, S. K. E. (1983). Human movement organisation and learning as revealed by variability of movement, use of kinematic information, and Fourier analysis. In *Memory and control of action* (ed. R. A. Magill). North-Holland, Amsterdam.

Mathieu, L. (1984). A phenomenological investigation of improvisation in music and dance. Unpublished Ph.D. thesis, New York University.

May, R. M. (1976). Simple mathematical models with very complicated dynamics. *Nature* **261**, 459–67.

Mersenne, M. (1635). *Harmonie Universelle.*

Milano, D. (1984). The psychology of improvisation. *Keyboard* **10** (Oct.), 25, 30–5.

Miller, G. A., Galanter, E., and Pribram, K. (1960). *Plans and the structure of behaviour.* Holt, Rinehart and Winston, New York.

Milner, B. (1962). Les troubles de la memoire accompagnant des lesions hippocampiques bilaterales. In *Phsyiologie de l'Hippocampe.* Cent. Natl. Recherche Scientifique, Paris.

Morasso, P. (1983). Three dimensional arm trajectories. *Biological Cybernetics* **48**, 187–94.

Murphy, F. (1982). The cornet style of Leon Bix Beiderbecke (1903–1931). Unpublished Ph.D. thesis. La Trobe University, Melbourne.

Nagler, M. N. (1974). *Spontaneity and tradition: a study in the oral art of Homer.* University of California Press, Berkeley.

Namikas, G. (1983). Vertical process and motor performance. In *Memory and control of action* (ed. R. A. Magill). North-Holland, Amsterdam.

Nelson, O. (1966). *Patterns for improvisation.* Nelson Music, Hollywood.

Nettl, B. (1974). Thoughts on improvisation . *Musical Quarterly* **60**, 1–19.

Nettl, B. and Foltin, B. Jr. (1972). *Daramad of Chahargah.* Information Coordinators, Detroit.

Nettl, B. and Riddle, R. (1974). Taqsim Nahawand: a study of 16 performances by Jihad Racy. *Yearbook of the International Folk Music Council* **5**, 11–50.

Newell, K. M. (1981). Skill learning. In *Human skills* (ed. D. Holding). Wiley, Chichester.

Oliveros, P. (1971). *Sonic meditations.* Smith Publications/Sonic Art Editions, Baltimore, Md.

Owens, T. (1974). Charlie Parker: techniques of improvisation, 2 Vols. Unpublished Ph.D. thesis. University of California at Los Angeles.

Paillard, J. (1980). The multichanneling of visual cues and the organisation of visually guided response. In *Tutorials in motor behaviour* (eds. G. E. Stelmach and J. Requin). North-Holland, Amsterdam.

Park, M. (1985). Music and shamanism in Korea: a study of selected ssikkŭm-gut rituals for the dead. Unpublished Ph.D. thesis, University of California at Los Angeles.

Parry, M. (1930). Studies in the epic technique of oral versemaking: I. Homer and Homeric style. *Harvard Studies in Classical Philology* **41**, 73–147.

Parry, M. (1932). Studies in the epic technique of oral versemaking: II. the Homeric language as the language of poetry. *Harvard Studies in Classical Philology* **43**, 1–50.

Parsons, W. (1978). *Music for citizen's band.* W. Parsons, La Jolla, Calif.

Partchey, K. C. (1973). The effects of feedback, models, and repetition on the ability to improvise melodies. Unpublished D.Ed. thesis. Pennsylvania State University.

Pew, R. W. (1974). Human perceptual-motor performance. In *Human information processing: tutorials in performance and cognition* (ed. B. H. Kantowitz). Erlbaum, NJ.

Pew, R. W. and Baron, S. (1978). The components of an information processing theory of skilled performance based on an optimal control perspective. In *Information processing motor control and learning* (ed. G. E. Stelmach). Academic Press, New York.

Pike, A. (1974). A Phenomenology of jazz. *Journal of Jazz Studies* 2, (1), 88–94.

Poulton, E. C. (1957). On the stimulus and response in pursuit tracking. *Journal of Experimental Psychology* 53, 57–65.

Powers, W. T. (1973). *Behaviour: the control of perception*. Aldine, Chicago.

Pressing, J. (1980). Music, altered states of consciousness, and psi. In *Proceedings of the Psychic Orientation Conference* (ed. A. Gabay). La Trobe University, Melbourne.

Pressing, J. (1984a). Cognitive processes in improvisation. In *Cognitive processes in the perception of art* (ed. W. R. Crozier and A. J. Chapman), pp. 345–63. North-Holland, Amsterdam.

Pressing, J. (1984b). A history of musical improvisation to 1600. *Keyboard* 10 (11), 64–8.

Pressing J. (1984c). A history of musical improvisation: 1600–1900. *Keyboard* 10, (12), 59–67.

Prigogine, I. (1967). *Introduction to thermodynamics of irreversible processes.* Interscience, New York.

Prigogine, I. and Nicholis, G. (1971). Biological order, structure and instabilities. *Quarterly Review of Biophysics* 4, 107–48.

Propp, V. I. (1927/1968). *Morphology of the folk tale* (trans. L. Scott). University of Texas Press, Austin.

Quantz, J. J. (1752/1966). *On playing the flute* (trans. E. Reilley). Free Press, New York.

Rabbitt, P. M. A. and Vyas, S. M. (1970). An elementary preliminary taxonomy for some errors in laboratory choice RT tasks. *Acta Psychologica* 33, 56–76.

Radano, R. M. (1985). Anthony Braxton and his two musical traditions, the meeting of concert music and jazz (2 vols). Unpublished Ph.D. thesis, University of Michigan.

Reck, D. B. (1983). A musician's tool-kit: a study of five performances by Thirugokarnam Ramachandra Iyer, 2 Vols. Unpublished Ph.D. thesis. Wesleyan University.

Rich, E. (1983). *Artificial intelligence*. McGraw-Hill, New York.

Richardson, C. P. (1983). Creativity research in music education: a review. *Council for Research in Music Education* 74, (Spring 1983), 1–21.

Roads, C. (1979). Grammars as representations for music. *Computer Music Journal* 3, 48–55.

Ryle, G. (1949). *The concept of mind*. Hutchinson, London.

Sadie, S. (ed.) (1980). *The new Grove dictionary of music and musicians.* Macmillan, London. Listings under improvisation, aleatory, cadenza, continuo, division. prélude non mesuré.

Sage, G. S. (1977). *Introduction to motor behaviour: a neuropsychological approach*. Addison-Wesley, Reading, Mass.

Saltzman, E. L. and Kelso, J. A. S. (1983). Toward a dynamical account of motor memory and control. In *Memory and control of action* (ed. R. A. Magill). North-Holland, Amsterdam.

Schickhaus, K-H. (1978). *Neues Schulwerk für Hackbrett*. Josef Preissler, Munich.

Schmidt, R. A. (1983). On the underlying response structure of well-learned motor responses: a discussion of Namikas and Schneider and Fisk. In *Memory and control of action* (ed. R. A. Magill). North-Holland, Amsterdam.

Schneider, W. and Fisk, A. D. (1983). Attention theory and mechanisms for skilled performance. In *Memory and control of action* (ed. R. A. Magill). North-Holland, Amsterdam.

Schouten, H. (no date given). *Improvisation on the organ* (trans. by J. L. Warren). W. Paxton, London.

Schuller, G. (1968). *Early jazz: its roots and musical development*. Oxford University Press, New York.

Serafine, M. L. (1983). Cognition in music. *Cognition* 14, 119–83.

Shafer, R. M. (1969). *Ear cleaning*. Universal, London.

Shaffer, L. H. (1978). Timing in the motor programming of typing. *Quarterly Journal of Experimental Psychology* 30, 333–45.

Shaffer, L. H. (1980). Analysing piano performance: a study of concert pianists. In *Tutorials in motor behaviour* (ed. G. E. Stelmach and J. Requin). North-Holland, Amsterdam.

Shaffer, L. H. (1981). Performances of Chopin, Bach and Bartok: studies in motor programming. *Cognitive psychology* 13, 327–76.

Shaffer, L. H. (1984). Timing in solo and duet piano performances. *Quarterly Journal of Experimental Psychology* A36, 577–95.

Shepherd, G. M. (1983). *Neurobiology*. Oxford University Press, New York.

Sher, C. (1983). *The world's greatest fake book*. Sher Music, San Francisco.

Shiffrin, R. M. and Schneider, W. (1977). Controlled and automatic human information processing: II. perceptual learning, automatic attending, and a general theory. *Psychological Review* 84, 127–90.

Signell, K. (1974). Esthetics of improvisation in Turkish art music. *Asian Music* 5, (2), 45–9.

Signell, K. (1977). *Makam: modal practice in Turkish art music*. Asian music Publications, Seattle.

Silverman, M. L. (1962) Ensemble improvisation as a creative technique in the secondary instrumental program. Unpublished Ed.D. thesis. Stanford University.

Sloboda, J. A. (1982). Music performance. In *Psychology of music* (ed. D. Deutsch). Academic Press, New York.

Slonimsky, N. (1975). *Thesaurus of scales and melodic patterns*. Duckworth, London.

Smith, G. E. (1983). Homer, Gregory, and Bill Evans? the theory of formulaic composition in the context of jazz piano improvisation. Unpublished Ph.D. thesis, Harvard University.

Smith, W. M. and Bowen, K. F. (1980). The effects of delayed and displaced visual feedback on motor control. *Journal of Motor Behaviour* 12, 91–101.

Sparrow, W. A. (1983). The efficiency of skilled performance. *Journal of Motor Behaviour* **15**, 237–61.

Sperber, M. (1974). Improvisation in the performing arts: music, dance and theatre. Unpublished Ed.D. thesis. Columbia University.

Squire, L. R. (1982). The neuropsychology of human memory. *Annual Review of Neuroscience* **5**, 241–73.

Stocks, J. (1939). *Reason and intuition* (ed. D. M. Emmett). Oxford University Press, New York.

Stumme, W. (1972). *Über improvisation.* B. Schott, Mainz.

Sudnow, D. (1978). *Ways of the hand.* Harvard University Press, Cambridge, Mass.

Suehs, H. C. (1979). The development, implementation, and assessment of a course of study for instruction in certain improvisational techniques in the performance of Baroque music from 1679 to 1741. Unpublished Ph.D. thesis, Catholic University of America at Washington.

Sumarsam (1981). The musical practice of the gamelan sekaten. *Asian Music* **12**, (2), 54–73.

Summers, J. J. (1981). Motor programs. In *Human skills* (ed. D. Holding), Wiley, Chichester.

Suzuki, S., Mills, E. and Murphy, T. (1973). *The Suzuki concept: an introduction to a successful method for early music education.* Diablo Press, Berkeley, Calif.

Terzudo, C. and Viviani, P. (1979). About the central representation of learned motor patterns. In *Posture and movement* (eds. R. Talbot and D. R. Humphrey). Raven, New York.

Thompson, S. (1946). *The folktale.* Holt, Rinehart and Winston, New York.

Torrance, E. P. (1966) *Guiding creative talent.* Prentice-Hall, Englewood Cliffs, NJ.

Touma, H. H. (1971). The *maqam* phenomenon: an improvisation technique in the music of the middle east. *Ethnomusicology* **15**, 38–48.

Treitler, L. (1974). Homer and Gregory: the transmission of epic poetry and plainchant. *Musical Quarterly* **9**, 333–72.

Turvey, M. T. (1977). Preliminaries to a theory of action with reference to vision. In *Perceiving, acting and knowing: toward an ecological psychology* (eds. R. Shaw and J. Bransford). Lawrence Erlbaum, Hillsdale, NJ.

Ueltzen, D. R. (1986). Improvisation in Kirchengesang und mit dem Kirchenlied und am Gesangbuch für das Jahr 2000. *Gottesdienst und Kirchenmusik* **3**, 71–7.

Vaughan, M. M. (1971). Music as model and metaphor in the cultivation and measurement of creative behaviour in children. Unpublished Ed.D. thesis. University of Georgia.

Vīķis-Fribergs, V. (1984). Creativity and tradition in oral folklore or the balance of innovation and repetition in the oral poet's art. In *Cognitive processes in the perception of art* (eds. W. R. Crozier and A. J. Chapman). North-Holland, Amsterdam.

Viviani, P. and Terzudo, C. (1980). Space-time invariance in learned motor skills. In *Tutorials in motor behaviour* (eds. G. E. Stelmach and J. Requin). North-Holland, Amsterdam.

von Foerster, H. (1960). On self-organising systems and their environments. In

Self-organising systems (ed. M. C. Yorits and S. Cameron). Pergamon, New York.

Von Holst, E. (1954). Relations between the central nervous system and the peripheral organs. *British Journal of Animal Behaviour* **2**, 89–94.

Wade, Bonnie (1973). Chiz in Khyal: the traditional composition in the improvised performance. *Ethnomusicology* **17**, 443–59.

Webster, R. P. (1977). A factor of intellect approach to creative thinking in music. Unpublished Ph.D. thesis. University of Rochester, Eastman School of Music.

Weidner, R. F. (1984). The improvisation techniques of Charles Tournemire as extracted from his five reconstructed organ improvisations. Unpublished Ph.D. thesis, Michigan State University.

Welford, A. T. (1974). On the sequencing of action. *Brain Research* **71**, 381–92.

Welford, A. T. (1976). *Skilled performance.* Scott, Foresman, Glenview, Ill.

West, L. J. (1967). Vision and kinesthesis in the acquisition of typewriting skill. *Journal of Applied Psychology* **51** (2), 161–6.

Westcott, M. R. (1968). *Towards a contemporary psychology of intuition*, Holt, Reinhart and Winston, New York.

Whitmer, T. (1934). *The art of improvisation.* M. Witmark and Sons, New York.

Wilberg, R. B. (1983). Memory for movement: discussion of Adams and Saltzman and Kelso. In *Memory and control of action* (ed. R. A. Magill). North-Holland, Amsterdam.

Winograd, T. (1975). Frame representations and the declarative-procedural controversy. In *Representation and understanding* (ed. D. Bobrow and A. Collins). Academic Press, New York.

Zelaznik, H. N., Hawkins, B., and Kisselburgh, L. (1983). Rapid visual feedback processing in single-arming movements. *Journal of Motor Behaviour* **15**, 217–36.

Zonis, Ella (1973). *Classical Persian music: an introduction.* Harvard University Press, Cambridge, Mass.

8

Experimental research into musical generative ability*

MÁRIA SÁGI and IVÁN VITÁNYI

One of the projects carried on for about 15 years in the Institute for Culture of Hungary has been concerned with analysing human creative faculties; in particular, artistic creativity. We have been concerned to discover the place, role, and modes of creativity in Hungarian culture, and we have attempted to relate different levels of creativity to economic, social, and educational factors. Our empirical studies have been extended to differnt arts, including music, fine arts, fiction, and poetry.

This chapter describes part of our research into musical creativity. Music is a particularly suitable idiom for our purposes. Its abstract character makes it easy to react to on many different levels. Also, music has deeply penetrated many different social groups, thus 'pre-conditioning' a wide range of subjects for giving relevant responses. In addition, the wide use in Hungarian education of the Kodály method has placed great importance on the practical development of musical creativity.

The music-psychological research to be described below was provoked by the view widespread in the literature both of the psychology and the sociology of art that two kinds of artistic experiences can be distinguished: that of the creator and that of the receiver. This is a view we do not share. Proponents of this view tend to argue that only a narrow group in contemporary society takes a creative part in music (for example from Hungary's population of 10 million, taking into account all the composers of popular songs and rock music, only about 2 to 3000; that is 0.02 to 0.03 per cent).

A contrasting view is provided by Weber's (1921) and Blaukopf's (1972) ideas on the role of sound systems. According to them, the systems of musical structures adopted by a composer form a language, a semiotic system to which the most ingenious composer can merely add something and which he is unable to create himself.

* A short summary of part of this study was published earlier in *Contribution to the Sociology of the Arts* (1983), ISA Research Committee 37, pp. 242–9. Research Institute for Culture, Sofia.

Of course, there are different levels of composing ability. In particular, we can distinguish between *constructive* and *generative* forms of composing ability. We do not wish to dwell at length on the general theoretical issues of creativity because our aim is to describe our empirical investigation. Let us simply note that we agree with authors like Taylor (1959) who distinguish levels of creativity. We consider creativity as consisting of two main types: constructive creativity (which is—in the stricter sense of the term—artistic creativity) and generative creativity.

We speak about constructive creative ability in music where the composer gives a final form to an original opus by means of conscious work, employing and (partly) reshaping the elements and rules known to him. By generative composing we mean a largely unconscious or intuitive variational application of the elements and rules which does not result in a final opus of unchangeable form but merely in a new variant. We have adapted this term from Chomsky's (1965) 'generative linguistic ability'. Generative linguistic ability means that with the knowledge of a definite number of elements and of a definite number of generative rules all the speakers of a language can produce an indefinite number of sentences. That is exactly how generative musical ability acts: with a definite number of elements (stock of sounds) 'and a definite number of generative rules' an indefinite number of melodies can be constructed.

Historical evidence of generative musical ability is readily available. We see this in the way that folk-songs take shape, are transformed, and are sung time and again by folk-singers. We may legitimately ask, however, if, through the destruction of traditional popular art, the generative musical ability of mankind may not have been destroyed as well. Has the pervasive music-supplying apparatus of radio, television, cinema, music-halls, and restaurants killed the ability of man to compose music for himself? This was the question to which the following investigation sought a reply.

Procedure

Exploration

Prior to undertaking the musical tasks subjects were engaged in a personal discussion to put them at ease. The subjects gladly discussed their lives, past and present, their general views on life, their relations to the world and the arts, and their general and artistic tastes.

Examination of generative musical ability

Subjects were asked to make immediate sung improvisations to poems.

One was Sándor Petőfi's (mid-19th century) '*Falu végén kurta kocsma*' ('Little inn outside the village') in the style of a folk-song.

Falu végén kurta kocsma,	At village end a small saloon,
Oda rug ki a Szamosra,	That is where Szamosra hangs out,
Meg is látná magát benne,	He would even be able to see himself in it,
Ha az éj nem közeledne.	If night was not approaching.
Az éjszaka közeledik,	Night is coming,
A világ lecsendesedik,	The world grows quiet,
Pihen a komp, kikötötték,	The ferryboat rests, they have tied it out,
Benne hallgat a sötétség.	In it the darkness remains silent.
	(translation by Dr Thomas Kabdebo)

Two other poems were chosen to represent the Hungarian poetry of the twentieth century: Endre Ady's poem '*A Kirsztusok mártirja*' ('The Martyr of the Christ').

	Literal translation
Vad, nagyszerü rajongást oltott	The brooklet's bank has infused in me
Az Érnek partja én belém	A worship wild and passionate,
Csupa pogányság volt a lelkem,	Of paganism my soul was brimful
Gondtalan vágy és vak remény	Carefree desire and blind of hope.
Forgott körültem zagyva módon	Turning confusedly around me
Lármával, vadul a világ	The world was clamorous and wild.
És én kerestem egyre-egyre	I was searching unfalteringly
Valami nagy Harmóniát.	In it some major Harmony.

and eight lines of Attila József's '*Óda*' ('Ode').

Óh, hát miféle anyag vagyok én,	O what kind of matter am I
hogy pillantásod metsz és alakit?	that your glance cuts and shapes me?
Miféle lélek és miféle fény	What kind of soul and what kind of light
s ámulatra méltó tünemény,	and what kind of amazing phenomenon am I
hogy bejárhatom a semmiség ködén	that in the mist of emptiness I can walk around
termékeny tested lankás tájait?	the gentle slopes of your fertile body?
S mint megnyilt értelembe az ige,	And like the word entering into an enlightened mind
alászállhatok rejtelmeidbe.	I can enter into its mysteries . . .
	(translation by Dr Thomas Kabdebo)

The fourth poem was the lyric of a hit song.

Subjects were also asked to make improvisations to simple harmonic progressions; first to the familiar I–IV–V–I, then to the more sophisticated progressions, including some typical of Bartók (see Examples 8. 1–7).

The sense of tonality of the subjects was examined by asking them to improvise completions to three melodies (see Examples 8. 8–10). Each was

Example 8.1

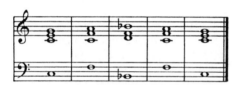

Example 8.2

Example 8.3

Example 8.4

Example 8.5

Example 8.6

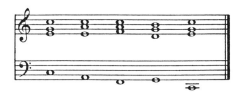

Example 8.7

in a different mode: pentatonic, major, and acoustic (or overtone). The latter, often used by Bartók, produces scales such as C–D–E–F♯–G–A– B flat–C.

pentatonic

Example 8.8. Bartók.

major

Example 8.9. Mozart.

acoustic

Example 8.10. Bartók.

Tests of tonal awareness

Some additional receptive tests of tonal awareness were administered, but the results of these tests are not considered here.

The subjects

The experiment was conceived on a large scale, with 220 subjects in 11 samples, after a pilot study with 20 peasants from a Hungarian village, Aradva'nypuszta.

Our hypothesis is that any person, whether musician or not is capable of composing music such as a song verse, using the musical patterns and structures provided by his/her daily musical environment (radio, TV, singing, etc.). Some musicologists have challenged our view. This is why our sample included untrained subjects from different age groups and social strata. A few control groups were selected from those studying or having studied music.

The impact of European musical culture arose as a separate issue which was studied by examining control groups consisting of students in Budapest of non-European (Asian, African, Latin American) origin.

The 11 samples are shown in Table 8.1.

Table 8.1   *Subject samples used in the experiment.*

Group No.	Age	Laymen	Age	Those having studied music
1/2	13	pupils	13	music pupils
3	17	middle school pupils	–	–
4	17	apprentices	–	–
5	20–25	industrial workers	–	–
6/7	20–25	university students	20–25	conservatory students
8	about 40	industrial workers	–	–
9/10	about 60	industrial workers	about 60	industrial workers singing in choirs
11	20–25			non-European students

Although the experiment involved a great deal of work (each person was tested for two to three hours), we succeeded in examining 20 persons in each of the 11 samples.

Before the beginning of the experiments a dispute over principles arose: many musicologists said we were embarking upon an impossible enterprise, that it was inconceivable that laymen might be able to perform the task. However, the result of the investigation has corroborated the correctness of our assumption.

Three thousand four hundred and twenty tunes, the length of folk-songs were recorded. If all subjects had succeeded in completing all the musical tasks, 3740 tunes could have been recorded. However, in several cases the subjects could not complete some of the tasks; for instance, they could not improvise tunes to the poems of Ady and József. This also happened when the chords proved too difficult to inspire a tune. The subjects were never forced to produce melodies since a negative result was also considered an important indicator in the experiment.

The tape-recorded music was transcribed into musical notation by 10 professional musicians whose transcriptions (both notes and bar lines) were checked by two independent judges; first by a colleague, then by a specialist, a former collaborator of Bartók. This was followed by a qualitative analysis of the tunes based on Bartók's method of folk-song classification. The analyses thus obtained were collated with the musical tastes obtained from the questionnaires and with the tests of tonal awareness. The entire work lasted eight years, from 1972 to 1980, including the analysis of the material in some 1300 pages and the writing of a 600-page book. (The book is now in press and will be published by the Hungarian Academy of Sciences.)

The scope of this chapter does not allow us to give a full description of the experiment but we can present our conclusions concerning the existence of a concrete level of generative musical creativity by means of the improvisational tests.

Results

In our experiment we endeavoured to study the phenomenon of musical creative ability by using new methods. Our work displayed all the positive and negative aspects of a pilot study and this was why keen attention had to be paid to methodology. In such situations the first tasks to be performed include the testing of the method applied and, if possible, its validation. If we have been able to prove, to a reasonable extent, that it is possible and worthwhile to follow this path, our work would have achieved its main purpose.

We feel that certain achievements can already be seen. In the following we shall summarize these results and inferences, and in certain cases we would like to add a few reflections which are not strictly entailed by the results, but which we are encouraged to propound in view of the relatively large amount of accumulated material.

Generative abilities in the universe of music

First of all, we have to note that the persons questioned willingly undertook the improvisation tasks and completed them with very few exceptions (although, naturally, at different levels of accomplishment). They were much less inclined to reproduce ready-made melodies: they apparently regarded this as a rather school-like task. Thus we can affirm in good conscience that generative musical ability is alive in the different strata of Hungarian society, even if most of the individuals investigated have not been able to practise it beforehand.

The discovery of the existence and survival of musical generative ability has considerable implications for views of the relations between music and man and between music and society (that is, for the psychology and sociology of music).

As a result, we have attained a new and different understanding of the individual's everyday musical activity and musical reception in the stricter sense of the term. With regard to the former, we must take into consideration what we call 'inner musical activity'. In a part of our experiment not included in this study we dealt in greater detail with inner musical activity; we found that most people produce music by themselves for one or two hours a day, mainly by varying what they know or by combining the known tunes according to their tastes. In addition, if we also take into account music we just hear each day as background, it becomes evident music is practically a permanent part of most people's everyday mental activity.

This issue is seen in a new light if we know that this musical activity, is creative in character if only on a low level, or has at least a creative aspect: the mind freely uses ready-made elements— sometimes complete tunes or entire works of music, sometimes mere fragments of musical works.

At this point we come to the problem of how this activity is related to musical reception. In the traditional view, reception is a one-way process: one recognizes, assimilates, and learns a given piece of music and then, during one's inner musical activity, one simply repeats the perceived material or loses it. We do not want to reject this possibility, because we started from the premise that the two levels of creative activity operate on two different levels (the generative and the constructive). Musical creative art is constructive, inner musical activity is generative, in character. However, we wish to claim that one is capable of assimilating only music whose elements one has learned and which one can use in a creative manner. We could not create Petőfi's poems, but we do understand not only his words and the rules of for interrelating them, but also his specific system of signs. On this basis we could, indeed, reproduce most of the details. However, we react to a poem written in an unknown language in an entirely different way; here only the musical cadence of the text can have an effect on us, but, since we inevitably compare it to our own idioms, we might misunderstand even that.

The concrete level of generative musicality

It was not our purpose merely to prove musical generative ability, but also to measure its concrete form and level. The collected data may serve as a basis for drawing certain general conclusions. We shall endeavour to describe the most general features valid for almost all the groups and which, therefore, best characterize the musical disposition of the subjects of our experiment.

Morphological features

We shall draw some general conclusions about the structure of the tunes improvised for the poems. The majority of the responses are characterized by strophic musical thinking on a level extending to the production and understanding of four-line musical forms. As soon as this limit has to be exceeded, they become uncertain.

Most subjects sang a strophic tune to the excerpt from the Petőfi poem. Forty-three subjects closely followed the strophic structure in the second verse (that is, they repeated the tune of the first verse with very little alteration); 47 endeavoured to achieve this but did not quite succeed; 54 sang two different verses of four lines each; another 30 considered the whole of the excerpt (eight lines) as a four-line tune and sang one musical line for each two lines of the poem. Thus, 174 of the 198 subjects were found to be capable of creating a more or less adequate form. The tendency to use the strophic structure is well illustrated by the fact that subjects tended to repeat the same musical line at different points in their song. Thirty per cent of the subjects used just four musical lines, 52 per cent used three, four or five lines for construction. The proportion of subjects using six, seven, or eight lines, or just one line, was 18 per cent.

The excerpt from the poem by Ady was more difficult. The test passage, of eight lines, was interpreted as such by only 44 of the 132 subjects; 63 subjects formed two four-line verses, while 20 created four two-line verses. Therefore, it seems that an eight-line strophe is more difficult to grasp, and even more difficult to structure, than a four-line verse. Many of the seemingly eight-line structures were quite loose in form and were not regular strophes.

Finally, the excerpt from the poem by Attila József was interpreted as an eight-line structure by most (70 of 117) subjects, for whom it was too difficult to establish a suitable system of interrelations between the lines. Thirty-two people created two four-line verses, while 15 created four two-line verses.

This may be due to two interrelated reasons. One is that most subjects could not really grasp the content and the message of the poems by Ady and József, their reasoning, their lyric world; this lack of understanding was indicated by frequent misreadings. The other is that, simultaneously with this, they could not grasp the structure of the poem and create an adequate form.

Thus, it may be said that the ideal form for most experimental subjects is the four-line song form; this is what they can best grasp, learn, and create. Those who know it better, repeat the first verse. The less accomplished cannot do this, but they endeavour to do so. And when they are faced with more difficult contents and poetic forms, they attempt to approach them from the angle of this ideal form; therefore they solve the task in an inadequate manner.

Melodic features

Very much like for the structure, a clear picture was gained also for melodics: 60–70 per cent of the improvisations made for the Petőfi, Ady, and József poems were in the minor or major scales, minor character always having priority, as shown in Table 8.2.

Table 8.2   *Use of major and minor modes*

	Poem		
	Petőfi	Ady	József
Total responses	198	132	117
Major	38	18	17
Minor	64	45	32
Major and minor mixed	24	41	26
Total major and minor	126	104	75
as % of all responses	63	74	63

If we deduct the control groups (the musicians and foreign students) from the full sample, that is, if we only consider the improvisations of the Hungarian non-musicians, the proportion of the minor and major tunes is even higher (Petőfi songs 65 per cent, Ady songs 81 per cent, Attila József songs 66 per cent). Whereas non-professionals tend to stay in the same mode, young professionals tend to switch between different modes.

In the case of the Petőfi song, many subjects produced improvisations which had a folk-song character. The number of strictly pentatonic tunes (see Appendix, p. 286, Example 8.11) (10) was the highest here, which, together with the tunes having a mainly pentatonic character (25) accounted for 17 per cent of all the tunes. Modal tunes were similarly high in number, primarily those in the Dorian and Aeolian modes (that is, those nearest to minor), and so were those in the Phrygian and Mixolydian modes, which mainly occurred in turns and cadences. In the case of young workers we also met Lydian-acoustic turns (with raised fourth). All these modes are characteristic of folk-songs.

We obtain a similar picture when considering the stylistic characteristics of the tunes. The total of folk-song-based improvisations reached 32 per cent (see Appendix, p. 287; Examples 8.12 and 8.13). But by including those conceived in the style of the popular Hungarian art (see Appendix, p. 288, Example 8.14), the ratio reached 51 per cent. One may hesitate about how to categorize intonations typical of Hungarian popular songs; if these are attached to the two former types it may be said that 72 per cent of the subjects related their improvisations to a style that in some way originates from current Hungarian national music culture. About half of the remaining 28 per cent endeavoured to use non-Hungarian (that is, non-Oriental) intonations (see Appendix, p. 288, Example 8.15) which are related to European art music, while the other half—not being able to tackle the problem—produced a few melodic fragments based on seconds.

A different picture is obtained from improvisations to the Ady poem. Here the highest rate is represented by tunes in minor-like and major-like scales (78.7 per cent), presumably because this poem did not make a folk-song-like impression. Therefore, the number of pentatonic tunes and phrases, as well as of modal tunes and phrases, descreased considerably. However, the rate of compositions with a mixture of minor and major increased, from 18 per cent in Petőfi songs to 39 per cent in Ady songs. In the majority of the cases this reflected uncertainty which led to the dissolution of the classical major-minor polarity. The result of this seems to be a tendency to turn towards tunes that reflected a 12-note scale, not only in the case of the musicians, but also in that of the musically untrained middle school students and the apprentices.

Similar differences are found with regard to styles. Only nine of the tunes were folk-music-like in character (7 per cent) and only seven had the character of composed folk-songs (5 per cent). The impact of Hungarian popular song and operetta increased (26 per cent), as well as that of school songs, marches, pop, and religious songs (see Appendix, p. 289, Example 8.16). None of these styles is particularly appropriate from the Ady poem; they may all derive from the endeavour to present the contents of the poem in music different from that used for the Petőfi poem and for this purpose an intonation subjects happened to remember was applied. Only 24 tunes (18 per cent) show the composer actually tried to find a modern tonality.

The tunes created for the Attila József poem yield again different pictures. The rate of minor-like and major-like tunes again decreased, to approximately the level of those improvised to Petőfi songs, but presumably for other reasons. We may be justified in presuming that the József poem had an even more remote content for the majority of the experimental subjects. They understood all the words but they could not grasp the sentences. However, there were some who obtained a feeling of the ballad, more so than in the case of the Ady poem, and this might be the reason for the repeated increase in the number of pentatonic and modal tunes and phrases, and for the unexpected appearance of other archaic structures (possibly from musical subconsciousness). This is how Lydian modes, Phrygian cadences, and whole-tone and acoustic scale fragments appeared; one experimental subject produced a pentatonic structure based on the 3/2/3/2 intervals (A–F sharp–E–C sharp–B descending structure with fourth structuring). The rate of tunes nearing dodecaphony had increased even compared to the Ady songs. The other reason for the decrease in the number of melodies using major–minor tonality was the increasing number of improvisations close to speech, almost pre-modal owing to uncertainty, based on seconds and varying one or two tones.

An even more complex picture is shown by the analysis of the styles. The rate of styles that are in no way suitable for formulating the musical material of this poem increased considerably. The rate of second-by-second tune fragments is 27 per cent, the same structure somewhat more fancifully conceived is 3.3 per cent, march tunes make up 5.6 per cent, pop 10 per cent, and all these combined constitute nearly half of the improvisations (47 per cent). This is followed by tunes of the Hungarian art song and operetta type (23 per cent) and by the composed folk-song (8 per cent) which can not be considered fit for the 'Ode' either. The rest is inspired by folk-songs, including songs reaching back to ancient tunes (8 per cent), and some initiatives resembling modern composed music (14 per cent). (See Appendix, p. 289, Example 8.17.)

On tune completion (Examples 8.8–10 above) we found that the same number of people (58 per cent) could complete both the major tune (Mozart) and the pentatonic melody (Bartók). In the case of the acoustic tune, not one single subject managed to complete the music without deviating from the tonality.

Tonal-functional thinking on an elementary level

A general characteristic of improvisation related to minor–major tonality is a stereotyped level of tonal-functional thinking. Sixty-two per cent of the Petőfi songs, 57 per cent of the Ady songs, and 40 per cent of the Attila József songs fit a simple functional structure, either the simplest T–S–D–T cadence (I–IV–V–I), or the T–D or T–S variants of functions.

We obtained similar results from improvisations to sequences of chords (or harmonic sequences, in other terms). As shown in our following analysis, the subjects could improvise on different levels to the seven sequences of chords (Examples 8.1–7 above). The improvisations were rated according to the degree to which they corresponded to the accompanying chords, according to traditional rules of harmony.

Based on the level of solution the seven sequences of chords could be separated into the following groups:

(1) An outstanding place is due to the harmonic sequence shown in Example 8.1, the classical I–IV–V–I cadence. Here, not only is the proportion of good solutions high (45 per cent), but the number of tunes harmonically unrelated to the chords is low (38 per cent). Also the number of variants that may be considered real improvisations is the largest; such tunes do not simply follow one or the other part, but create elaborations by arpeggiating the chord (18 per cent) and by flourishes. (See Appendix, p. 290, Example 8.18.)

(2) The second group includes harmonic sequences examples 8.2, 8.5, and 8.7. Example 8.2 comes into this group presumably because all the parts create suitable and understandable descending-ascending motifs. Example 8.7 is in this group because the addition of VI (in I–IV–V–I) extends harmonic sequence Example 8.1 in a manner that is familiar from hit songs; and Example 8.5 because the minor-character given by the Naples chord renders it accessible due to its romantic connotation. The number of good solutions in these three harmonic sequences is high. Example 8.2 inspired 41 per cent successful improvisations, 8.5 44 per cent, and 8.7 39 per cent. Despite this, we must distinguish these harmonic sequences from Example 8.1, because in these cases the proportion of unrelated and bad solutions is larger (38, 44, and 36 per cent) and even the acceptable responses include a larger number of tunes that merely follow the top part (that is, in unison) rather than being real improvisations.

(3) The third group includes harmonic sequences Examples 8.3, 8.4, and 8.6, which proved to be the most difficult ones. The rate of acceptable answers was 35 per cent for Example 8.6, 33 per cent for 8.3, and 31 per cent for 8.4. Sixty-four, 67, and 69 per cent of the experimental subjects could only sing notes completely unrelated to the chords. In the case of sequence 8.3, the problem was presumably caused by the flattened seventh degree; in Example 8.6 the source of problems (although popular in romantic music) was chromatics. A special place is occupied by sequence 8.4 which suggests Lydian-acoustic modality and therefore remains uninterpretable for most of the experimental subjects. In these three sequences of chords even the good solutions follow the parts, with only a few exceptions.

Rhythm

The analysis of the rhythmic structure of the improvisations requires a preliminary note. All three poems or excerpts involve parlando-like rhythmic structures. None of our examples would adequately fit a giusto (strict) rhythmic tune. Thus, we could achieve only a partial evaluation of sensitivity to rhythm, but this was enough to draw some conclusions.

The highest rate of parlando rhythm was created for the Petofi excerpt: a total of 103 (51 per cent). The vast majority of these had good prosody interpreting the 'ancient eight' in a 6+2 division. This provided for several intonations, between the explicitly old-style folk song and the style of the Hungarian popular song. Seventy songs (27 per cent) were prepared in a strict rhythm: however, the majority did not suit the poem, but were done with wrong prosody. The three-fourths rhythm was often used, though it can only forcibly be applied to the poem. The same can be said of march-like and hit song rhythms, as well as of repeated crotchets or quavers. It is, however, noteworthy that bound rhythms were primarily used by young people, and among them mainly by those attending special music elementary school and by the students of the vocational school. Finally, only 13 per cent belonged to the mixed category, who changed from free to bound rhythms and back.

In the Ady excerpt the proportion of improvisations in strict rhythm was the same (34 per cent). These were used mainly by the young, but now from all the categories. The proportion of free rhythms was 27 per cent, and most improvisations conformed to the prosodic and rhythmic requirements of the poem. The rate of mixed rhythms increased (39 per cent). Half of these (19 per cent) were still characterized by suitable prosody; these were basically parlando songs with bound scanning sections. The other half (nearly 20 per cent) endeavoured to impose some known style of Hungarian popular song (or of opera arias) on the poem, but the music turned out to be incompatible with the text due to the complexity of the latter.

Finally, in the performance of the 'Ode', the rates were again different. Here the rate of strict rhythms increased to 43 per cent, that of mixed rhythms remained unchanged (37 per cent), and that of the free-parlando rhythms decreased (25 per cent). Despite all this, the best rhythmic solutions were those in the free category and this was chosen most often by the music students. Others (peasants from Aradva'nypuszta, members of the workers' choirs) formulated parlando-recitativo hymn-like songs, or opera excerpts, selected ways with which they could best approach the poem according to their own knowledge. In this case, the mixed rhythms meant mainly infeasible tasks and a resort to scanning (the tune mostly moved in seconds here). The strict rhythm was again the 'solution' of the young in hit-like, march-like isorhythmic, or triplet-like style.

All this indicates that the subjects have a strong inclination for parlando-strict polarity which corresponds not only to the traditions of Hungarian folk-song but also has its equivalents in Hungarian popular song as well as in the style of hit music. This duality, naturally, also applies to art music but here there are far many more transitions and sepithese in genre than in current music. However, for the experimental subjects this wealth is unattainable; thus, when they are faced with a task that cannot be solved either with a folk-song-like parlando or a march, they become uncertain. It is especially important to note that parlando is so closely linked to folk-songs (and to Hungarian popular songs) that it can hardly be applied to the Ady and József poems. The young (even pupils of music elementary school) are less acquainted with folk-song than older people, and that is why their improvisation is dominated by a march-like and a hit-like character.

Conclusions

Altogether, these data demonstrate a certain parallel with Bernstein's (1970) sociolinguistic investigations and might lay the foundation of a kind of sociomusicological attitude. Bernstein makes a distinction between a tied-to-context and an elaborated method of use of the language. The situation in music is similar—the difference being that music as a language is less generalized or is generalized in a different way.

Our observations concerning the state or generative musical ability relate to our investigations regarding the development of popular music. In our opinion, generative ability determines also the spectrum of receptive experience. We listen in a distinct way to music that does not exceed the limits of our own generative musical ability. And so we can distinguish three degrees of musical receptive capacity:

(1) In the first degree, nearly the whole of the music listened to is interpreted in terms of structures that can be handled by the generative musical ability of the receivers themselves. This will be realized, for instance, in popular and beat music. Here the receiver can become identified with music. He feels as if he were able to make it himself.

(2) In the second degree, receptive generative musical ability does not comprise the whole of the composition received, only some of its elements. That is how for instance a listener with little formal musical education listens to, say, Beethoven's Symphony No. 5. The listener, being able to translate only a few elements—for example, the melody—to his own language, will understand the symphony only partially. The practice of everyday musical life proves, however, that he can enjoy it even in this case.

(3) Finally, in the third degree, the 'vocabulary' of the listener's generative musical ability and the composition listened to have nothing in common: in such cases no receptive experience comes about. These are the impressions of a listener brought up on Classical and Romantic music when hearing the works of, say, Webern or Bartók (not to speak of Boulez,

Stockhausen, or Ligeti). He does not meet a single familiar structure: he feels as though he were in a barren desert.

Our research not only revealed the attraction of the younger generation to pop music but also proved that this new type of investigation was a much more negotiable and applicable method in music psychology than the usual investigation of musical tastes. We can say that almost all the 11 groups had a specific musical characteristic or aspect which accorded with their different social backgrounds, and these musical attitudes definitely tally with the actual musical tastes and practices of the social strata in question.

References

Bernstein, B. (1970). Social Class, language and socialization. In *Current Trends in Linguistics* (ed. A. S. Abramson). Mouton, The Hague.

Blaukopf, K. (1972). Musiksoziologie: eine Einführung in die Grundbegriffe mit besonderer Berücksichtigung der Soziologie der Tonsystems. VI. Auflag. Verlag Arthur Niggli, Niederteufen.

Chomsky, N. (1965). *Aspects of theory of syntax.* MIT Press, Cambridge, Mass.

Taylor, I. (1959). The nature of the creative process. In *Creativity: an examination of the creative process* (ed. Paul Smith). Hastings House, New York.

Weber, M. (1921). *Die rationalen und soziologischen Grundlagen der Musik.* Drei Masken Verlag, München.

9

Young children's musical representations: windows on music cognition

LYLE DAVIDSON and LAWRENCE SCRIPP

Soon after children begin to speak, they begin to make marks on paper. At first, these marks form primitive depictions of everyday objects—flowers, houses, the family dog, and pictures of mummy and daddy. Later, marks change their meaning. For example, scribbled marks, which formerly stood for a stream, might now each represent a 'list' of things to get at the store. Gradually individual letters are formed and words begin to take shape. When children enter formal schooling, much effort is devoted to mastering the conventions of the written language, the importance of keeping the letters in a straight line, the common forms of spelling, word order, and grammar. Eventually, children's ability to make meaning from and express themselves in written language becomes a sign of understanding, an index of intellectual ability and perhaps even of station in life.

In music, the case is very different. Parents know that young children take great delight in listening to music, singing songs, and inventing songs of their own. However, they rarely suggest that their children write out songs they know. Performance ability alone is taken as the index of musical ability. Unlike language, mastery of the written form of music is neither viewed as necessary for musical ability, nor as an index of musical understanding. However, in music, as in language, the ability to represent relationships among elements in various ways is a more powerful measure of understanding than relying on performance or speech alone.

This raises many questions for those interested in young children and music. Is it possible that young children's invented marks or pictures could contain any musical meaning? Or is it possible that writing the words of a song could also convey some rhythmic grouping, melodic contour, or musical structure? Without training in standard music symbol systems, children are forced to invent symbol systems in order to indicate the musical features of a song or phrase. Thus, interpreting children's early symbolic representations of music is the initial task. It is only by finding ways to understand these unique symbol systems that we can begin to look at the range of sophistication in their representational knowledge of music and for possible patterns of development.

While some findings have been reported about the child's representational knowledge of music during these early years (Bamberger 1980, 1982; Upitis 1985), recent researchers in developmental and cognitive psychology have shown more interest in the music perception and performance skills of young children. Drawing from Piaget's notion of discrete and ordered stages of cognitive development, researchers in music report considerable evidence for different levels of perceptual development (Gordon 1965; Petzold 1966; Zenatti 1969; Dowling 1982) and performance development (Werner 1948; Pflederer 1964; McKernon 1979; Davidson 1985) in pre-adolescent children. It is our contention that for a more complete knowledge of children's understanding of music, their representations of music are critical 'windows' for viewing their musical cognitive development. For example, by asking children to write down a song they know 'so that someone else can sing it', we can find evidence of those musical features children think are most important for remembering 'how the tune goes'. Viewing the same children's musical representations over time, we can witness the development of their understanding of pitch, rhythm, or phrase relationships in the songs they know.

Consider the closing phrase of the common nursery tune 'Row, Row, Row Your Boat' (Fig. 9.1).

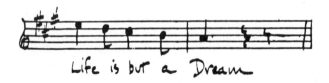

Fig. 9.1. Closing phrase of the song 'Row, Row, Row Your Boat'.

As a participant in our longitudinal study of young children's music notations, Janet provides remarkably clear representations of this musical phrase (Fig. 9.2). At age five Janet enactively traces only the rhythmic groupings of the 'fast and slow notes' while later (age six) she provides precise seriated lines that represent the melodic contour of the phrase ('the small lines are the higher notes'). Finally (age seven), she *simultaneously* suggests the rhythmic grouping and the melodic contour of the song (using the added dash to indicate rhythmic grouping and the layout of the words in a downward slope for the melodic contour), and additionally provides the text of the phrase.

This example illustrates three premises of this chapter. First, young

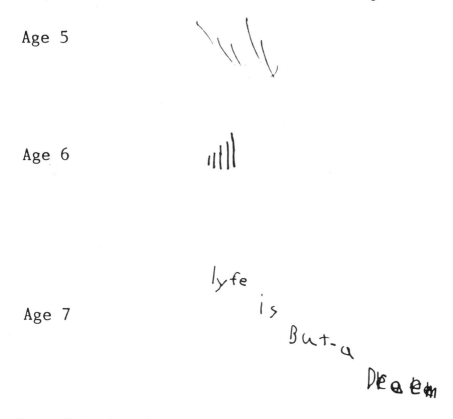

Fig. 9.2. Closing phrase of the song 'Row, Row, Row Your Boat' as represented by Janet at ages 5, 6, and 7.

children, untrained in music notation, can invent rich and articulate representations of the songs they know. Like many other children between the ages of five and seven, Janet effectively represents a wide range of musical features in her notations. Second, children's music notations reveal crucial insight into their understanding of music at various stages of musical cognitive development. Powerful developmental trends can be seen in Janet's and other children's notations as they increasingly specify and combine the rhythm and pitch dimensions of a single phrase. Between the ages of five and seven their notations become strikingly articulate and multi-dimensional. Third, taking both representational and performance development into account, musical pitch emerges as the primary component of children's musical cognitive development by the age of seven. Janet, typical of most young children we saw, increasingly focused on pitch relationships in her music notations and performance.

The study of young children's notations reported in this chapter offers a wide-ranging view of their representations of music. While several recent studies have considered older children's (ages 8–12) spontaneous representations of rhythmic fragments (Bamberger 1980, 1982) and instructional effects in children's notations (Walker 1981; Upitis 1985), no previous study has explicitly looked at the early longitudinal development of younger children's spontaneous musical notations across various rhythmic, melodic, and structural contexts. Before looking at this new evidence we will first consider in more detail what music psychologists have found in music perceptual, performance, and representational development in children. Drawing on general models of cognitive development, we will piece together a 'three-dimensional view' of music cognition in which children's representations will play a vital role.

Towards a three-dimensional view of young children's musical development

In the past, studies of musical development have been largely influenced by behaviourist, associationist, and atomist psychology. As a result, music psychologists traditionally tended to focus on extremely local stimulus-response tasks in music perception and performance. In music perception tests (Seashore 1919), for example, children were typically asked to discriminate two narrowly differentiated frequencies as 'same' or 'different' without regard to their musical temperament (within a standard scale) or their melodic context. Similarly, in music performance, research (Hattwick and Williams 1935) focused on children's ability to match individual pitches or to reproduce extremely short melodic phrases. Although this early research documented changes in children's perceptual or performance acuity with isolated pitches or melodic fragments, it offered little insight into children's ability to discriminate or produce pitch or rhythm patterns within broader, more realistic musical contexts.

More recently, studies in music perception and performance have taken a more global, cognitive approach. Current research in music perception, for example, has focused on children's developing ability to recognize melodic patterns within wider and more tonal contexts (Gordon 1965; Dowling 1982). Children were asked to recognize short melodies as 'same or different' depending on pitch transpositions or alterations of the contour (directionality) of the phrase. Results indicate that children at the age of five typically do not recognize two melodic fragments as the 'same' if the pitches are not identical in both fragments. However, by the age of eight, an important 'cognitive shift' occurs. Children now can recognize pitch relationships betwen two melodies as the 'same' even though the actual individual pitches of each melody are not shared (Pflederer 1964; Dowling 1982). Children's perception of music by the age of eight is now understood as operating within an increasingly stable *tonal system* where the musical scale and a tonic reference are used to store melodic 'information'.

A 'cognitive shift' occurs in children's performance abilities as well. Whereas young toddlers approach the task of singing melodies by means of loosely structured pitch 'contour schemes' (Davidson 1985), six- or seven-year-olds sing familiar and invented songs with increasingly discrete and stable pitch reference (Werner 1948; McKernon 1979). The music transcriptions in Fig. 9.3 show performance development typical of most young children between the ages of four and seven. Jeannie, at the age of four, sang the melody of 'Twinkle, Twinkle, Little Star' without reference to the major scale system. By the age of six, however, her singing rivals adult performance standards.

Fig. 9.3. Two versions of 'Twinkle, Twinkle, Little Star' by Jeannie.

Taking two dimensions together—perception and performance—we can characterize children's musical development as progressing rapidly through parallel stages of increasingly systematic knowledge. This development is measured by the emergence of a stable tonal framework. This is in contrast to rote imitation of musical fragments or perception of isolated pitches. From this 'two-dimensional' point of view we can see that untrained children between the ages of four and seven develop into surprisingly sophisticated musical listeners and performers.

Still, important questions remain regarding the depth of children's musical understanding. For example, although children may be able to simultaneously perform the rhythms, pitches, and text of a familiar song, we know very little about which of these components children themselves regard to be most important to represent. In fact we have no idea whether young children primarily attend to more central components (rhythm and pitch) or to the relatively peripheral aspects (words or story-line) of the music they sing. Nor do we know how these patterns may change with age. Questions such as these are not easily answered with the research techniques traditionally used in studying young children's music perception and performance development. By turning to yet another dimension, children's initial representations of their performance knowledge, we may be able to better understand the roots of their developing musical comprehension.

Music and representational development in children

Psychologists researching cognitive development in other domains have interpreted children's representations from several different points of view. Children's drawings, for example, have been used as evidence for levels of mental development (Werner 1948). From this point of view representational development occurs as a result of general mental development which Werner believes proceeds 'from a state of relative globality and lack of differentiation to a state of increasing differentiation, articulation and hierarchic integration' (1957). Piaget, particularly with his study of children's knowledge of spatial relations (Piaget and Inhelder 1956), used young children's representations to show precisely ordered levels of cognitive development. Piaget argues that children's representations are the product of what children 'know' rather than what they 'see'. To substantiate this claim, in later research, he asked young children to make drawings of a set of seriated vertical lines from memory, and reported positive development in their drawings *without perceptual intervention* six months to one year later (Piaget and Inhelder 1973). These drawings suggest that children later had access to a more intellectually advanced 'cognitive lens' which allowed them to *refocus* on their stored mental images. Other psychologists report that children's representations can also reflect stages of cognitive strategies (Bruner 1973) and levels of cognitive development within artistic domains (Goodnow 1977; Gardner 1980). Olson (1970) reports the importance of children co-ordinating pencil and papr skills with their perceptual skills in order to explore the link between cognitive skills and their representation.

Clearly children's representations are of critical value to a wide range of psychologists studying cognitive development within various domains. Similarly, children's music representations are crucial to our understanding of their musical cognitive development. Only very recently have music psychologists begun to view this 'third dimension' of children's musical cognitive development.

Cognitive processes and children's representation of simple rhythms

By asking young children and musically untrained adults to perform simple rhythms and then later represent them, Bamberger (1980, 1982) allows us to glimpse the 'cognitive structures' children use to express their understanding of music. Bamberger's research suggests that writing down rhythms involves a 'figural-formal transaction' (Bamberger and Schon 1977). That is, when representing these rhythmic fragments, notators may attend to the more figural properties (for example the motivic groupings formed by adjacent 'fast' and 'slow' notes) or to the more formal/metric properties (for example the organization of the surface patterns with respect to an underlying pulse) of the target phrase. Bamberger reports a developmentally ordered typology of symbols used by her subjects in respect to either side of this 'transaction'.

Bamberger reports that four- and five-year-old children typically represent simple rhythms (1980) using primitive enactive scribbling to trace the action of the rhythmic performance. Later on, children (age six or seven) use early 'figural' representations that group the surface units by duration, or notations that merely record the number of events in the phrase. Only after training is there evidence for a 'cognitive shift' towards a system where figural grouping can become subsumed by a formal/metric system classifying beat units, rhythmic patterns, and their co-ordinations. Bamberger reports:

Results indicate that musically untrained adults and older children (9–12) seem to develop the capacity only to make figural drawings: metric/formal drawings are made almost solely by those with the trained ability to read standard music notation. (1980, p. 172)

Bamberger's work provides an intriguing first view of young children's music representational development. We can see categorically different processes in young children's notations as they discover ways of restructuring their performance knowledge of simple rhythms. Through this cognitive 'window' we begin to see how musically untrained children (without knowledge of a conventional code) represent the complex and sometimes conflicting musical dimensions of surface patterns, underlying metric pulse, and their possible co-ordinations in 'simple' rhythmic phrases.

However, Bamberger's research also raises vexing questions concerning children's musical cognitive development. Considering children's music representations within the larger framework of cognitive development, we need to ask why young children without musical training are unable to develop beyond the 'figural' representations of simple rhythms while 'formal' development apparently occurs in other domains (Flavell 1963; Furth 1969). Within the domain of music, on the other hand, we need to know why children's music representations of rhythm apparently lag behind the more developed levels of their pitch perception and performance described earlier. Because we only have evidence detailing children's representations of short rhythms, we have no way of directly comparing the development of tonality in children's perception and performance with their representational development. In sum, Banberger's work offers an enlightening point of departure for assessing children's music representations. A wider-ranging study is needed in order to get a more complete picture of children's music representational development.

In the next sections we will report findings from the Harvard Project Zero notations study (Wolf *et al.* 1986), the first longitudinal study to look at children's (ages five to seven) music notations across a wide range of musical contexts. We begin by describing in some detail the structure of the research.

The research design: children's representations of musical content across various contexts

In this study we asked 39 musically untrained children to perform a wide variety of tasks. In the spring of each of three years, we requested the children (over two separate sessions) to reproduce short rhythmic or melodic patterns, recall a familiar song ('Row, Row, Row Your Boat'), and learn a short, unfamiliar song. At the beginning of each session it was explained that all the items were to be written down in their 'own music book'. To ensure that each child had a secure performance knowledge of the items, a pattern of phrase of the song was repeated either until the child made a correct performance or until the level of performance had stabilized. Afterwards, children were asked, 'Write the song down on your paper so that someone else who doesn't know the song can sing it back.' For those who objected to the task of writing down a song they'd known since they were 'babies', it was suggested that they should write down the song carefully for children from 'other countries' who might not know the song. They were also told they might use any mark they wished to write down the music if it helped them remember the sound of the rhythms or melodies. The children were allowed as much time as they needed to write in their 'music books'.

Immediately upon completing their notations, children were asked to perform each item while reading from their 'music books'. The experimenter explained that he wanted to 'see if the music book would work for someone who couldn't remember the clapping or the singing'. Later on in the session the experimenter asked each child to read back the notations in the 'music book' in random order to determine whether or not children were using

·their own notation rather than recalling the target items by rote. At the end of the final session, each child was asked to explain or demonstrate 'how the music book works'. Each session was about 20 minutes long.

The materials for the tasks were simple. Two cassette tape-recorders were used, one to play the pre-recorded musical examples, and one to record the child's performances for future transcription and scoring. Children were each given a 12" × 18" piece of white drawing paper and a choice of coloured felt-tipped markers with which to notate their performances. When the task was completed (and after the child had left) the experimenter freely added comments to the notation (in pencil) or recorded remarks that might serve to clarify the child's process of making the notation.

Rather than simply focussing on one set of materials, this research design allows us to analyse children's representational as well as performance development across various musical contexts: rhythm patterns, pitch patterns, a familiar song, and a new song (see figure 9.16). These four different contexts share the same pitches or rhythms. In designing our study we structured our tasks to provide answers to the following broad questions:

(1) What is the general nature of young children's (five to seven) musical representations?

(2) What musical dimensions are young children able to extract from the melodic fragments or familiar songs they are asked to write down?

(3) What evidence is there for development in young children's music notations from the ages of five to seven?

(4) How does context affect children's notations of music?

In following sections we will analyse the notational responses to the familiar song task. First, we will show how young children use an extremely wide range of invented and borrowed graphic symbols to create increasingly sophisticated notational systems. Second, we will examine their ability to extract and code various musical dimensions without the use of standard musical symbols in their music representations. Finally, we will present evidence of representational development in children's ability to increasingly specify various musical dimensions such as phrase strucure, musical units, rhythmic pulse and grouping, and pitch contour. This allows us to appreciate the remarkably rich and articulate knowledge of music which many of these young children can express through their invented notations.

Borrowed symbols and invented systems: young children's first notations of song

Children approached the task of writing down a familiar song with great earnestness. For five-year-olds, the task of choosing an appropriate symbol for representing music involves a good deal of personal investment. Many openly confided they didn't know how to do it and it was not uncommon to observe children pause several minutes in silence before writing down their first mark. Careful not to prompt young children towards a particular set of graphic symbols, we witnessed an extraordinary range of symbol use. More importantly, we saw how they adapted and organized various families of graphic symbols into *symbol systems* that map various musical dimensions of their songs.

We have grouped the children's notations of song into five symbol systems: the *pictorial*, *abstract patterning*, *rebus*, *text*, and *combination/ elaboration* symbol systems. Although these systems can be identified largely by their ingredient graphic symbol types, our analysis will focus primarily on which features of the song were coded and how they were organized within the notation.

The pictorial system

This system features a variety of pictures, icons, and images that young children use to record the song 'Row, Row, Row Your Boat'. These evocative 'picture drawers' represent the song with a drawing that can effectively render the title of the song, the look of a 'music book' or a 'person singing', or perhaps the entire story-line condensed into one salient image. Because these 'picture notations' do little more than record the song as a global event or action, this system usually remains a primitive and ineffective system of notation. Indeed, the pictorial system probably best meets the common adult expectations of the 'artistic', yet notationally untutored, child.

Emily's notation is a particularly good example of the limitations of her particular symbol system (Fig. 9.4). After observing Emily carefully drawing a rich landscape of rippling water, clouds, and a prominent boat, we asked her how 'to read the song' from this picture. Patiently explaining 'the book isn't finished yet', she turned the paper over, folded it in half, and began drawing the notes that 'belong' in her 'music book'. Although the picture of the boat may remind us of the title of the song and the notes drawn inside tell us that it is a music book, there is little here to help us remember how the tune goes. Alas, these notes appear to have all the 'look' but little of the substance of standard music notation.

The abstract patterning system

This system usually features lines and dots which children use to represent the melodic units ('notes') of the song and record the rhythmic groupings, underlying pulse, melodic contour, or phrase structure. Due to the ambiguous nature of these symbols, it is often difficult to tell at first which

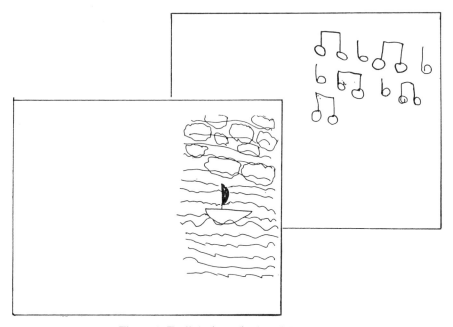

Fig. 9.4. Emily's (age 6) pictorial system.

musical dimensions of the song are being coded, but it is clear that these 'abstracters' are primarily concerned with the rhythmic and melodic *relationships* of the notes of the song rather than being content with merely representing the story-line or the text.

As is typical with 'abstracters', no conclusive interpretation of Janet's notation (Fig. 9.5) can be made without a transcript. What at first appears to be an arbitrary set of seriated vertical lines turns out to be an elegant system for recording pitch relationships in the song. And, once we understand that the smaller 'sticks' indicate the higher notes, we can track through the entire system with little difficulty. We see that the structural boundaries of the musical phrases are indicated not only by gaps in the notation (that is, musical 'rests'), but also by the corresponding intervallic pitch relationships recorded throughout the song (for example, the last note of phrase 1 appears to be equivalent to the first note of phrase 2 or, more remarkably, the first note of phrase 1 seems equivalent with the last note of phrase 3 and the first note of phrase 5). In fact, after Janet performed her notation while pointing at the lines, she spontaneously announced that the last phrase 'is just like the first one'!

The rebus system

This system usually features elaborate and flexible *alternations* of icons,

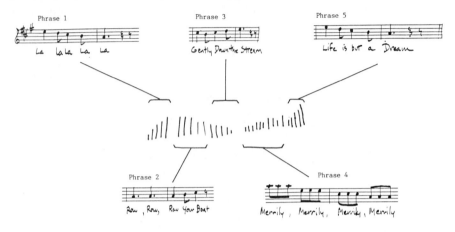

Fig. 9.5. Janet's (age 6) abstract patterning system with corresponding phrases of 'Row, Row, Row Your Boat' in standard notation.

conventional signs, and words children use to record the text of the song. While 'rebus makers' effectively depict the text or illustrate the lyrical content of the song, they can also occasionally reveal the underlying pulse (word stress) or pitch direction (contour) of the tune.

At first glance, it appears that Aaron (Fig. 9.6) has freely selected letters, words, and icons only to track the lyrics of the song. With closer inspection, however, we see that there are occasional omissions of the text, which suggest a focus on the rhythmic organization of the words as well. In phrase 2, for example, Aaron redundantly draws three 'rowing boats' and spells out the word 'boat' while leaving out the word 'your'. Apparently Aaron is concerned more with notating the underlying *pulse* (or stress) of the rhythm than with merely recording all the 'units' of the text. Phrase 5 shows a similar understanding of musical pulse as the stressed words are depicted and the 'weak beats' appear to be deliberately left out. In phrase one, he shows sensitivity to the longer duration of the final 'la' and explains that the last 'la' is 'different from the rest'. Typical of rebus makers, Aaron inconsistently yet imaginatively suggests various salient dimensions of the song in his notations.

The text system

This system features the words, letters, or imitations of conventional language symbols children use to record the text of the song. Although these children seem primarily concerned with simply 'writing down the words', they also often take advantage of graphic layout devices to code

Fig 9.6. Aaron's (age 6) rebus system.

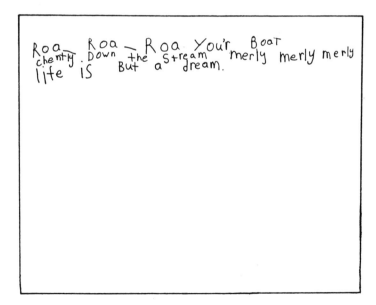

Fig. 9.7. Eleanor's (age 6) text system.

the verse structure, the direction of pitch, or the rhythmic grouping of the song.

Eleanor's notation (Fig. 9.7) is typical of most text notators. Eager to show off her newly learned writing skills, she quickly wrote down the words of the song. Although her transcription of the lyrics is almost impeccable, more importantly, the notation also clearly reveals her attention to the phrase structure of the song. Looking closely at the text system we see that she uses 'carriage returns' and additional space between 'stream' and 'merly' to show the individual lines of the text. Also she provides elongating marks after the first few words ('*Roa*') and demonstrates their purpose to the experimenter by gesturing the pulse and sustain while singing the opening phrase. Like most text systems, however, this notation has fallen considerably short of a consistent, systematic representation of rhythmic or pitch dimensions of song.

The combination/elaboration system

This system features *simultaneous* use of abstract symbols and words to represent the text and musical dimensions together. Unlike the pictorial and rebus system, this system does not utilize pictures or icons, nor does it primarily focus on the lyrical content of the song. 'Elaborators' are children who consistently employ abstract symbols to modify the text to show how the words are to be sung. 'Combiners' are children who record both the text and abstract patternings of the 'notes' as two separate and equally necessary ingredients of the song.

Mary's notation (Fig. 9.8) demonstrates both approaches children used in constructing their combination/elaboration system. Like most 'elaborators' Mary records the text first and later modifies these 'notes' with marks (arrows) showing relative pitch direction. Like most 'combiners' she works through one entire system first and then fashions a separate series of marks to be read simultaneously with the first. In this case Mary uses abstract symbols to represent the 'long and short notes' of the song. As with all children using combination/elaboration notation, Mary is embarking on an ambitious path: the integration of the melodic and lyrical content.

In sum, what is more impressive in these examples of children's symbol systems is the sophistication with which they approach the task of

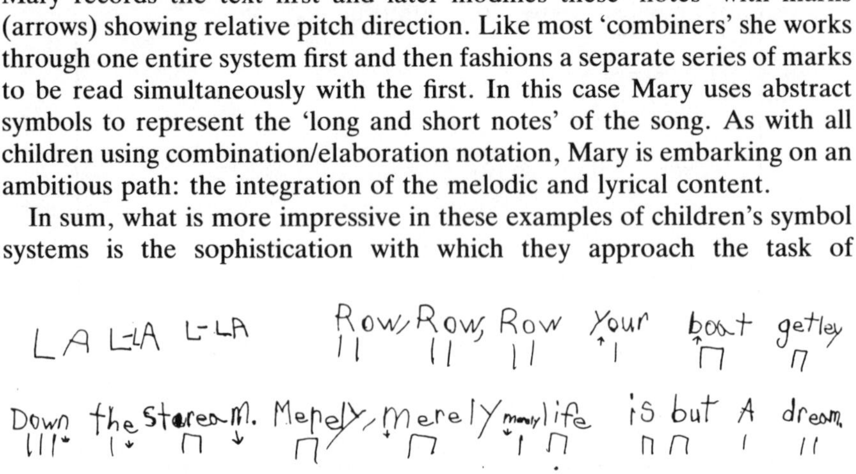

Fig. 9.8. Mary's (age 6) elaboration and combination system.

representing music. Using highly individual symbol systems these children can successfully code not only the song title, the story, and the text, but also the melody's more salient musical features—its underlying rhythmic pulse, pitch contour, or phrase structure. In the most gifted of notators we see children attending to several musical dimensions *at once*, constructing highly elaborated or elegantly patterned descriptions of the song. Recognizing the wide range of symbol use and the degree of sophistication with which children employ these symbols to write down a familiar song, new questions can be addressed: What changes in symbol use occur with age? Can these changes be ordered into developmental sequences?

Signs of development: preliminary evidence for children's emerging musical cognition in their representations of song

The sections that follow present evidence for development trends in young children's representational knowledge of music between the ages of five and seven. In this section we will only look at children's developing notations of the familiar song 'Row, Row, Row Your Boat'. In later sections, we will look at children's notation of a single phrase across various musical contexts.

Our data show that children between the ages of five and seven not only change radically in their choice of symbol systems to represent songs, but also show a dramatic increase in the level of sophistication of their notations. Examples from our entire sample of children's songs can be organized in the following developmental sequence:

Age 5—children (who may not have the option of writing words) primarily use pictures and abstract symbols to show musical structure or the units of the phrase.
Age 6—children primarily use abstract or language symbols and sometimes organize the units to show either underlying pulse, rhythmic grouping, or melodic contour.
Age 7—children combine and modify language with abstract symbols and consistently show multiple features of the music with particular attention to melodic contour.

Janet's and Mary's song notations (Fig. 9.9) between the ages of five and seven provide clear examples of this developmental sequence.

Mary's initial pictorial system exemplifies the average child's notation at the age of five. Although she makes a clear distinction between the introductory phrase and the rest of the song, little attention is given to the musical units within the phrases of the song.

Janet's precocious abstract notation at age five and Mary's elaborate rebus at age six are both typical of the average six-year-old's attention to

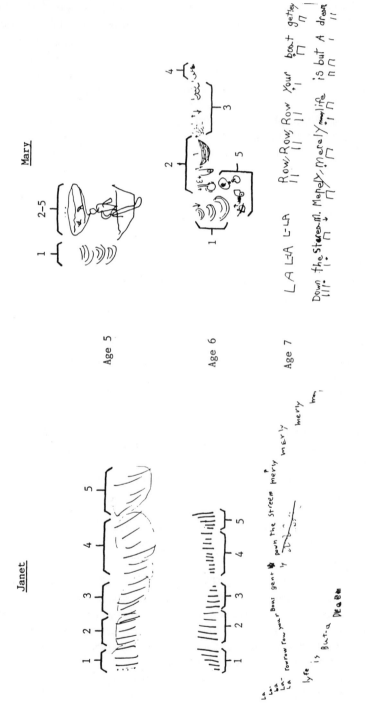

Fig. 9.9. Janet's and Mary's notations of the song 'Row, Row, Row Your Boat' at ages 5, 6, and 7 (phrases numbered as in standard notation).

the rhythmic organization of the units of the song. Here Janet provides an enactive tracing of the musical units with some semblance of their rhythmic pulse (phrase 1) or grouping (phrases 2 and 5); Mary clearly depicts the words of the text that receive the underlying pulse or stress (phrases 1, 3, and 5).

Both Janet and Mary anticipate the average seven-year-old child's attention to melodic contour at age six but without using language symbols. More typically, the average seven-year-old uses the combination/elaboration symbol system to record the text of the song while *simultaneously* providing indications of melodic contour.

The symbol system sequence

Janet and Mary are both examples of particularly fluent and richly sophisticated notators. As different as their 'tracks' of development at first appear, the notations of these two children suggest that the pictures or abstract patterns used to represent songs at age five will later be superseded by words combined or modified with abstract symbols. Data from the entire sample (*n*=39) over three years provide considerable evidence for this developmental trend in children's symbol system use.

An analysis of figure 9.10 shows that most children (69 per cent) use either the *pictorial* or *abstract patterning* systems to represent songs at age

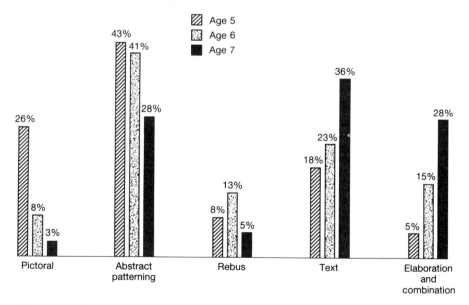

Fig. 9.10. Change in use of symbol systems for representing the song 'Row, Row, Row Your Boat' by children ages 5–7.

five while a majority of children (64 per cent) are using either the *text* systems or *combination/elaboration* systems by the age of seven. Statistical analysis supports the notion of these ordinal trends in symbol system choice with age [Friedman Chi-square = 9.94, 2 df, $p<0.007$, $n = 39$].

Probing further into this 'symbol system' sequence, two findings are particularly important to our understanding of the children's music representational development. First, since we assumed that most five- and six-year-old children would draw pictures to represent the song, the predominant use of abstract patterning systems throughout these early years was totally unexpected. Although young children receive considerable instruction with language literacy skills and are encouraged to draw, many feel compelled to use a totally different set of invented symbols to represent music. This suggests that the average five- or six-year-old perceives music as a separate domain, requiring its own particular symbol system uniquely suited to the task of representing musical features.

Second, although young children increasingly abandon pictorial systems and employ their newly acquired writing skills to transcribe the text of the song, many find language symbols insufficient for the task of representing the song. Surprisingly, children insist on representing important musical features as well as the words of the song. This is particularly signficant at age seven when there is a dramatic increase of elaborating marks or abstract patternings in conjunction with text.

This sequence illuminates significant trends of symbol system development. In the next section we will look at development in levels of extraction of musical dimensions in children's notations and possible correlations with symbol system or performance development.

Representational development in song

Analysing children's representational development in song, we coded children's notations according to the musical dimensions they were able to extract and represent. In the dimension of musical pitch, we predicted a simple sequence of development. We assumed that children would at first code the *units* (notes) of the phrase (level 1), and later indicate the *melodic contour*, or directionality, of these units (level 2), with a few older children eventually mapping the *intervallic boundaries* of these melodic contours (level 3). Although we did not expect many children to code exact pitch relationships, that is, *regulated pitch* (level 4), this was the next logical step in pitch representation. This was confirmed throughout the various contexts of our pitch tasks.

In rhythm, the sequence predicted was unconfirmed by our data. Originally we assumed that children would first code *units* (level 1), followed by the *grouping* of the units (level 2), the *underlying pulse* of the phrase (level 3), and finally the rhythmic grouping regulated by pulse, that is, *pulse plus grouping* (level 4). This sequence was based on Bamberger's (1982) research which suggested that untrained children first attend to 'figural' features of rhythm (the grouping of fast and slow notes) while only a few later attempt a more 'formal' regulation of the rhythmic figures. We were unable to confirm this finding. Surprisingly, we found many children representing the underlying (metric) pulse or stresses of the text before providing any indication of the (figural) grouping of these units. As a result, our notational sequence for rhythm allows for selecting *either* grouping or underlying pulse as an intermediate step towards simultaneously constructing both pulse and surface groupings of rhythms.

The following examples (Fig. 9.11) of the introductory phrase of our song shows how children achieved various notation levels in rhythm and in pitch.

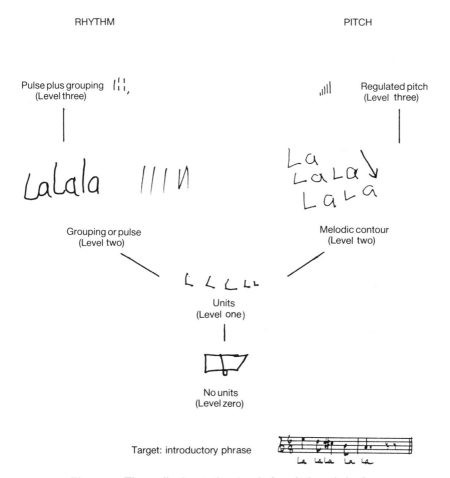

Fig. **9.11.** The ordinal notation levels for pitch and rhythm.

Overall, we scored children's notations according to the level of the rhythm or pitch they consistently (three out of five phrases) encoded in their representations of song. A summary measure of notational consistency in rhythm and in pitch was achieved by calculating an average score produced by these levels. Looking at the mean notation scores in Fig. 9.12 we see that, on the average, children at ages five and six were able to represent the song only at the level of musical units. At age seven, however, there is a dramatic increase in representational skills as children demonstrate higher levels of rhythmic structure (that is, grouping or pulse) or pitch relationships (for instance, melodic contour or relative interval boundaries) in their notations of song.

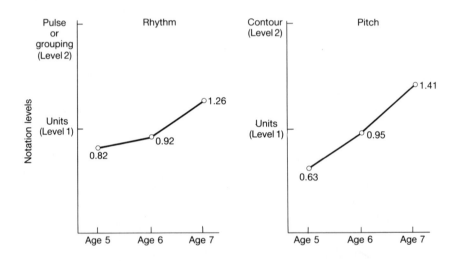

Fig. 9.12. Mean notation scores for rhythm and pitch in song by children ages 5–7.

Development in levels of representation of pitch can be clearly contrasted with representation of rhythm. Repeated measures one-way ANOVA suggests highly significant improvement in pitch notation levels [Friedman Chi-Square 20.55, df 2, $p<0.00005$] while improvement in rhythm notation levels appears to be relatively weaker [Friedman Chi-Square 6.62, df 2, $p<0.05$] over the three-year period. From these results it appears that young children are increasingly able to develop notations that consistently show the melodic contour rather than the surface rhythms or underlying pulse of the song.

Instead of looking at children's choice of graphic symbols as a measure of their notational sophistication, we can view children's music representational development in song independent of their choice of symbol systems. If we factor out children's symbol system choices, we are in a better position to assess the relationship between young children's level of performance and levels of representational skills using familiar songs.

Analysis of the relationship between symbol system choice and level of notational sophistication shows decreasing correlation with age. In Fig. 9.13, we see that the more 'advanced' symbol systems (for example text or elaboration and combination systems) predict better notation scores in rhythm and pitch at age five but correlate less strongly a year later. In other words, one can expect five-year-olds to achieve higher levels of notation only if they are using a more sophisticated symbol system. In contrast, by the age of seven there are no significant correlations between children's notation scores and their choice of symbol system. In other words, the level of notation achieved and the symbol system used become increasingly independent for older children.

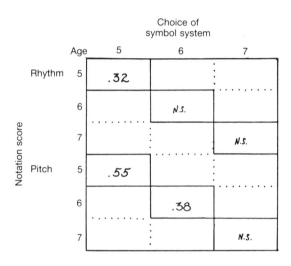

Fig. 9.13. Matrix showing significant ($p<0.05$) rank correlation coefficients (Kendall Tau) between symbol system choice and notation scores in children's notations of song.

Surprisingly, children's choice of symbol system in representing songs comes to have little bearing on development in notation. The more sophisticated the level of children's representations, the less of a factor the choice of specific symbol system becomes. In other words, the vehicle of expression becomes less visible with development.

Musical performance and representational development in song

Throughout the three-year study, we observed the development of children's performance knowledge of the song 'Row, Row, Row Your

Boat'. For rhythm, children were scored according to their ability to reproduce accurately the *number of units*, steady *underlying pulse*, the *surface grouping*, or the co-ordination of *underlying pulse plus the rhythmic grouping* of a phrase of the song. With respect to pitch, the children were scored according to their ability to match the *initial pitch*, the *melodic contour*, the *interval boundary*, and the *key* (scale) of the phrase.

From Fig. 9.14 one can assess performance development in rhythm and pitch in terms of the percentage of items accurately matched by children between the ages of five and seven. Performance in both rhythm and pitch improves over the three-year period but, as we take a closer look at these overall performance scores, we see strikingly different profiles of development. In contrast to reproducing the rhythm, the task of accurately singing the pitches of a familiar song proves to be initially far more difficult. Whereas five-year-old children, on the average, reproduced the rhythm measures with 85 per cent accuracy, approximately half of the pitch measures were matched accurately. With age, however, this gap narrows considerably, suggesting that either rapid and substantial improvement in pitch accuracy occurs in contrast to rhythm, or that rhythmic development is more precocious and thus its growth is less dramatic over the course of our study.

Statistical analysis supports the notion of rapidly improving pitch in children's performance development. Repeated measures one-way ANOVA and Duncan Multiple Comparison procedures (Cody and Smith 1985) suggests highly significant [$p<0.001$] improvement in both rhythm and pitch over the three-year period. Comparisons between years show significant [$p<0.05$] improvement in rhythm between the ages of six and seven while pitch dramatically progresses in each of the three years. As in representational development, longitudinal growth in young children's performance accuracy in song between the ages of five and seven apparently is best viewed within the dimension of pitch.

At no point in the three-year study did performance skills correlate significantly with children's choice of symbol system to represent music. Apparently, the ability of children at ages five through seven to accurately sing a tune or clap a rhythm in no way predicts their choice of graphic symbols to notate the music. This finding allows us to better appreciate music research as a domain uncontaminated by conventional symbol systems that may influence young children's ability to represent their understanding of that domain. Furthermore, it underscores the initial independence of children's notational and performance abilities.

In Fig. 9.15 one can view the developing relationships between performance and representational knowledge of the song. When the dimensions of pitch and rhythm are combined, we see significant correlations between performance skills and level of representational knowledge only at the age of seven. This suggests that children, as they

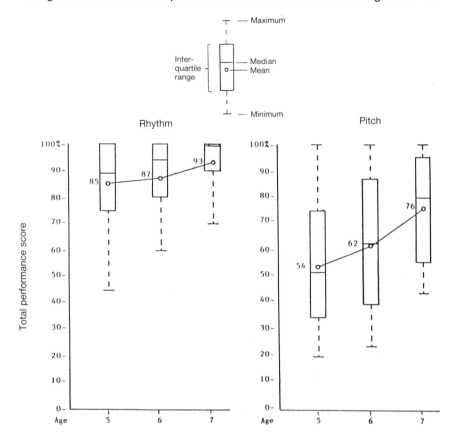

Fig. 9.14. Performance scores for rhythm and pitch in song by children ages 5–7.

develop, are increasingly able to draw on their performance knowledge in their representations. However, looking at pitch and rhythm separately, we see that pitch development in notation and performance increasingly correlates with age, whereas correlations are decreasing with respect to rhythm. This suggests that children's understanding of pitch is more closely linked to their developing representational knowledge of song than is their understanding of rhythm.

In sum, although there is substantial evidence for developmental trends in children's choice of symbol systems and in the level of sophistication of children's notation of songs, it appears that these are both increasingly independent 'tracks' in young children's representational development. However, as children's representations become more sophisticated, their level of representation increasingly corresponds to their performance knowledge of the song. This suggests, by the age of seven, the emergence

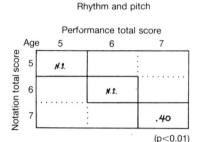

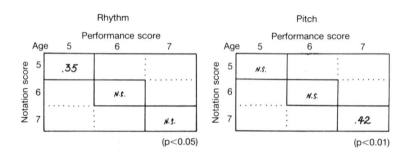

Fig 9.15. Matrices showing rank correlation coefficients (Spearman) between performance and notation scores in rhythm and pitch in children's song.

of a 'cognitively unified' domain of musical intelligence (Gardner 1984), where children's knowledge of musical performance and representation become increasingly yoked together. In both representational and performance knowledge of song, the dimension of pitch appears as the most stabilizing and powerfully predictive measure of children's musical development.

In the next section we look at children's notation of a single phrase across various musical contexts. Looking closely at their use of graphic symbols, we see young children's increasing sensitivity to the context of a phrase. Analysing the level of sophistication in their representations of a single phrase, we witness the increasingly powerful and consistent coding of musical features regardless of musical context. We also find more evidence establishing pitch as the primary factor in young children's developing musical cognition.

Making the difference: a closer look at young children's representations across musical contexts

Although we have seen developmental stages in children's notations of song, a closer view of their development is needed in respect to a wider range of musical contexts. Children's music representations may profoundly differ according to *performance attributes* (is the phrase sung or clapped?), *structural presentation* (is the phrase an isolated pattern or embedded within a song?), or *familiarity* (is the phrase familiar or newly learned?).

In our sessions we asked children to perform and notate a single five-note phrase in five distinctly different contexts : (A) as an *isolated rhythmic fragment*, (B) as an *isolated melodic fragment*, (C) as an *added introductory phrase to a familiar song*, (D) as a *concluding phrase of a familiar song*, and (E) as a *concluding phrase of an unfamiliar song*. As we can see from Fig. 9.16, these five contexts contain virtually identical pitch and rhythmic musical motives.

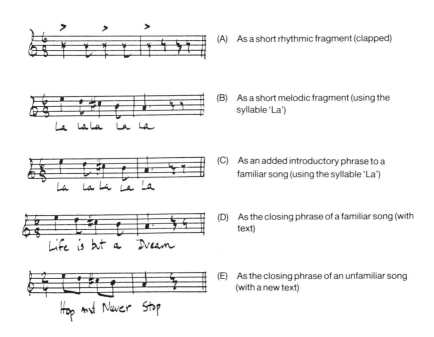

Fig. 9.16. The five musical contexts of a single musical phrase.

Using this single phrase as a control, we explore the ways in which young children are responsive to musical context. In particular, we contrast developmental trends in notation within the context of isolated rhythmic or pitch fragments with trends occurring within the structure of a whole song. Also, we want to know the effect of text on children's musical representations. Comparisons between no text (clapping), a generic text (the syllable 'la'), the text in a familiar song, and the text of a recently learned song allow us to see how text may confound young children's attention to the musical features of a song. Finally, we can see which musical features children are apt to represent *regardless* of musical context. This last question may help us understand which dimensions of music are most important to (or less easily ignored by) young children.

Choosing graphic symbols for a single phrase: evidence for the increasingly 'context sensitive' musical child

Analysing notations of a single phrase, we again see the broad developmental trends discussed in the analysis of children's notations of a familiar song. These trends include the dramatic decrease of icons and pictures, the increase of words and mixed symbols with age, and the relatively consistent use of abstract lines and dots (Fig. 9.17). More importantly, we see evidence for increasing sensitivity to musical context.

Children use *icons* less often with age, perhaps because they consider musical context when they choose these symbols. From Fig. 9.17 below we see that chldren ages five and six are just as likely to use icons to represent the single phrase in the context of isolated rhythm or pitch pattern as they are within a familiar or newly learned song. In other words, young children consider these symbols unconstrained by musical context and increasingly inappropriate for music representation.

This finding substantially contrasts with the children's increasingly 'context-sensitive' use of *abstract lines and dots* and *letters and words*. At first, children use these symbols equally often across the various musical contexts, but, in the succeeding years, there is a great deal of fluctuation of use, depending on the musical context. In particular, children use lines and dots more often for short rhythm patterns (with no pitch or text), less often for isolated or introductory melodic phrases (with generic text 'la la la'), and least often for verses (using the lyrics) of a familiar or unfamiliar song. This effect is increasingly pronounced with age. Children also use letters and words with increased context sensitivity but in opposite contexts: these symbols appear more often in phrases of the song, less often in isolated pitch patterns, and rarely in rhythm patterns.

Although language symbols appear as an obvious choice for representing a phrase within the context of a familiar song, we also see the sudden emergence of *mixed symbols* (usually combining words with abstract symbols or signs) with seven-year-olds, particularly in the context of isolated melodic patterns. Observing the relatively profuse use of mixed symbols in pitch patterns compared with relatively scant use with the identical phrase used as an introduction to the song, we see evidence for young children's increasing sensitivity to the structural aspects of song.

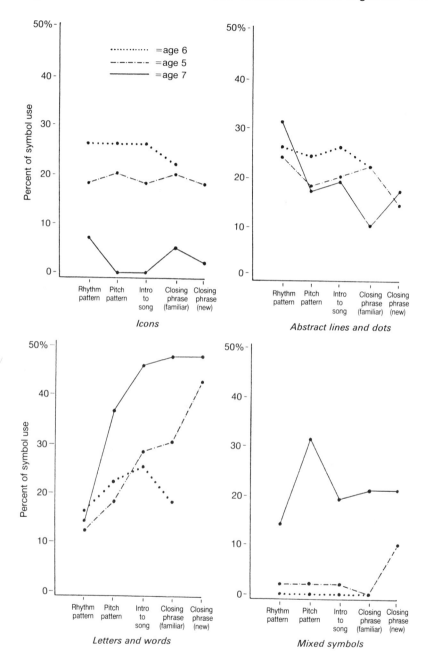

Fig. 9.17. Use of the four major graphic symbol types in a single phrase across five musical contexts by children ages 5–7.

Summarizing children's use of graphic symbols *by age*, we see an increasingly wider range of sensitivity to musical context. At the age of five, children's range of symbol use is surprisingly broad, yet relatively context-independent. At this age children use a large repertoire of symbol types of grasp the musical phrase. By the age of seven, however, a remarkably distinct profile of children's sensitivity to musical context emerges as children consistently choose language or abstract symbols (and their combinations) according to the context of the phrase. Looking across *context* at this age, we see children predominantly using abstract symbols for rhythm patterns, abstract and language symbols for pitch patterns, and mixed symbols for phrases within new or familiar songs.

As we trace Mary's notations of the single phrase through three years we encounter a clear example of this developmental sequence. In her notations we see a consistent use of abstract symbols for the rhythm patterns at all ages, while language and mixed symbols increasingly appear in the remaining contexts (Fig. 9.18).

Controlling for the structural context of the phrase, we see the symbols chosen for phrases as isolated patterns are markedly different from those chosen for phrases functioning within the song. We see a contrast in graphic symbols chosen for rhythmic fragments as opposed to pitch patterns. Continuing this analysis of a single phrase across the five contexts, we can take a closer look at children's ability to represent pitch and rhythmic content.

Evidence for the increasingly divergent paths of rhythm and pitch in representational development

In our previous analysis of young children's representational development we contrasted their growth in notating the rhythmic and pitch dimensions of a familiar song. On the average, we saw the power of children's notations in both rhythm and pitch significantly expand from musical units (at age five) towards the organization of these units into rhythmic pulse or grouping and melodic contour (at age seven). We noticed also that growth in music representation and performance was particularly powerful in pitch. In our present analysis of the single phrase across five musical contexts we will see a telling clarification of this finding.

Comparing children's notations of musical dimensions across contexts we find that developmental trends in rhythm and pitch very different (Fig. 9.19). Whereas rhythmic levels are relatively unstable across contexts, pitch levels are much more stable. And, while representational development in rhythm occurs in spurts across years, growth patterns in pitch are unambiguous and increasingly substantial. Additionally, these tendencies are increasingly pronounced with age.

Although children at age five can organize the rhythmic units in the context

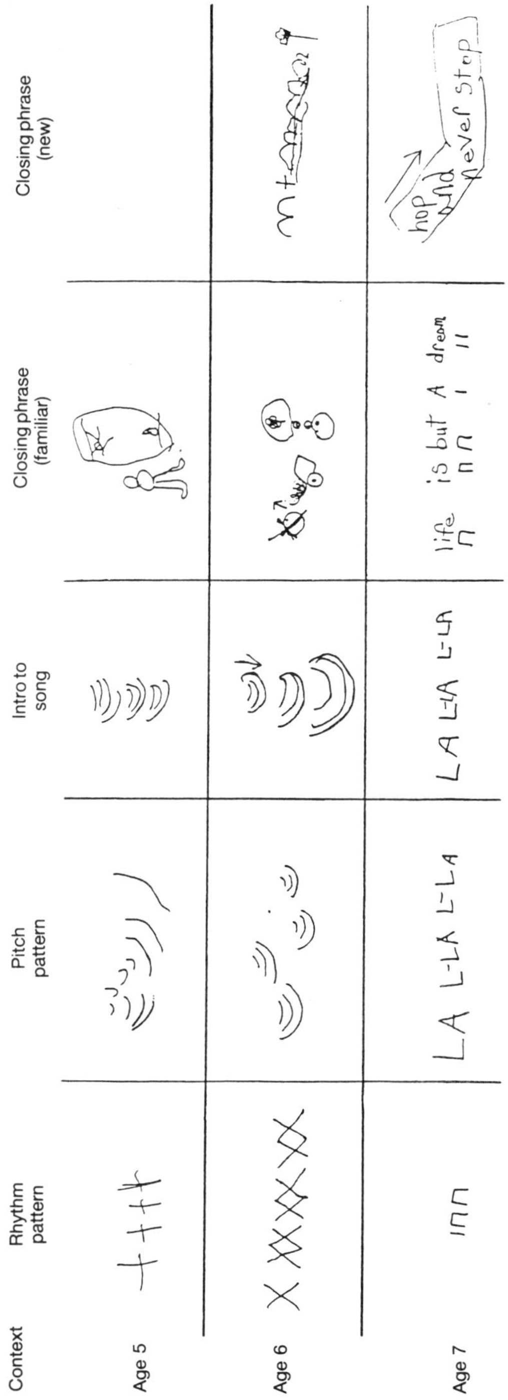

Fig. 9.18. Mary's notation of a single musical phrase across five contexts at ages 5–7.

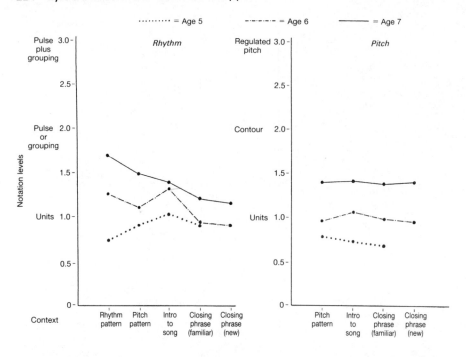

Fig. 9.19. Mean notation scores for rhythm and pitch in a single phrase across five musical contexts by children ages 5–7.

of a song, later they reveal their most sophisticated understanding of rhythmic features within the context of isolated rhythm patterns. Accordingly, statistical analysis of rhythmic notations using one-way repeated measures ANOVA reveals highly significant development [$p<0.0001$] over the three-year period *only* for isolated rhythm patterns. In this context it is not unusual to see seven-year-olds representing rhythmic grouping and the underlying pulse *simultaneously*. However, as soon as the dimension of pitch is introduced to the phrase, the notation of rhythmic pulse or grouping appears less often. This decline continues as the rhythmic features of the phrase competes with those features of pitch, text, and song structure. Although seven-year-olds continue to develop higher levels of rhythmic complexity in their musical representations, these only occur in the context of isolated rhythm patterns.

On the other hand, children's developing representations of pitch appear regardless of musical context. Whether the phrase occurs as an isolated melodic pattern, as an added introduction phrase with generic syllables, or as a phrase in a familiar or unfamiliar song, children attend to pitch equally well at every level of development. When compared to rhythm, pitch development appears universally stable and increasingly robust with age. Statistical analysis in pitch notations using one-way repeated measure ANOVA shows highly significant [$p<0.002$] growth over the entire three-year period in all of the contexts.

This stable representation of pitch is most impressive at the age of seven. The average child is no longer content to code units of the phrase without providing some indication of melodic contour. Many children are now concerned with higher levels of organizing and formatting pitch as they invent ways of regulating the placement of notes so that intervallic or even scalar relationships can be represented. Furthermore, representing this level of pitch is important to the child in every musical context.

As we trace Janet's notations of the single phrase at age five and six, we see a clear example of the preference children generally give to pitch (Fig. 9.20). At age five, Janet represents the units of the phrase in the context of isolated patterns while tracking the underlying pulse (context (C)) or rhythmic grouping (context (D)) in song. At age six, she is primarily concerned with showing melodic contour except with isolated rhythm patterns. At age seven, she again consistently represents the melodic contour of the phrase, while occasionally adding indications of rhythmic grouping.

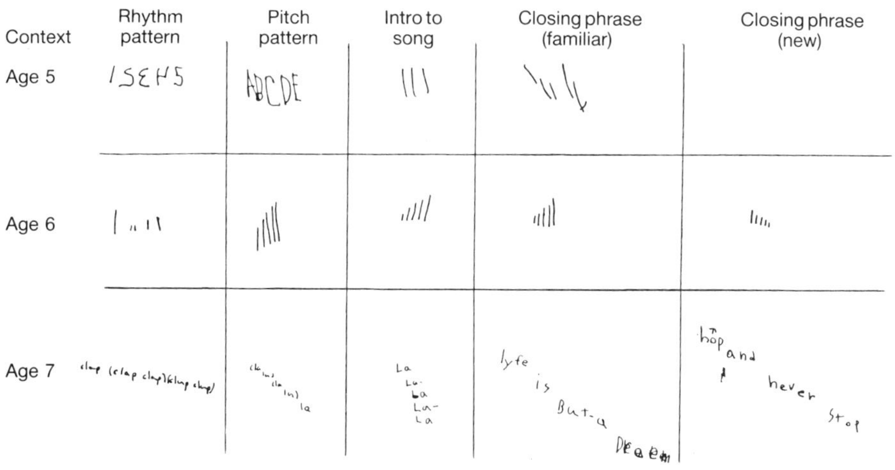

Fig. 9.20. Janet's notation of a single phrase across five musical contexts at ages 5–7.

Correlational analysis provides another way of viewing the diverging patterns of association between levels of rhythm and pitch representation. As seven-year-olds develop more complex representations of the phrase, notations of pitch in all contexts are highly correlated, while rhythm notation levels are not. This strongly suggests that once children are able to record melodic contour in one context they are likely to retain this level of pitch representation throughout various contexts.

Remarkably, only children's notations of *isolated* rhythm patterns are highly correlated with the level of sophistication of pitch. Those who represent more sophisticated notational levels of isolated rhythm patterns tend to be the same ones who do well at representing pitch in their notations of short melodic fragments or phrases of songs. These findings reveal a distinctive profile of their musical understanding. Although clearly these children *can* represent the complex patterning of rhythmic relationships, when pitch is present they more often *choose* to notate the melodic contour. This switch of attention places rhythm and pitch in a figure-ground relationship, that is, the rhythmic 'figure' in isolation becomes 'ground' when pitch is introduced into the context of the phrase.

Looking briefly at the relationship between performance skills and ability to represent rhythm and pitch across contexts, we see additional evidence for the developing link between children's performance abilities and their representations of music. As children grow older and develop more sophisticated representations of pitch, they appear increasingly able to draw upon their performance knowledge. Surprisingly, this is not the case with their representation of the rhythmic content of the phrase. At first, correlations between performance scores and notation scores are practically nonexistent. By the age of seven, however, children's performance scores almost all significantly correlate with notation levels of pitch across virtually every context. Again, this is not the case with rhythm.

In sum, this 'across context' analysis of children's ability to attend to increasingly sophisticated levels of rhythm and pitch in their notations provides a rare 'composite' image of their implicit understanding of music. By looking at their notations of a single phrase across a wide range of musical contexts, we see the representation of pitch as their primary focus of attention. Although children can produce remarkably sophisticated representations of isolated rhythmic patterns during this time, we witness the dramatic emergence of pitch as the musical ingredient most consistently important to young children.

Again we witness the divergent paths of rhythm and pitch in young children's representational development. Although rhythm appears as the initial focus of focus of children's notations, pitch emerges as the increasingly cohesive underpinning of representational development. Not only is development more striking within pitch, but representational development with pitch can now be seen as extremely stable within a wide range of musical contexts and graphic symbols. We also find that representation of pitch—particularly in the context of songs—is increasingly tied to the performance knowledge of young children.

Conclusion

Originally, in this chapter, we were concerned with the relationship of representational development to perceptual and performance development in the domain of music. For the most part, earlier studies in musical development concentrated on perception and performance. Although this research shows that young children progress considerably in their ability to recognize or discriminate melodic patterns, or in their ability to produce or imitate short melodic fragments, it may be that children's musical cognitive development is best viewed by their symbolic representations of music. Simply put, although dogs can recognize melodic calls and birds can create and reproduce tuneful ditties, human musical development is uniquely tied to symbolic 're-presentations' of the music we hear and perform. Therefore, through young children's first musical representations we can begin to view the uniquely human inception of musical cognitive development.

The age range of five to seven has been documented by many development psychologists (White 1970) as a period of considerable change in most children's learning and perception modes. Past research in musical perception and performance shows that music cognition is no exception. In our study of children's representation of musical features across a full range of contexts, we have documented dramatic developmental trends in their use of symbols, the level of sophistication of their notations, and their selective attention to musical features depending on the context. These trends appear particularly between the ages of six and seven. These findings root music cognition more firmly within the framework of general cognitive development than originally thought. Children not only reveal an increasingly systematic representation of musical features, they also increasingly draw on their performance knowledge when inventing their notations.

More importantly to psychologists of music, by studying the divergent paths of development in rhythm and in pitch we gain a more precise understanding of the course of musical development between the ages of five and seven. As these children's notations become more sophisticated, our results suggest the emergence of pitch as a prime ingredient of musical cognitive development. Pitch emerges as the most robust component of musical cognitive development, independent of musical context or symbol choice in representation, and increasingly associated with development of performance skills. We speculate from these findings that, as pitch development occurs with age, it becomes increasingly independent of the language, kinaesthetic, or number skills that confound our assessment of musical development in young children. For example, although performing the words of a well-known song may at first help control the rhythmic surface of the performance, it does not predict the ability to sing these words with pitch. On the other hand, as children get older, the ability to reproduce 'pitch in song' increasingly predicts the ability to notate pitch in all contexts. Pitch, therefore, appears to be an essential 'core' ingredient of

In music education, we view these results as important to our understanding of the developing child. This study reveals that young children, without explicit musical training in notation, can represent an increasingly sophisticated understanding of the music they perform. While recognizing the *success* of performance training at an early age (for instance Suzuki training), we must also pay attention to the musical *understanding* of young children. For example, music teachers might be better off assessing children's sensitivity to musical features by looking at their invented representations of music rather than at their reproduction of music symbols. Also, music educators might restructure the focus and timing of musical training in accordance with these developmental findings. We would emphasize the assessment of pitch development as a critical focus in young children's musical training.

Finally we strongly urge the continued exploration of young children's understanding of music. The early development of music perception, performance, and symbolic representation can only help us better understand the early roots of human cognition. Contained in children's spontaneous notations of short nursery songs are glimpses of growing minds at work. As we better understand children's extraordinary invented symbol systems for music, we discover how they mindfully abstract and reconstruct an increasingly rich and integrated world of musical understanding.

Acknowledgements

This research was supported in part by grants from the Carnegie Corporation, Rockefeller Foundation, and the Spencer Foundation. The work was carried out in the Cambridge, Mass, Public Schools and at the Cambridge Friends School. We are grateful to the teachers, children, and parents who helped us to pursue our interest in musical cognition. For their careful and critical readings of early drafts, we thank Howard Gardner and Jeanne Bamberger. John Willet's command of non-parametric statistical techniques aided us greatly in our data analysis. We are also indebted to Martha Davis-Perry, Joan Meyaard, Dennie Wolf, Joe Walters, and Rena Upitis for their suggestions and assistance.

References

Bamberger, J. (1980). Cognitive structuring in the apprehension and description of simple rhythms. *Archives de Psychologie* **48** , 177–99.

Bamberger, J. (1982). Revisiting children's drawings of simple rhythms: a function for reflection in action. *U-Shaped behavioural growth* (ed. S. Strauss). Academic Press, New York.

Bamberger, J. and Schon, D. A. (1977). The figural-formal transaction: a parable of generative metaphor. Unpublished paper, Division for Study and Research in Education at the Massachusetts Institute of Technology.

Bruner, J. (1973). The growth of representational processes in childhood. *Beyond the information given*. Norton, New York.

Cody, R. and Smith, J. (1985). *Applied statistics and the SAS programming language*. North-Holland, New York.

Davidson, L. (1985). Tonal structures of children's early songs. *Music Perception* 2, No. 3 361–74.

Dowling, W. J. (1982). Melodic information processing and its development. *The psychology of music* (ed. D. Deutsch). Academic Press, New York.

Flavell, J. H. (1963). *The developmental psychology of Jean Piaget*. Van Nostrand, New York.

Friedman, M. (1937). The use of ranks to avoid the assumption of normality implicit in the analysis of variance. *Journal of the American Statistical Association* 32, 675–701.

Furth, H. (1969). *Piaget and knowledge*. University of Chicago Press, Chicago.

Gardner, H. (1979). Developmental psychology after Piaget: an approach in terms of symbolization. *Human development*. Academic Press, New York.

Gardner, H. (1980). *Artful scribbles: the significance of children's drawings*. Basic Books, New York.

Gardner, H. (1983). *Frames of mind: the theory of multiple intelligences*. Basic Books, New York.

Gardner, H., Howard, V., and Perkins, D. (1974). Symbol systems: a philosophical, psychological, and educational investigation. *Media and symbols: the forms of expression, communication, and education* (ed. David Olson). University of Chicago Press, Chicago.

Goodman, N. (1976). *Languages of art*. Hackett, Cambridge, Mass.

Goodman, N. (1978). *Ways of worldmaking*. Hackett, Cambridge, Mass.

Goodnow, J. (1977). *Children drawing*. Harvard University Press, Cambridge, Mass.

Gordon, E. (1965). *Musical aptitude profile*. Houghton Mifflin, Boston.

Hattwick, M., and Williams, H. (1935). Measurement of musical development II, *University of Iowa Studies in Child Welfare*, Vol. 11, No. 2, pp. 63–6. Iowa City: University of Iowa Press.

Hollander, M., and Wolfe, D. (1973). *Nonparametric statistical methods*. Wiley, New York.

McKernon, P. (1979). The development of first songs in young children. *New Directions for Child Development* 3, 43–58.

Olson, D. (1970). *Cognitive development: the child's acquisition of diagonality*. Academic Press, New York.

Petzold, R. G. (1966). *Auditory perception of musical sounds by children in the first six grades*. Cooperative Research Project No. 1051, University of Wisconsin.

Pflederer, M. (1964). The responses of chlidren to musical tasks embodying

Piaget's principle of conservation. *Journal of Research in Music Education* **12**, (4) 251–68.

Piaget, J. and Inhelder, B. (1956). *The child's conception of space.* Norton, New York.

Piaget, J. and Inhelder, B. (1973). *Memory and intelligence.* Routledge and Kegan Paul, London.

Seashore, C. E. (1919). *Measures of musical talents.* The Psychological Corporation, New York.

Serafine, M. L. (1984). The development of cognition in music. *The Music Quarterly* **70**, 218–33.

Upitis, R. (1985). Children's understanding of rhythm: the relationship between development and musical training. Unpublished Ph.D. thesis. Harvard University. University Microfilms International, London.

Walker, R. (1981) Teaching basic musical concepts and their staff notations through cross-modal matching symbols. *Psychology of Music* **9**, (1), 31–8.

Werner, H. (1948) *The comparative psychology of mental development.* International Universities Press, New York.

Werner, H. (1957). The concept of development from a comparative and organismic point of view. In *The concept of development* (ed. D. Harris). University of Minnesota Press, Minneapolis.

White, S. H. (1970). Some general outlines of the matrix of developmental changes between five and seven years. *Bulletin of the Orton Society* **20**, 41–57.

Wolf, D., Davidson, L., Davis, M., Walters, J., Hodges, M., and Scripp, L., (1986). Beyond A, B and C: a broader and deeper view of literacy. In *The psychological bases of early education* (ed. A. Pellegrini). Wiley, London.

Zenatti, A. (1969). *Le développement génétique de la perception musicale.* Monographies Françaises de Psychologie, No. 17.

Zuckerkandl, V. (1969). *Sound and symbol: music and the external world.* Princeton University Press.

10

Cognitive constraints on compositional systems

FRED LERDAHL

In this chapter I explore the relationship between composing and listening. I begin with a problematic story, draw some general conclusions, introduce relevant concepts from Lerdahl and Jackendoff (1983) and related work, propose some cognitive constraints on compositional systems, discuss 'pitch space', and explain why serial (or 12-tone) organizations are cognitively opaque. Most of these topics deserve fuller treatment than is given in these pages. My concern here is just to lay out a basic, if wide-ranging, argument.

I am not interested in passing judgement on the composers and compositions that are mentioned, particularly not on the remarkable work by Boulez that I use as a representative example. The thrust of my argument is psychological rather than aesthetic. But since aesthetic issues inevitably impinge on the discussion, I treat them briefly at the end.

Hidden organization in *Le Marteau sans Maître*

Boulez's *Le Marteau sans Maître* (1954) was widely hailed as a masterpiece of post-war serialism. Yet nobody could figure out, much less hear, how the piece was serial. From hints in Boulez (1963), Koblyakov (1977) at last determined that it was indeed serial, though in an idiosyncratic way. In the interim listeners made what sense they could of the piece in ways unrelated to its construction. Nor has Koblyakov's decipherment subsequently changed how the piece is heard. Meanwhile most composers have discarded serialism, with the result that Koblyakov's contribution has caused barely a ripple of professional interest. The serial organization of *Le Marteau* would appear, 30 years later, to be irrelevant.

This story is, or should be, disturbing. There is a huge gap here between compositional system and cognized result. How can this be?

One might suppose that the impenetrability of *Le Marteau's* serial organization is due to insufficient exposure. After all, the piece was innovative; listeners must become accustomed to novel stimuli. Such has been the traditional defence of new art in the face of incomprehension. One might refine this view by pointing out that there is little repetition in *Le Marteau*. The lack of redundancy perhaps overwhelms the listener's processing capacities. Comprehensibility, then, is arguably a consequence both of the degree of conditioning to the materials and of the number and variety of events per unit time. (Is it a coincidence that *Le Marteau* was composed in the heyday of behaviourism and information theory?)

But this explanation is inadequate. For one thing, competent listeners to *Le Marteau*, even after many hearings, still cannot even begin to hear its serial organization. For many passages they cannot even tell if wrong pitches or rhythms have been played. The piece is hard to learn by ear in a specific sense; its details have a somewhat statistical quality. Conditioning, in short, does not suffice. For another thing, *Le Marteau* does not feel structurally complex in the way, for example, that compositions by Beethoven or Schoenberg do. Vast numbers of nonredundant events fly by, but the effect is of a smooth sheen of pretty sounds. The listener's processing capacities, in short, are not overwhelmed.

This is not to deny the influence of exposure and redundancy on comprehensibility. But these factors do not go far enough; they do not address issues of specific organization. Cognitive psychology has shown in recent decades that humans structure stimuli in certain ways rather than others. Comprehension takes place when the perceiver is able to assign a precise mental representation to what is perceived. Not all stimuli, however, facilitate the formation of a mental representation. Comprehension requires a degree of ecological fit between the stimulus and the mental capabilities of the perceiver.

Experienced listeners do not find *Le Marteau* totally incomprehensible, but neither, I would argue, do they assign to it a detailed mental representation. This is why the details of the piece are hard to learn and why the piece does not in the end feel complex. The serial organization that Koblyakov found is opaque to such structuring.

Of course a musician of Boulez's calibre would not use a compositional system without drawing crucially upon his musical intuition and experience. Music-generating algorithms alone have always produced primitive outputs; not enough is known about musical composition and cognition for them to succeed. Boulez had the intellectually less ambitious goal of developing a system that could just produce a quantity of musical material having a certain consistency. He then shaped his materials more or less intuitively, using both his 'ear' and various unacknowledged constraints. In so doing, he listened much as another listener might. The organization deciphered by Koblyakov was just a means, and not the only one, towards an artistic end.

The degree to which *Le Marteau* is comprehensible, then, depends not on its serial organization but on what the composer added to that organization. On the other hand, the serial procedures profoundly influenced the stimulus structure, leading to a situation in which the listener cannot form a detailed mental representation of the music. The result is a piece that sounds partly patterned and partly stochastic.*

Compositional and listening grammars

It will be useful to put these observations in schematic form. Let me introduce the notion of a *musical grammar*, a limited set of rules that can generate indefinitely large sets of musical events and/or their structural descriptions. Such a grammar can take the form of (a) or (b) in Fig. 10.1. (The rectangles stand for sets of rules, the ellipses for inputs and outputs of rules.) In (a), the rule system generates the events of a passage or piece, and in the process provides some sort of specification (the 'input organization'). In (b), the sequence of events is taken as given, and the role of the rule system is to assign a structural description to the sequence.

Our discussion of *Le Marteau* suggests that there are two kinds of musical grammar at work here. The first is the *compositional grammar*, consciously employed by Boulez, that generated both the events of the piece and their serial organization as discovered by Koblyakov. This grammar is an instance of (a) in Fig. 10.1. The second kind is the *listening grammar*, more or less unconsciously employed by auditors, that generates mental representations of the music. This grammar is an instance of (b) in Fig. 10.1; the events themselves are present when *Le Marteau* is played.

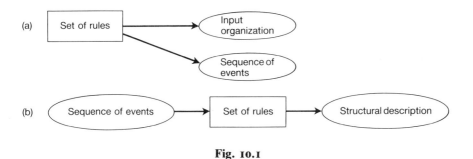

Fig. 10.1

---

* In *Structures*, Book I (1952), Boulez flirted with 'algorithmic composition', and in *Pli selon pli* (1958–61) he incorporated aleatoric elements; so *Le Marteau* lies *en route* in his dialectic of determinism and chance (see Boulez 1964). His interest in algorithmic composition continues to the extent that for a while there was a research group at IRCAM pursuing it. For six months in 1981 I was part of that group, though in my project the purpose of the computer program was not to compose but to assist composers in composing, much as a word processor assists writers (see a brief description in Lerdahl 1985). Many of the ideas expressed in this essay grew out of that experience, for which I remain deeply grateful.

Fig. 10.2 summarizes these remarks. The diagram shows that the compositional grammar generates the sequence of events and the manner in which they are specified. Only the sequence of events, however, is available as input to the listening grammar: the listener hears the acoustic signal, not its compositional specification. The listening grammar then generates the mental representation that comprises the 'heard structure' of the piece. Note that Fig. 10.2 incorporates both (a) and (b) of Fig. 10.1.

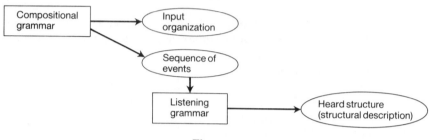

Fig. 10.2

This account is complicated by the fact that, as noted above, Boulez created *Le Marteau* not only through serial procedures but through his own inner listening. In the process he followed constraints that, while operating on the sequence of events produced by the compositional grammar, utilized principles from the listening grammar. This more elaborate picture is drawn in Fig. 10.3.

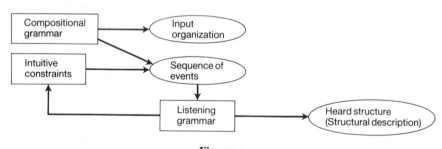

Fig. 10.3

Observe that none of the arrows in the diagram are inputs to the 'compositional grammar'. This component is inaccessible to the rest of the system. Hence it becomes quite possible for the 'compositional grammar' to be unrelated to the other rules, the 'listening grammar' and 'intuitive constraints'. If this happens, the 'input organization' will bear no relation to the 'heard structure'. Here, then, lies the gap between compositional system and cognized result with which we began.

This situation exists not only for *Le Marteau* but for much of contemporary music. I could have illustrated just as well with works by Babbitt, Carter, Nono, Stockhausen, or Xenakis. This gap is a fundamental problem of contemporary music. It divorces method from intuition. Composers are faced with the unpleasant alternative of working with private codes or with no compositional grammar at all. Private codes remain idiosyncratic, competing against other private codes and creating no larger continuity—so that, for example, 30 years later the serial organization of *Le Marteau* becomes irrelevant even to other composers.

Natural and artificial compositional grammars

Where does a compositional grammar come from? The answer varies, but a few generalizations may be helpful. Let us distinguish between a 'natural' and an 'artificial' compositional grammar. A natural grammar arises spontaneously in a musical culture. An artificial grammar is the conscious invention of an individual or group within a culture. The two mix fruitfully in a complex and long-lived musical culture such as that of Western tonality. A natural grammar will dominate in a culture emphasizing improvisation and encouraging active participation of the community in all the varieties of musical behaviour. An artificial grammar will tend to dominate in a culture that utilizes musical notation, that is self-conscious, and that separates musical activity into composer, performer, and listener.

The gap between compositional and listening grammars arises only when the compositional grammar is 'artificial', when there is a split between production and consumption. Such a gap, incidentally, cannot arise so easily in human language. People must communicate; a member of a culture must master a linguistic grammar common to both speaking and hearing. But music has primarily an aesthetic function and need not communicate its specified structure. Hidden musical organizations can and do appear.

A natural compositional grammar depends on the listening grammar as a source. Otherwise the various musical functions could not evolve in such a spontaneous and unified fashion. An artificial compositional grammar, on the other hand, can have a variety of sources—metaphysical, numerical, historical, or whatever. It can be desirable for an artificial grammar to grow out of a natural grammar; think, for example, of the salutary role that Fux (1725) played in the history of tonality. The trouble starts only when the artificial grammar loses touch with the listening grammar.

In the Western tradition the trouble began with the exhaustion of tonality at the turn of the century. Anything became possible. Faced with chaos, composers reacted by inventing their own compositional grammars. Within an avant-garde aesthetic it became possible to believe that one's own new system was the wave of the future. Boulez's generation was the last to believe this. To a younger generation these systems have come to seem merely arbitrary. The avant-garde has withered away, and all methods and styles are available to the point of confusion.

One can react to this situation by giving up on compositional grammars and relying solely on ear and habit—on the 'intuitive constraints' of Fig. 10.3. But composing is too difficult for such a solution; there are too many possibilities. Or one can react by reverting to earlier 'natural' styles, a move that condemns one to a parasitic relationship with the past. Both reactions are common these days, and both are motivated by the desire to avoid the gap between composing procedure and what is heard.

My own reaction as a composer has been less to avoid than to confront this gap. These were my initial ground rules: (1) a compositional grammar is necessary; (2) it need not be nostalgic; (3) our musical culture is too fragmented and self-conscious for a natural grammar to emerge; but (4) an artificial grammar unresponsive to musical listening is unacceptable. It was inevitable, I concluded, that early attempts at artificial grammars—say, from the 1920s to the 1950s—were defective in their relation to listening. Not enough was known about musical cognition; the basic questions had not even been framed. Beginning around 1970, however, a new perspective became possible through the simultaneous decline of the avant-garde and rise of cognitive psychology. Contemporary music had lost its way. What other foundation was there to turn to than the nature of musical understanding itself? In other words, I decided that a compositional grammar must be based on the listening grammar. Fig. 10.4 illustrates this by adding a dashed arrow to the flow chart of Fig. 10.3. In principle this arrow integrates the compositional grammar into the overall framework, rather than leaving it isolated from input.

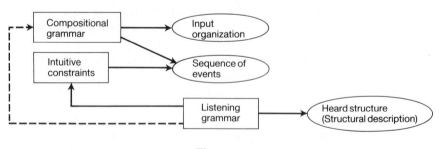

Fig. 10.4

But for this proposal to have substance, a great deal must be known about the listening grammar. Hence it became necessary to develop a detailed theory of musical cognition (Lerdahl and Jackendoff 1983). Such a theory, I reasoned, could provide the basis for artificial compositional grammars that could be intellectually complex yet spontaneously accessible to mental representation. The commonality of compositional and listening grammars could produce a rich yet transparent music.

Theoretical overview

This is not the place to describe the specifics of Jackendoff's and my theory. I propose only to outline some of its general features. The reader should bear in mind, however, that the theory is concrete and detailed.

Our theory models musical listening within the framework of some standard methodological idealizations. Assuming (1) an experienced listener, (2) the psychoacoustical organization of the physical signal into a 'musical surface' comprising a sequence of discrete events, and (3) a final-state knowledge of the sequence, the theory predicts structural descriptions from musical surfaces by means of a set of rules that ideally corresponds to the 'listening grammar' of Figs. 10.2–4. See Fig. 10.5; and note that the theory is 'generative' in the sense of (b) in Fig. 10.1. The predictions of the rules are testable by introspection and, in principle, by experiment.*

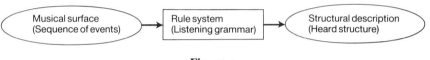

Fig. 10.5

As a practical matter the theory focuses on Classical tonal music, but most of the rules appear to have a more general psychological basis and therefore to be applicable to other idioms as well. The extent of the universality of the rules is an empirical question. Again for practical reasons, the rules assign structural descriptions only to the hierarchical aspects of musical structure, neglecting 'associational' dimensions such as motivic processes and timbral relations (but see Lerdahl 1987). By 'hierarchy' is meant the strict nesting of elements or regions in relation to other elements or regions. The theory claims that, if the signal permits, the listener unconsciously infers four types of hierarchical structure from a musical surface: *grouping structure*, or the segmentation of the musical flow into units such as motives, phrases, and sections; *metrical structure*, or the pattern of periodically recurring strong and weak beats associated with the surface; *time-span reduction*, or the relative structural importance of

---

* Deliège (1985) has experimentally verified—and, in a few cases, improved upon—the local grouping preference rules of the theory. Todd (1985) has used the time-span reductional component of the theory to model expressive timing at cadences in performance. Palmer and Krumhansl (in press) have found empirical support for predictions made by the metrical and time-span components.

events as heard within contextually established rhythmic units; and *prolongational reduction*, or the perceived pattern of tension and relaxation among events at various levels of structure. Both kinds of reduction are described by structural trees. The prolongational component incorporates aspects of Schenker's (1935) theory.

For the most part these four hierarchies interact as shown in Fig.10.6. From the grouping and metrical structures the listener forms the rhythmic units, or *time-span segmentation*, over which the dominating-subordinating relationships of time-span reduction take place; and from the time-span reduction the listener in turn projects the tensing-relaxing hierarchy of prolongational reduction. Thus the mapping from musical surface to prolongational structure is indirect. In addition, both kinds of reduction depend for their operation on *stability conditions* among pitch configurations as considered 'out of time'. These conditions, which also can be described hierarchically (Krumhansl 1983; Bharucha 1984*b*), are internal schemata induced from previously heard musical surfaces and brought to bear on the in-time event sequences described by the reductions.

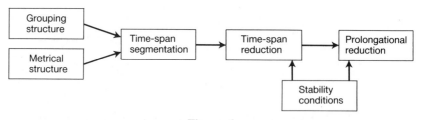

Fig. 10.6

For each of the four organizations there is a set of *well-formedness rules* that defines the conditions for hierarchy. Well-formed structures can be modified in limited ways by *transformational rules*. These two rules types are abstract in that they only define formal possibilities. By contrast, a third rule type, *preference rules*, registers particular aspects of presented musical surfaces and selects which well-formed or transformed structures in fact apply to those surfaces. The preference rules, which do the bulk of the work of the theory, do not generate categorically right or wrong analyses but instead predict descriptions as more or less coherent. When the preference rules reinforce one another, the analysis is stable and the passage in question is judged as stereotypical: when they conflict, the analysis is unstable and the passage is judged as ambiguous or vague.

In summary, the theory asserts that (1) the listener has at his disposal a number of hierarchical organizations possessing certain formal properties, and (2) the listener unconsciously attempts to assign the most stable overall description (or descriptions) by means of preferential principles that activate and interact in response to specific features of musical surfaces.

Constraints on event sequences

What does Jackendoff's and my theory have to say about closing the gap between compositional system and cognized result? Let me explore this question by proposing, in this and the following two sections, a number of psychologically plausible constraints on compositional grammars. These constraints will give substance to the dashed arrow in Fig.10.4. Then I will use the constraints to explain why serial organizations are not easily learnable.

We begin with a presupposition of the theory, namely that the musical surface breaks down into individual events. Certain recent musical developments (pioneered for instance by Ligeti) have tended to blur distinctions between events. Sensuously attractive though this blurring may be, it inhibits the inference of structure.

> *Constraint 1*: The musical surface must be capable of being parsed into a sequence of discrete events.*

It is hardly fortuitous that our theory concentrates on hierarchies. Most of human cognition relies on hierarchical structuring (Miller *et al.* 1960; Simon 1962; Neisser 1967). Studies in music psychology have indicated that the absence of perceived hierarchy substantially reduces the listener's ability to learn and remember structure from musical surfaces (Deutsch 1982). It does not suffice for the input organization to be structured hierarchically; such in fact is the case for *Le Marteau* (Koblyakov 1977). It is the relationship to the listening grammar that matters.

> *Constraint 2*: The musical surface must be available for hierarchical structuring by the listening grammar.

As suggested above, there are four ways that the listening grammar can structure event sequences hierarchically. Let us return to Fig. 10.6 and consider what is needed at the musical surface for these organizations to come into play.

Segmentation into groups is accomplished at local levels largely by detection of *distinctive transitions* in the musical flow. A distinctive transition corresponds at a less fine-grained level to the principles by which events themselves are perceived as discrete rather than continuous. It is a change in some musical dimension, such as greater distance in attack points or shift in dynamics, timbre, or register, with respect to an immediate context that is relatively invariant. From this it follows that constant change will not give rise to salient distinctive transitions; nor of course will

---

* This formulation skirts the issue of simultaneous sequences of discrete events, an area that has been researched as 'auditory stream segregation' by Bregman and his associates (see McAdams and Bregman 1979 for a review).

no change at all. Babbitt and Reich have something in common after all. The steady-state quality of both their musics is due to a paucity of distinctive transitions, hence of grouping boundaries.

> *Constraint 3*: The establishment of local grouping boundaries requires the presence of salient distinctive transitions at the musical surface.

The other factor creating local groups is repetition or, more generally, *parallelism* of musical units. Repetition is an obsession of minimalism. But without distinctive transitions such groups produce only 'flat' hierarchies; that is, the repetitions are not heard within larger groups to any depth of embedding. Groups of groups tend to arise rather through the reinforcing action of distinctive transitions and parallelisms, often supplemented by a third principle of *symmetry* (the approximately equal division of a larger time span). At global levels parallelism becomes the overriding grouping principle: listeners try to hear parallel passages in parallel places in the overall structure.

> *Constraint 4*: Projection of groups, especially at larger levels, depends on symmetry and on the establishment of musical parallelisms.

Much contemporary music avoids symmetry and parallelism. Indeed, in the 1950s and 1960s literal repetition was widely regarded as aesthetically inexcusable. But symmetry and especially parallelism are basic ingredients of any complex grouping structure. The reliance on these principles in Classical tonal music and in various ethnic musics is not necessarily a sign of lack of invention but is an essential technique for the creation of deeply embedded groups.

We turn now to metrical structure. A well-formed metre is a looping pattern of equidistant beats occurring at multiple hierarchical levels. A beat at any metrical level is felt to be strong if it is also a beat at the next larger level. Depending on the musical idiom, the criterion of equidistance may be loosened, but not to the extent of abandoning all sense of periodicity. A musical idiom typically has available a limited repertory of well-formed metrical possibilities.

When hearing a musical surface, the listener seeks an optimal fit between the accents perceived directly from the signal and the repertory of available metrical structures. These *phenomenal accents* arise from local stresses such as sforzandos, changing bass notes and chords, contextually long events, and so forth. Insofar as possible, the onsets of phenomenal accents are aligned with relatively strong beats. In other words, the listener looks for maximal periodicity in the musical signal.

Great regularity in phenomenal accents produces a rhythmic quality of stability and squareness. In much rhythmically vital music, however, many phenomenal accents are forced to align with weak beats, creating cross-accents or syncopations. But if there is very little regularity to the phenomenal accents, the listener may not be able to infer any metrical structure. Most music is metrical, and the immediate location of events is established largely in relation to this or that strong or weak beat. An inability to assign a metrical grid weakens the precision of location of events, resulting in a quality of suspended rhythm.

> *Constraint 5*: The establishment of a metrical structure requires a degree of regularity in the placement of phenomenal accents.

Much contemporary music, even if notated traditionally, avoids regularity of phenomenal accents and does not give rise to a sense of metre. Complicated rhythms can cancel as well as create structure. An interesting case is Carter's practice of establishing two or more simultaneous tempos. Each such tempo corresponds to a single metrical level, or pulsation, but usually does not evoke a hierarchy of strong and weak beats. Carter contracts metrical depth in order to focus on multiple speeds. However, two or three simultaneous tempos cannot be taken in as readily as the four or five metrical levels that are commonplace in a march or waltz. Musical cognition has a bias for hierarchical organization. Simultaneous tempos instead produce independent organizations competing for attention. The difficulties in attending to more than one such organization are well known (Cherry 1953) and are ameliorated only if the vertical correspondences are coherent (Sloboda 1985), a condition that only partly obtains in this case. The situation is analogous to that of harmonically controlled versus uncontrolled polyphony.

The grouping and metrical structures come together (via well-formedness rules) to form the time-span segmentation. Details aside, it should be intuitively obvious that events are heard and thought of within such units. We normally speak of an event at small levels in terms of this or that beat, at larger levels in terms of this or that phrase or section. If the grouping or metrical structure is impoverished, then so too is the time-span segmentation.

> *Constraint 6*: A complex time-span segmentation depends on the projection of complex grouping and metrical structures.

Various passages of *Le Marteau*, in which no metrical structure is apparent and the groups are not deeply embedded, provide a contrary illustration. Because of the consequent lack of hierarchical time-span segmentation, the sense of these passages is of a flurry of events followed by a pause, then another flurry and another pause, like beads on a string. Each flurry tends to become one complex 'event' rather than an organized sequence of events. The phrase is replaced by a sonorous object extended in time. (This is one way of explaining why, despite its generally fast tempos, *Le Marteau* feels slow.)

The notion of an extended sonorous object filled with inner movement is a compelling one, especially in light of recent developments in computer music. Here lies an unexpected link beteween *Le Marteau* and Boulez's recent work, *Répons*. But from the perspective of musical cognition, one must ask how the inner movement of an object receives structure. We have returned to Constraint 1, the issue of musical surfaces as discrete events. If the listener can assign any rich internal structure to the sonorous object, it must be perceived as consisting of 'subobjects'. But if the subobjects are to be experienced as aspects of one object, they cannot be too discriminable or allow salient structuring.

The time-span segmentation must be highly structured for a complex event hierarchy to emerge—something not achieved, and perhaps not tried for, in *Le Marteau*, *Répons*, or indeed most contemporary music. Since 'events' in music are usually pitch events, event hierarchies are normally pitch hierarchies. A unified pitch hierarchy is an instance of tonality (broadly defined), the stability conditions for which will be discussed in the next two sections. For now let us assume stability conditions and review the projection of event hierarchies from musical surfaces.

The two kinds of reduction are complementary descriptions of event hierarchies. In the time-span reduction, the listener compares the relative stability of events within each time-span segment. The less stable event in a segment is judged as subordinate to, or as an elaboration of, the more stable event. This process continues recursively from local to global levels of the time-span segmentation until an entire time-span tree is built up. The relative stability of events within a span is determined partly by rhythmic position, for example whether an event occurs on a strong beat or cadences a group. But the main determinant of domination or subordination within a span is the set of stability conditions.

> *Constraint 7*: The projection of a time-span tree depends on a complex time-span segmentation in conjunction with a set of stablility conditions.

A little thought-experiment will demonstrate the necessity for both the time-span segmentation and the stability conditions for the hearing of an event hierarchy. Imagine the pitches of *Le Marteau* plugged into the rhythms of Beethoven's Fifth Symphony. The hierarchical time-span segmentation would largely be erased by the lack of any concomitant pitch articulation, and, in any case, the absence of stability conditions would prevent the inference of any pitch hierarchy. Or, conversely, imagine the pitches of the Fifth Symphony plugged into the rhythms of *Le Marteau*. The potentially hierarchical pitch structure would be garbled by the lack of supportive time-span segmentation (including the absence of any metrical structure or patterned grouping structure). In short, rhythm and pitch must work in concert if there is to be any time-span reduction.

The prolongational reduction derives from the time-span tree and, again, from the stability conditions. Although this is the most important of the ways in which events relate to one another, its description is rather technical and abstract, and so will be avoided here. Suffice it to say that in this component events connect hierarchically in terms of progression and continuity, creating *prolongational regions* that act in structural counterpoint to the time-span segmentation (see Lerdahl and Jackendoff 1983 for a detailed treatment).

>   *Constraint 8*: The projection of a prolongational tree depends on a corresponding time-span tree in conjunction with a set of stability conditions.

Before continuing, it would be well to emphasize how interdependent the contraints are that have been listed so far. Most of them call on their immediate predecessors. Thus a hierarchy of events (Constraint 2) requires a musical surface that has been parsed into events (Constraint 1); the recursive segmentation of the surface into rhythmic units (Constraint 6) cannot take place without the establishment of grouping and metrical structures (Constraints 3–5); the relative structural importance of events (Constraint 7) cannot be assessed without the time-span segmentation (Constraint 6); and the representation of how events depart and return (Constraint 8) demands an evaluation of their function in the rhythmic structure (Constraint 7). The requirement of projecting event hierarchies to the listener has brought a great deal in its wake.

Constraints on underlying materials

We turn now to the stability conditions underlying the two reductions. Generally, a stability condition says, 'Musical context aside, this structure is judged as more stable than that.' Stability conditions interact like preference rules, sometimes reinforcing and sometimes conflicting with one another. In Classical tonality, for example, a triad in root position is more stable than a triad in first inversion, and a I chord is more stable than a V chord. These conditions reinforce one another when the judgement is between a I and a V^6, but conflict when the judgement is between a I^6 and a V. In actual music such conflicts are resolved by context: on the assumption that the two events come up for comparison in the same unit (time-span segment or prolongational region), the reductional preference rules decide which event is more stable on the basis of rhythmic position, linear function, and other factors.

Stability conditions are contingent on the basic materials and properties out of which the event structure of a piece is made. In Classical tonal music, for instance, the basic materials include the diatonic scale, which has certain internal and transpositional properties that can project judgements of relative stability (of which more below). Musical idioms vary in these respects. It is possible though rare for the basic materials not to be used in a way that gives rise to stability conditions: one can imagine a treatment of the diatonic scale where all scale degrees are functionally equivalent and the circle of fifths is not employed. Similarly, both Bach and Schoenberg used the well-tempered chromatic scale, but only the former carved it up so as to induce clear judgements of relative stability among pitch configurations; the latter instead sought a noncentric musical universe in which the 'twelve tones . . . are related only with one another' (Schoenberg 1941). However, since learning and memory depend on hierarchical structuring (Constraint 2), and since event hierarchies depend on stability conditions (Constraints 7 and 8), it follows that stability conditions are cognitively advantageous.

What are the constraints on stability conditions? First, there must be a fixed collection of sonic elements (normally pitches; but see Lerdahl 1987). The assumption of such collections might go unremarked except that in electronic music they are fairly rare. When there is a virtual infinitude of sonic possibilities, it is hard for a composer to select and stick with a limited collection. Non-selection, however, means no syntax.

> *Constraint 9*: Stability conditions must operate on a fixed collection of elements.

A fixed collection should not be thought of as completely rigid. First, an element of a collection need only be perceived categorically (Burns and Ward 1982); otherwise a slightly mistuned pitch would cause havoc. Second, as long as the categories remain the points of reference, there can be embellishing or sliding within or between categories (as in microtonal inflexions in Indian music or string glissandos in Western music).

The elements of a collection can be placed along a dimension to form a scale. The intervals of a scale have general size limitations: they must be large enough for adjacent elements to be easily discernible, but not so large as to use up excessive space along the continuum.

> *Constraint 10*: Intervals between elements of a collection arranged along a scale should fall within a certain range of magnitude.

Constraints 9 and 10 are analogous to Constraint 1 (the requirement of discrete events). Both cases provide the building blocks for further organization, Constraints 9 and 10 for stability conditions and Constraint 1 for event hierarchies. A fixed collection with moderate interval sizes allows other stability conditions to emerge. In surveying some of these, let us assume that the collections are pitch collections—as opposed, say, to drums or synthesized timbres.

Most pitch collections take advantage of the 2:1 frequency ratio of the octave, so that in one respect pitches reduce to 'pitch classes'. There are 88 pitches on the piano but only 12 pitch classes. Thus, in addition to giving a recurring structure to the overall collection, the octave decreases to a more manageable size the memory load for elements of the collection.

> *Constraint 11:* A pitch collection should recur at the octave to produce pitch classes.

The octave can be divided up in innumerable ways. A common route has been to make a collection beginning with other small-ratio intervals and progressing gradually to intervals with larger ratios. From the present perspective, this route is advantageous because the resultant intervals provide a broad and graduated palette of *sensory* consonance and dissonance. Sensory consonance and dissonance can in turn form the basis for *musical* consonance and dissonance, where in a general sense consonance is equivalent to stability and dissonance to instability. Thus a seventh in Classical tonal music resolves to a sixth not just out of cultural convention but because the syntactical resolution is supported by sensory experience.

The claim is not that pitch configurations exhibiting relative sensory consonance must necessarily be more stable in musical contexts than those exhibiting relative sensory dissonance. The reverse can occur contextually, and shows up in the reductions where appropriate. Rather the claim is that the stability conditions will be relatively ineffectual unless they are supported by sensory consonance and dissonance. Stability conditions in which a seventh is supposed to be more stable than a sixth would contradict sensory experience and would not lead to event hierarchies of any depth of embedding.

Strictly speaking, these remarks hold for fundamentals with harmonic partials, such as produced by the voice and by all instruments in which the source is periodically excited. For intervals with very small ratios, the partials of the respective fundamentals are largely reinforcing, creating the sensation of consonance. Sensory dissonance, or 'roughness', arises when frequencies (whether of fundamentals or of partials) interfere within a critical bandwidth, which extends in most musical registers from a fraction of a semitone to a little less than a minor third (Plomp and Levelt 1965). The critical bandwidth is a consequence of the resolving power of the hearing mechanism in the peripheral auditory system. One could also invoke pattern-recognizing templates of the central auditory system, such as proposed in Terhardt (1974); these for present purposes lead to the same conclusion.

> *Constraint 12:* There must be a strong psychoacoustical basis for stability conditions. For pitch collections, this entails intervals that proceed gradually from very small to comparatively large frequency ratios.

However, as is well known, small interval ratios—whether in just or Pythagorean tuning—present problems for the transposition of intervals and chords. A reading of Partch (1949) might additionally suggest that the number of pitches and intervals in such a collection can become alarmingly large. An alternative route that avoids these problems is to divide the octave into equal intervals. The collection then permits equivalence under transposition, and the pitches and intervals to be learned are limited.

> *Constraint 13*: Division of the octave into equal parts facilitates transposition and reduces memory load.

But these advantages are offset by the fact that almost all equal divisions of the octave lead to interval ratios that are complex and that do not easily round off categorically to simple ratios. As a result the intervals give a small range of sensory consonance and dissonance, and Constraint 12 is not satisfied.

The 12-fold division of the octave (and to a lesser extent the 19-fold division; see Yasser 1932) is an exception: its intervals are sufficiently close to just intervals to be useful; that is, the deviations from just intonation are not large enough to cause serious roughness from otherwise consonant intervals. The slight loss in distinctions in sensory consonance and dissonance is compensated for by the possibility of unfettered transposition. The familiar chromatic scale has presumably survived so well because it meets the demands of both Constraints 12 and 13.

At this point two routes are available, one viewing the chromatic collection (or set) essentially as a whole, the other thinking of it as material for subsets that have various musical and psychological properties. Let us review these alternatives.

One can evoke stability conditions directly from the chromatic set through a selection and patterning of different degrees of sensory consonance and dissonance. For example, Debussy's and Bartók's harmonies often 'modulate' among chord types of varying degrees of dissonance. Schoenberg was at least tacitly occupied with such a notion both early and late in his career: early, notably in the First Chamber Symphony (1906), where the basic dissonant-to-consonant progression is from a chord built in fourths to a whole-tone chord to a triad; late, in the 12-tone works of the 1940s that include tonal features, particularly at cadential points. Hindemith's (1937) theory of 'harmonic fluctuation' is based on a similar idea, generalized on a supposedly psychoacoustic foundation to embrace all possible sonorities. It is profitable to view harmonic progression in the work of Machaut and other fourteenth-century composers in such a light. Much of my own work also fits in this category.

The other route is taken by the Classical tonal system, in which the referential sonority is always the triad. Various versions of the triad alone do not project adequate differences in sensory consonance and dissonance.

Stability conditions among triads are instead achieved through the use of subsets of the chromatic set, notably the diatonic. (Historically, of course, the diatonic scale precedes the chromatic, and until Wagner it was musically paramount as well. It can be illuminating, however, to view the diatonic in terms of the chromatic.)

Balzano (1980, 1982) shows through a group-theoretic analysis that only certain equal-interval sets—the 12-fold among them—lead to subsets incorporating the psychologically important criteria of intervallic 'uniqueness', scale-step 'coherence', and transpositional 'simplicity'. All three criteria have to do with location in 'pitch space'. The first criterion demands a unique 'vector of relations' for each pitch in a subset, so that the listener can orient himself unambiguously in relation to the other pitches. For example, each scale degree of the asymmetrical diatonic subset of the chromatic set has a non-duplicating intervallic relation to the other scale degrees. In contrast, the octatonic subset (alternating half- and whole-steps), which has been widely used in this century, is not 'unique', since its vector repeats four times in an octave (this is the 'charm of impossibilities' described in Messiaen 1944). The second criterion ensures that the intervals of a scale proceed in an orderly manner, so that, for instance, the same distance is not traversed by one step in one part of a scale but by two or more steps in another part. The harmonic minor scale, not to mention more extreme examples, would thereby be disqualified, since the augmented second between the sixth and seventh scale degrees is equal in distance to the minor thirds that elsewhere take two steps to traverse; this presumably explains why the scale is avoided melodically in much diatonic music. The third criterion ensures orderly transposition of a subset. The diatonic subset, for example, drops one pitch and adds another as it transposes along the circle of fifths, so that distance in transposition correlates with the number of pitches shared in two diatonic scales.

> *Constraint 14*: Assume pitch sets of n-fold equal divisions of the octave. Then subsets that satisfy uniqueness, coherence, and simplicity will facilitate location within the overall pitch space.

Balzano surprisingly demonstrates that in the 12-fold chromatic set only the pentatonic and diatonic subsets satisfy all three criteria. He advances this rather than traditional psychoacoustical explanations as the reason for the cultural ubiquity of these scales; and he recommends that the few other n-fold divisions of the octave that permit these features (such as the 20-fold set) be explored for their musical potential. However, none of the other candidates approximates just intonation. The real cognitive appeal of the chromatic set, I would argue, is that only here do Constraints 12, 13 and 14 all converge intact. The structural features of the pentatonic and diatonic subsets would appear to be correspondingly special. (For discussion relating to this section, see Sloboda 1985; Dowling and Harwood 1986.)

Pitch space

I referred above to 'pitch space'. I want now to examine this notion with the purpose of extracting a few more constraints on stability conditions.

A number of cognitive psychologists, notably Longuet-Higgins (1978) and Shepard (1982), have proposed multidimensional representations for pitch relations.* The basic idea is that in a tonal framework pitches are cognized as relatively close to or far from one another, and that these distances can be represented geometrically. To take the simplest case, pitches are heard as proximate in terms of both pitch height and pitch class, so at least a two-dimensional representation is necessary. Another dimension can be added to account for fifth-relatedness; and so on. One can think of these representations as internalized maps. Just as cities are close to or far from home and can best be reached via some roads rather than others, so it is with tonal relations.

> *Constraint 15*: Any but the most primitive stability conditions must be susceptible to multidimensional representation, where spatial distance correlates with cognitive distance.

The geometric pitch spaces proposed in the psychological literature seem promising, but I have lingering doubts. First, granting the insights provided by Balzano (1982) and Shepard (1982), it remains odd that the chromatic collection is taken as the basis for the diatonic music they seek to explain. A second and related point is that, in pursuit of geometric symmetry, these models tend to come up with more regularity than diatonic music warrants. For example Longuet-Higgins's (1978) array has a major-third axis, and Shepard's (1982) double helix is made up to two strands of whole-tone scales. But only the semitone and perfect-fifth interval cycles are relevant to diatonic music, which is in many ways asymmetrical. Other interval cycles do not begin to assume musical significance until nineteenth-century chromaticism.

These questions lead me to suggest a complementary pitch space that has a reductional rather than a geometric format. This space is musically obvious yet has explanatory power. I take the lead from Deutsch and Feroe (1981), who speak of different pitch 'alphabets'—chiefly the chromatic, diatonic, and triadic—that the tonal listener 'highly overlearns' from previously heard musical surfaces. This in itself is an important point, since without repeated exposure to such regularities, listeners could not spontaneously organize new input in terms of them.

---

* Actually, there is a long tradition in music theory for such models, dating back to Weber (1824) and his eighteenth-century predecessors; see Werts (1983). Schoenberg's (1954) chart of regions, which has been cited in the psychological literature, can be traced through Riemann back to Weber.

Constraint 16: Levels of pitch space must be sufficiently available from musical surfaces to be internalized.

Deutsch and Feroe show that memory load is greatly reduced if tonal melodies are structured by means of their alphabets. As their formalism suggests, such alphabets are hierarchically related as in Fig. 10.7: the octave level *a* elaborates into the perfect-fifth level *b*, which elaborates into the triadic level *c*, which elaborates into the diatonic level *d*, which elaborates into the chromatic level *e*. In addition, pitches at higher levels in the hierarchy are more stable than pitches that do not appear until successively lower levels. This correlates with Krumhansl's (1979) experimt results. So Fig. 10.7 includes a partial representation of stability conditions.

Level *a* :	C											C
Level *b* :	C					G						C
Level *c* :	C			E		G						C
Level *d* :	C	D		E	F	G		A		B		C
Level *e* :	C	D♭	D	E♭	E	F	F♯	G	A♭	A	B♭	B	C

Fig. 10.7

This pitch space circumvents the reservations mentioned above. First, the overall orientation is not chromatic. Non-well-tempered distinctions can be incorporated merely by expanding the content of level *e*, leaving the other levels untouched. Second, level *e* expresses an equal interval cycle and other unwanted equal divisions of the octave are absent.

As chords and diatonic collections change, so too must the hierarchy in Fig. 10.7. For example, in the framework of a IV chord in C major, levels *a*, *b* and *c* would shift respectively to F–F, F–C–F, and F–A–C–F. If the diatonic collection changes to that of F major, level *d* would also shift, with B flat replacing B. The structure of this shifting pitch space demands further representation, perhaps geometic in format, but we will not pursue this here.

Each level in Fig. 10.7 can be thought of as a scale with stepwise motion occurring between adjacent members. An octave is a step away at level *a*, as is a fifth at level *b*; an arpeggiation proceeds by step at level *c*; diatonic and chromatic progressions are by step at levels *d* and *e*. A skip is a progression between two elements that requires more than one step for traversal. This step/skip distinction is important for establishing cognitive distance, and was implicit in Constraint 14 above.

Fig. 10.7 can further be seen as expressing preferred melodic routes via the Gestalt laws of proximity and good continuation. A preferred route is one that is 'complete', where completeness is defined as a stepwise progression at any level that begins and ends at elements represented at the next higher level. Thus a complete chromatic progression must begin and end on diatonic pitches, and so on. Anything else—a chromatic appoggiatura, for instance—is felt as 'incomplete'. Generally, incompleteness is more acceptable at the start than at the end of a progression; unstable elements must be subsequently 'anchored' (Bharucha 1984).

> Constraint 17; A reductionally organized pitch space is needed to express the steps and skips by which cognitive distance is measured and to express degrees of melodic completeness.

The notion of completeness ties in significantly with current music theories that are otherwise dissimilar. Meyer's (1973) and Narmour's (1977) implication-realization theory depends exactly on the space in Fig. 10.7: a stepwise motion at any level implies the next step at that level; such an implication can be realized or not, as the case may be. And Schenker's (1935) central conception of the *Zug*, a diatonic progression bounded by pitches of the prolonged harmony, falls out as a special case of completeness at levels *c* and *d* in Fig. 10.7. Other Schenkerian concepts (coupling, arpeggiation, the initial ascent, the *Urlinie*, the *Bassbrechung*) can be illuminated in related fashion. Completeness appears to be the basic voice-leading principle in Classical tonal music.

Two general psychological points may be inserted here. First, even if—as at the fifth, triadic, and diatonic levels—intervals along a level are psychoacoustically unequal, they are cognitively equal because they are steps at that level. Second, because each of these levels constitutes a category in terms of which the next level is understood, Miller's (1956) restrictions on memory load ('seven plus or minus two') are easily met, something not accomplished by the single category of the chromatic set.

Finally, Fig. 10.7 reflects certain psychoacoustic facts. In general, a descent from level *a* to level *e* brings increasing sensory dissonance. Level *a* gives the 'virtual pitch' (or root) of the collections in levels *b* and *c* (Terhardt 1978). Level *b* serves as the harmonic norm for medieval music and various ethnic musics, level *c* for Classical tonal music. Level *d* provides the melodic basis for many musical idioms, with level *e* offering inflectional possibilities. Thus between levels *c* and *d* there appears a conceptual line separating harmony and melody. This differentiation may in part stem from the critical bandwidth, since for most registers steps at level *c* fall outside the bandwidth and steps at level *d* fall inside.

Fig. 10.7 embodies all of the constraints on stability conditions enumerated in the last two sections: fixed collections with appropriate interval sizes (Constraints 9 and 10); octave equivalence at level *a* (Constraint 11); increasing sensory dissonance from level *a* to level *d* (Constraint 12); equal division of the octave at level *e* (Constraint 13); uniqueness, coherence, and simplicity at level *d* (Constraint 14—and, incidentally, uniqueness and coherence at level c); multidimensional representation expressing cognitive distances (Constraint 15); levels of pitch space that are easily induced from a wide variety of musical surfaces (Constraint 16); and steps, skips, and degrees of melodic completeness at multiple reductional levels (Constraint 17). The cultural persistence of the many musical idioms relating to Fig. 10.7 may be due to this convergence.

Some of these constraints seem to me binding, others optional. Constraints 9–12 are essential for the very existence of stability conditions. Constraints 13–17, on the other hand, can be variously jettisoned. The resulting stability conditions may be weaker, but they can still lead to hierarchically rich music. For example, South Indian music approximates just intonation and does not modulate, thereby ignoring Constraint 13 and part of Constraint 14; Debussy, Bartók, and others have developed consonance-dissonance patterns directly from the total chromatic, thereby ignoring Constraints 14–17. It will be fascinating to discover how the new sound materials of computer music will be able to meet these constraints. In all probability the new materials will bring additional requirements into play. Meanwhile there remains ample leeway within the chromatic collection and within the constraints listed above for music as yet unimagined.

Cognitive opacity of serialism

Now we are in a position to see why serial organizations are inaccessible to mental representation. Rather than explore the subject through the idiosyncratic serialism of *Le Marteau*, I will refer to elementary aspects of the Classical 12-tone system, which has been more widely influential (Schoenberg 1941). I will give three causes for serialism's cognitive opacity.*

Before proceeding, I must emphasize that the issue is not whether serial pieces are good or bad. As with tonal music, some serial pieces are good and most are bad. Nor am I claiming that listeners infer no structure at all from musical surfaces composed with serial techniques. What listeners in fact infer from such surfaces is an interesting question, one that deserves theory and experiment in its own right. But this is not the issue here. The issue is why competent listeners do not hear tone rows when they hear serial pieces.

The first reason is that serialism is a permutational rather than

---

* It must be said that, if only from the evidence in Schoenberg's 12-tone sketches (Hyde 1980), Schoenberg's (1941) account of the 12-tone system is partly misleading. Plainly he used the system not just to generate rows but to create certain systematic but non-serial relationships among subsets. This, however, does not affect my argument, which concerns the cognitive opacity of serial structures (tone rows) as such.

elaborational system. Pitch relations in virtually all 'natural' compositional grammars are elaborational. Take for example the pitch sequence B–E–F sharp. It is easy to imagine any number of melodic embellishments internal to the sequence. This typically happens when children sing and performers improvise. Like the syntax of a sentence (Chomsky 1957), musical elaborations can continue recursively to an indefinite level of complexity; for example, sonata form is an expansion of the Classical phrase (Schenker 1935: Rosen 1972; Lerdahl and Jackendoff 1983). This feature enables pitch relations to be described hierarchically by a tree notation.

Serialism instead depends on specific orderings of the elements of a set. Distinctions arise from permutations of the elements; for example, the inversion of a 12-tone row has the same 12 pitch classes but in a different order. The order position of the elements is therefore essential to the identity of individual set forms. From this it follows that internal elaboration of any element by other elements will undermine a set form. Consider the row of Schoenberg's Violin Concerto (1936), shown in Fig. 10.8 with order numbers given above. The sequence B–E–F sharp appears at order numbers 3–5. If one wanted to elaborate E, say, with G or with B flat–A, creating the sequences B–E–G–E–F sharp or B–E–B flat–A–E–F sharp, the integrity of the row would be destroyed, since G, B flat, and A have order positions elsewhere in the row. A tone row is not an elaborational structure. (The same point could be made with reference not to elements but to the intervals between elements.)

Order number:	0	1	2	3	4	5	6	7	8	9	10	11
12-tone set:	A	B♭	E♭	B	E	F♯	C	C♯	G	A♭	D	F

Fig. 10.8

The little research that has been directed towards serialism (as in Francés 1958; Dowling 1972; Deutsch 1982; Bruner 1984) supports the contention that permutational structures are hard to learn and remember. Since other human activities are not organized in such a fashion, it is hardly surprising that the issue has in general been ignored by psychologists. The situation reminds me, though, of Chomsky's (1965) observation that many logically possible grammatical constructions never occur, such as forming interrogatives from declaratives by word reversal or by exchange of odd and even words. There is unfortunately no one on whom to test these linguistic counter-examples. Music offers a unique opportunity in this regard. Surely children can be found who have been raised on a steady diet of serial music. Do they identify tone rows? A negative answer will provide strong counter-evidence concerning the structure of musical cognition, and may suggest inherent limitations on cognitive organization in other domains as well.

Ironically, Schoenberg was much preoccupied with the issue of comprehensibility. I suspect this is one reason why in his 12-tone phase he adopted Classical motivic, phrasal, and formal structures. As a result, his serial music satisfies the rhythmic Constraints 3–6. But the permutational basis of his pitch organization assures a gap between the compositional and listening grammars.

It is of course possible to organize the combinations and sequences of individual rows on a hierarchical rather than permutational basis. Boulez, Babbitt, and others have done just that. But these higher-level hierarchies are extremely difficult to cognize in a hierarchical fashion because their underlying basis, the row, remains non-tree-like. There are further reasons as well, which brings us to the other causes of serialism's cognitive opacity.

The second cause is the avoidance of sensory consonance and dissonance as an input to the system (Constraint 12). This avoidance in turn stems from the historical collapse of the stability conditions underlying Classical tonal pieces. The pre-serial atonal period had established an aesthetic in which hierarchical pitch relations gave way to purely contextual, associative ones. The 12-tone system reinforced this trend through constant reshuffling of the total chromatic and through constant repetition of the intervallic patterns of the row. Concerned about the natural basis of his new aesthetic, Schoenberg (1911, 1941) invoked the doctrine of the 'emancipation of the dissonance': consonance and dissonance are not opposites but are on a continuum determined by the overtone series; dissonances are harder to comprehend than consonances; but aquaintance with the more remote overtones has made dissonant intervals just as comprehensible as consonant intervals; so now intervals may be treated as equally consonant (or dissonant). Babbitt (1965) goes a step further, debunking the overtone series as a basis for pitch systems and claiming that consonance-dissonance distinctions among intervals are entirely contextual in origin.

Neither Schoenberg nor Babbitt distinguishes between sensory and musical consonance and dissonance. Though the details of pitch perception are not fully resolved, there is no doubt about the objective existence of sensory consonance and dissonance. For intervals between pitches with harmonic partials, the degree of sensory dissonance bears an important relationship to the overtone series, by virtue of the degree of interference among partials within the critical bandwidth. Thus far Schoenberg, at least, is right. What one does with this musically is another matter. Classical tonality founds musical consonance and dissonance largely on sensory consonance and dissonance (partial exception must be made for the perfect fourth, the minor triad, and so on). Serialism, on the other hand, treats intervallic combinations in terms of the row and in effect defines musical consonance and dissonance out of existence (with the glaring exception of the octave: pitch classes are needed). But this strategy, while perfectly logical, does not neutralize sensory consonance and dissonance. The sensory dissonance of a seventh remains greater than that of a sixth, regardless of the musical purposes to which these intervals are put.

There is an important psychological consequence: by ignoring sensory distinctions, serialism creates musical contexts that are not apprehended hierarchically. One pitch or hexachord may be associated with another pitch or hexachord, but these relationships are not easily heard in a dominating-subordinating manner. The requisite intuitions of stability and instability are missing. And because hierarchies are not inferred, tone rows and their combinations are difficult to comprehend (Constraint 2).

The third cause is that serialism does not induce a pitch space where spatial distance correlates with cognitive distance (Constraint 15). Assume for simplicity that serial pitch space looks like the 'combinatorial' space shown in Fig. 10.9 for Schoenberg's Violin Concerto. Here the first six pitch classes of the inverted set, transposed up five semitones, are identical to the second six pitch classes of the prime set, though in a different order. For a variety of reasons such a space was useful to Schoenberg (see Schoenberg 1941). A complete 12-tone pitch space would include transpositions of this and other relationships, just as the tonal space of Fig. 10.7 would have to be enlarged for other chords and regions.

P0:	A	B♭	E♭	B	E	F♯	C	C♯	G	A♭	D	F
I5:	D	C♯	A♭	C	G	F	B	B♭	E	E♭	A	F♯

Fig. 10.9

One might suppose that a 'step' in such highly chromatic music is a semitone. But this is not reflected at all in the pitch space of Fig. 10.9. Or, more in the spirit of the row, one might say that a 'step' occurs from any pitch class to any horizontally adjacent pitch class. But in this case step distance varies wildly from one adjacency to the next, and there is no correlation with psychoacoustic (log frequency) distance. In short, serialism does not incorporate any psychologically coherent notion of step and skip. The listener consequently has difficulty locating a pitch as close to or far from another pitch.

Further causes of serialism's cognitive opacity could be adduced, such as its failure to provide consistent exposure from piece to piece to a limited number of 'alphabets' (Constraint 16). But the main points have been addressed. We turn now to some aesthetic issues that have been lurking behind this entire discussion.

Comprehensibility and value

There is no obvious relationship between the comprehensibility of a piece and its value. Many masterpieces are esoteric, while most ephemeral music is all too comprehensible. On the other hand, if a piece cannot be understood, how can it be good? Most would agree that comprehensibility is a necessary if not sufficient condition for value.

Care must be taken with this formulation in three respects. First, comprehension presupposes listening competence for the music in question. This competence varies with ability and especially with exposure, but is not less real for that. Second, comprehension pertains to the listening grammar rather than to the compositional grammar. A serial piece may be understood in non-serial ways. Third, we are talking about intuitive rather than analytic comprehension. Along the lines of Fodor (1983), the mind's music module must be able spontaneously to form mental representations of musical structure from musical surfaces. This is quite different from using the all-purpose reasoning faculty to figure out the structure of a piece.

With these provisos in mind, I think the above formulation stands. Appreciation depends on cognition. I now want to go an aesthetic step further.

> *Aesthetic Claim 1*; The best music utilizes the full potential of our cognitive resources.

This seemingly innocuous statement carries weight because a great deal is becoming known about how musical cognition works. I have outlined aspects of this understanding in the constraints presented above. Following them will not guarantee quality. I maintain only that following them will lead to cognitively transparent musical surfaces, and that this is in itself a positive value; and, conversely, that not following them will lead in varying degrees to cognitively opaque surfaces, and that this is in itself a negative value.

This stance can be refined through the notion of musical 'complexity', which is to be contrasted with musical 'complicatedness' (Lerdahl 1985). A musical surface is complicated if it has numerous non-redundant events per unit time. Complexity refers not to musical surfaces but to the richness of the structures inferred from surfaces and to the richness of their (unconscious) derivation by the listener. For example, a grouping structure is complex if it is deeply embedded and reveals structural patterns within and across levels. The derivation of such a structure is complex if all the grouping preference rules come into play and if they conflict with one another to a certain degree. (Total reinforcement of the rules would produce a stereotypical grouping structure; total conflict would create intolerable ambiguity.) I take complicatedness to be a neutral value and complexity to be a positive one. Many musical surfaces meet the various constraints, but only those that lead to complexity employ 'the full potential of our cognitive resources'.

All sorts of music satisfy these criteria—for example, Indian raga,

Japanese koto, jazz, and most Western art music. Balinese gamelan falls short with respect to its primitive pitch space. Rock music fails on grounds of insufficient complexity. Much contemporary music pursues complicatedness as compensation for a lack of complexity. In short, these criteria allow for infinite variety, but only along certain lines.

I find this conclusion both exciting and—initially, at least—alarming. It is exciting because psychology really does have something substantive to say about how music might be; here is the foundation I was seeking. It is alarming because the constraints are tighter than I had bargained for. Like the old avant-gardists, I dream of the breath of other planets. Yet my argument has led from pitch hierarchies (Constraints 7–8) to an approximation of pure intervals (Constraint 12), to diatonic scales and the circle of fifths (Constraint 14), and to a pitch space that prominently includes triads (Constraint 17).

However, the constraints do not prescribe outworn styles. Rather they provide a prototype (Rosch 1975). Let me first give an uncontroversial rhythmic example. A musical surface in which the note values are multiples of 2 is intrinsically more stable and easier to cognize than one in which the note values are multiples of 7 and 11. This does not mean that the latter surface is somehow impermissible. It instead amounts to the observation that, because of the resultant ease in forming a metrical structure, note values that are multiples of smaller prime numbers are easier to process and remember, and therefore that multiples of 2 (or 3) inevitably remain a cognitive reference point for more complicated rhythms. I claim that a similar situation holds for pitch: the structure in Fig. 10.7 (with its hierarchically organized octave, fifth, triad, and diatonic scale) remains a reference point for other kinds of pitch organization, not because of its cultural ubiquity but because it incorporates all of the constraints developed above. I take this as a given, with or against which a composer can play creatively. Of course one may opt for a less constrained pitch space. But if a composer chooses the space represented by Fig. 10.7, I am sure there are innumerable and radically new ways to use and extend it. The future is open.

My second aesthetic step was discussed above; I list it here only for completeness.

> *Aesthetic Claim* 2: The best music arises from an alliance of a compositional grammar with the listening grammar.

This claim does not exclude the artifice hidden in a Bach fugue or a Brahms intermezzo. Such artifice is rooted in the bedrock of a 'natural' compositional grammar. At our present musical juncture, however, composers would do well to heed the claim.

This claim carries with it a historical implication. The avant-gardists from Wagner to Boulez thought of music in terms of a 'progressivist' philosophy of history: a new work achieved value by its supposed role *en route* to a better (or at least more sophisticated) future. My second aesthetic claim in effect rejects this attitude in favour of the older view that music making should be based on 'nature'. For the ancients, nature may have resided in the music of the spheres, but for us it lies in the musical mind. I think the music of the future will emerge less from twentieth-century progressivist aesthetics than from newly acquired knowledge of the structure of musical perception and cognition.

References

Babbitt, M. (1965). The structure and function of musical theory. *College Music Symposium* **5**, 10–21. (Reprinted in 1972 in *Perspectives on contemporary music theory* (ed. B. Boretz and E. T. Cone). Norton, New York.)

Balzano, G. J. (1980). The group-theoretic description of 12-fold and microtonal pitch systems. *Computer Music Journal* **4**, (4), 66–84.

Balzano, G. J. (1982). The pitch set as a level of description for studying musical pitch perception. In *Music, mind, and brain* (ed. M. Clynes). Plenum, New York.

Bharucha, J. J. (1984*a*). Anchoring effects in music: the resolution of dissonance. *Cognitive Psychology* **16**, 485–518.

Bharucha, J. J. (1984*b*). Event hierarchies, tonal hierarchies, and assimilation: a reply to Deutsch and Dowling. *Journal of Experimental Psychology: General* **113** (3), 421–5.

Boulez, P. (1954). *Le marteau sans maître*. Universal Edition, London.

Boulez, P. (1963). *Penser la musique aujourd'hui*. Schott, Mainz. (Tr. 1971 by S. Bradshaw and R. R. Bennett. Harvard University Press, Cambridge, Mass.)

Boulez, P. (1964). Alea. *Perspectives of new music* **3** (1), 42–53.

Bruner, C. L. (1984). The perception of contemporary pitch structures. *Music Perception* **2** (1), 25–40.

Burns, E. M. and Ward, W.D. (1982). Intervals, scales, and tuning. In *The psychology of music* (ed. D. Deutsch). Academic Press, New York.

Cherry, E. C. (1953). Some experiments on the recognition of speech, with one and two ears. *Journal of the Acoustical Society of America* **25**, 975–9.

Chomsky, N. (1957). *Syntactic structures*. Mouton, The Hague.

Chomsky, N. (1965). *Aspects of the theory of syntax*. MIT Press, Cambridge, Mass.

Deliège, I. S. (1985). Les régles preferentielles de groupement dans la perception musicale. Unpublished Ph.D. thesis. Université de Bruxelles.

Deutsch, D. (1982). The processing of pitch combinations. In *The psychology of music* (ed. D. Deutsch). Academic Press, New York.

Deutsch, D., and Feroe, J. (1981). The internal representation of pitch sequences in tonal music. *Psychological Review* **88**, 503–22.

Dowling, W. J. (1972). Recognition of melodic transformations: inversion, retrograde, and retrograde-inversion. *Perception and Psychophysics* **12**, 417–21.

Dowling W. J., and Harwood, D. L. (1986). *Music cognition*. Academic Press, New York.

Fodor, J. A. (1983). *The modularity of mind*. MIT Press, Cambridge, Mass.

Francés, R. (1958). *La perception de la musique*. Vrin, Paris.

Fux, J. J. (1725). *Gradus ad parnassum*. Joannis Petri van Gehlen, Vienna. (Tr. and ed. 1965 by A. Mann. Norton, New York).

Hindemith, P. (1937). *Unterweisung im tonsatz*, Vol. 1. Schott, Mainz. (Tr. 1942 by A. Mendel. Associated Music Publishers, New York.)

Hyde, M. (1980). The roots of form in Schoenberg's sketches. *Journal of Music Theory* **24** (1), 1–36.

Koblyakov, L. (1977). P. Boulez, 'Le Marteau sans Maître,' analysis of pitch structure. *Zeitschrift für Musiktheorie* **8**, (1), 24–39.

Krumhansl, C. L. (1979). The psychological representation of pitch in a tonal context. *Cognitive Psychology* **11**, 346–74.

Krumhansl, C. L. (1983). Perceptual structures for tonal music. *Music Perception* **1** (1), 28–62.

Lerdahl, F. (1985). Théorie générative de la musique et composition musicale. In *Quoi? quand? comment?: la recherche musicale* (ed. T. Machover). Christian Bourgois, Paris.

Lerdahl, F. (1987). Timbral hierarchies. *Contemporary Music Review* **1**, (3–4), 135–60.

Lerdahl, F. and Jackendoff, R. (1983). *A generative theory of tonal music*. MIT Press, Cambridge, Mass.

Longuet-Higgins, H. C. (1978). The perception of music. *Interdisciplinary Science Reviews* **3**, 148–56.

McAdams, S. and Bregman A. (1979). Hearing musical streams. *Computer Music Journal*, **3** (4), 26–43. (Reprinted in 1985 in C. Roads and J. Strawn, eds., *Foundations of computer music*. MIT Press, Cambridge, Mass.)

Messiaen, O. (1944). *Technique de mon langage musical*. Alphonse Leduc, Paris.

Meyer, L. B. (1973). *Explaining music*. University of California Press, Berkeley.

Miller, G. A. (1956). The magical number seven, plus or minus two: some limits on our capacity for processing information. *Psychological Review* **63**, 81–96.

Miller, G. A., Galanter, E., and Pribram, K. (1960). *Plans and the structure of behaviour*. Holt, Rinehart and Winston, New York.

Narmour, E. (1977). *Beyond Schenkerism*. University of Chicago Press.

Neisser, Ulric. (1967). *Cognitive psychology*. Prentice-Hall, Englewood Cliffs, NJ.

Palmer, C., and Krumhansl, C. L. (in press). Independent temporal and pitch structures in determination of musical phrases. *Journal of Experimental Psychology: Human Perception and Performance*.

Partch, H. (1949). *Genesis of a music*. University of Wisconsin Press, Madison. (Republished 1974 by Da Capo, New York.)

Plomp, R., and Levelt, W. J. M. (1965). Tonal consonance and critical bandwidth. *Journal of the Acoustical Society of America* **38**, 548–60.

Rosch, E. (1975). Cognitive reference points. *Cognitive Psychology* **7**, 532–47.

Rosen, C. (1972). *The classical style*. Norton, New York.

Schenker, H. (1935). *Der Freie Satz*. Universal Edition, Vienna. (Tr. 1979 by E. Oster. Longman, New York).

Schoenberg, A. (1911). *Harmonielehre*. Universal Edition, Vienna. (Tr. 1978 by R. E. Carter, University of California Press, Berkeley.)

Schoenberg, A. (1941). Composition with twelve tones. In A. Schoenberg. *Style and Idea*. St Martins, New York, new expanded edn 1975.

Schoenberg, A. (1954). *Structural functions of harmony*. Norton, New York.

Shepard, R. (1982). Structural representations of musical pitch. In *The psychology of music* (ed. D. Deutsch). Academic Press, New York.

Simon, H. A. (1962). The architecture of complexity. *Proceedings of the American Philosophical Society* **106**, 467–82. (Reprinted 1972 in H. A. Simon, *The sciences of the artificial*. MIT Press, Cambridge, Mass.)

Sloboda, J. A. (1985). *The musical mind*. Oxford University Press, Oxford.

Terhardt, E. (1974). Pitch, consonance, and harmony. *Journal of the Acoustical Society of America* **55**, 1061–9.

Terhardt, E. (1978). Psychoacoustic evaluation of musical sounds. *Perception and Psychophysics* **23**, 483–92.

Todd, N. (1985). A model of expressive timing in music. *Music Perception* **3** (1), 33–57.

Weber, G. (1824). *Versuch einer Geordeneten Theorie*. Schott, Mainz.

Werts, D. (1983). A theory of scale references. Unpublished Ph.D. thesis. Princeton University.

Yasser, J. (1932). *A theory of evolving tonality*. American Library of Musicology, New York.

11

From collections to structure: the developmental path of tonal thinking

LYLE DAVIDSON and PATRICIA WELSH

Imagine three musicians composing a piece. Each is seated at a piano; manuscript paper is on the music rack; pens are alongside. The first musician plays some notes on the piano, erases a few notes he has already scribbled on the manuscript paper, and replaces them with new ones. He continues in this manner until he finally completes the melody. After completing it, he plays it on the piano, immediately starts revising it, rubbing out whole sections. He stops before finishing and goes for a walk. The second musician spends some time staring at the blank manuscript paper, plays a few notes over and over on the piano, and after a few false starts writes out the complete melody on paper. During the final playing of the melody on the piano his finger slips and he hits a 'wrong' note. Immediately, he is interested in his mistake. He incorporates the 'error' into his written melody, replacing the original note. The third musician scans the page, checks the pen, thinks a moment, and writes out the melody without hesitation, as if taking down dictation.

These three working styles represent those of well-known composers. It is easy to imagine Beethoven, Stravinsky, and Mozart hard at work, creating significant musical compositions, solving complex musical problems. But at the same time, it is difficult to imagine the thought processes which supported their efforts. We know only that each composer had a very different working style and the working styles themselves tell us very little beyond the fact that there are different ways of composing.

If we replay the scene, and specify the task, 'compose a melody which starts in one key, modulates to a specific key, and returns to the original key at the end', our interpretation of these working styles changes. We expect composers of the stature of Beethoven, Stravinsky, or Mozart to be able to dash off such a melody easily. However, it is easy to imagine inexperienced musicians having trouble with this task. Young musicians writing such a melody might show working styles very much like those described. Furthermore, the working styles now take on additional meaning. Under these circumstances, it is relatively easy to imagine the working style of the beginner, the intermediate, and the expert. Different working styles can reflect different levels of skill.

Tasks similar to this one are common in music schools. While the writing of melody is rarely studied, work in harmony and counterpoint focuses on specific aspects of composing within a tonal framework. These studies are a standard part of professional training for the classically oriented musician. However, little is known about the mental and cognitive processes which support different orientations to the musical task of writing a melody which modulates. There are two reasons for this. First, melody writing has not been systematically studied. Second, in music schools, musicians tend not to be interested in the processes involved in arriving at solutions to musical problems, but only in musically successful products.

Perception and production of tonality

While musicians are more interested in production, psychologists take a different tack. They focus on the perception of tonality by untrained individuals. Several studies have compared the recognition of melodic shapes which form tonal patterns to those which form atonal patterns (Frances 1958; Dowling and Fujitani 1971; Zenatti 1975; Cuddy and Lyons 1981). These studies consistently report that tonal patterns are easier to process, recognize, and recall than atonal patterns. Still other work suggests the presence of tonality plays a central role in our perception and cognition of richer musical contexts. Research indicates that the components of melodic textures are easier to grasp when they are in the context of closely related keys than in more distantly related keys (Sloboda and Edworthy 1981).

Apparently, little training is needed to establish highly useful tonal schemata when perception is required. Krumhansl (1979) shows that scales are highly stable mental structures even for untrained listeners. Her work also suggests that relationships between keys parallel those of the notes of the diatonic scale (Krumhansl *et al.* 1982). Taken together, these various studies indicate that tonality and scales are powerful psychological structures which play an important role in our comprehension and enjoyment of music.

It seems clear that adults spontaneously employ the principles of tonality when they perceive melodic structures. But we should not assume that they spontaneously use that same tonal knowledge when they invent or compose even simple melodies. Indeed, except for the work of Bamberger, we know very little empirically about how the perception of tonality is employed in the construction of tonal musical structures.

Bamberger (1986) finds that children construct tonal melodies on a set of bells in very different ways. For example, when constructing melodies from a chromatic collection of bells, some subjects physically separate the bells with pitches which do not 'fit' the tune they are attempting to play from those bells that sound notes in the tune. In doing so, they place the bells in the order in which they are played in the melody. Performance of the melody then means playing the bells in order from left to right. Another strategy these subjects use when making a tune is to select one bell for each sound of the melody. For example, the first three notes of 'Row, Row, Row Your Boat' would require three different bells using this strategy, even though all three notes are the same and could be played on a single bell.

In contrast to those subjects, subjects of another group first position the bells to make a scale, then play the tune in an action path which maps the sequence of pitches of the melody on to the pitches of the scale pattern. Similarly, these same subjects simply restrike one bell to produce repetitions of pitches. Bamberger suggests that these very different strategies for finding the notes for an already known tune reflect the different levels of musical knowledge held by novice and gifted children.

Domains as arenas for solving problems

Psychological research makes it clear that developmental studies of skill and cognition have much to offer for developing a more articulated understanding of a domain. Differences between the responses of subjects with different levels of ability provide windows on the subskills and foundations of specific skills involved in relatively simple tasks. For example, looking at the difference between novice and expert chess players has told us much about the nature of the knowledge required for the game, its representation, and how chess players use that representation to process new bits of information, make decisions, and orient themselves to subtle differences in patterns of information (DeGroot 1965, 1966). The tools of cognitive psychology and artificial intelligence have been used to look at other domains as well (Simon 1979).

The information gained in these studies is due in part to the use of protocols and protocol analysis and in part to the design of the questions guiding the interpretation of the protocols (Simon 1979). While this paradigm is not traditionally experimental, it has been extraordinarily useful in unravelling various aspects of cognition—for example, the creative process (Perkins 1981). Perkins observed poets in the process of writing poems, and he highlights the role of everyday perception, reflection, and production in the creative process.

Combining the approach taken by Perkins, and including a developmental component, we can define and unravel still more of the mysteries of tonality. A great deal can be learned by studying musicians in the process of writing a modulating melody. Comparing musicians who have a sophisticated knowledge of tonality with those who do not can shed light on the underlying constructs of tonality. A musically and psychologically interesting task, it provides an opportunity to see how novices and experts think in a key, weaken one tonal centre, and strengthen another.

In addition to identifying developmental profiles, we hoped to be able to identify various problem-solving strategies. One might expect to find strategies in musical composition similar to those reported in studies of general problem solving (Johnson-Laird and Wason 1977), especially since the use of 'means-ends analysis' (breaking the larger composition problem into a series of subproblems) is routinely taught as a strategy in harmony and counterpoint classes. One might anticipate other heuristic procedures for compositional problem solving as well.

We also wondered about the prerequisites for the tonal understanding necessary for a simple composing task. Is the ability to play an instrument sufficient to enable one to compose melodic shapes which reflect tonal knowledge? Does the tonal knowledge acquired with advanced performance ability transfer to the composition of a tonal melody?

Novice and expert solutions to a musical problem

We chose a composition task because it allowed us to observe the process of constructing tonal relationships. Many different ways of observing subjects composing modulating melodies were considered before the final version was designed. One approach considered was that of asking students who were studying composition to allow us to observe while they wrote melodies which modulated. This task would provide subjects who were accustomed to writing, but it would not allow us to control for individual differences which might arise between composition students over issues of metre, key, rhythm, length, phrase structure, or style. More importantly, it failed to recognize the possible biasing which personal writing habits might introduce into the task. For example, one composer might not be accustomed to writing tonal music at all while another might be acustomed to making melodies that were tonal but which moved only to certain keys and not others. For these reasons, we decided two things—first, not to include composers in the study and second, to control for variables which were not central to the issue of tonality. These variables included the length of the melody and the rhythmic durations to be used.

The rhythm of the melody was controlled by using a rhythmic structure modelled on the first section of the march by Schubert, Op. 27 No. 1. The rhythmic pattern, in 2/2 metre, was 14 measures long. The rhythmic shape allowed different interpretations of the phrase structure while providing the opportunity for constructing melodic motives. This rhythmic pattern

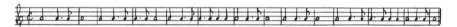

Example 11.1

created a 'shell' which the subjects filled in with notes they determined to be necessary to fulfil the requirements of the task.

It was also necessary to specify the nature of the modulation. If we left the modulation unspecified, we ran the risk of every one making a favourite and presumably well-practised key shift, or relying on their memory of a specific modulation from a specific piece as a model. Because we wanted to draw out the principles on which beginners and more experienced music students relied, we decided to ask for a relatively rare and unpractised modulation.

We controlled for the modulation by requesting a melody which would move from the tonic to the key a tritone away and back to the tonic. This provided three specific areas within the task where tonal thinking could be observed: the opening of the melody (to determine how the first key was established), the transition into the new key (to observe how the stability of the first key was undermined and the second key established), and finally, the ending of the melody (to determine how the return to the first key was negotiated). Interest was sharply focused on the areas in which the key was established or undermined. In this way, we could observe the ebb and flow of tonal support around specific points of reference.

Conditions of the study

Ten music students took part in the study. They were all performers and were assigned to one of two groups. Five students were in their first year of conservatory study (we shall refer to this group as 'beginners'). Their average age was 20, and they had studied an instrument, on average, for six years. The second and more experienced group of students had an average age of 22 and all had undergone two years of training at the conservatory (we shall call these students 'experienced').

At the beginning of the session individual students were seated at a piano and given a sheet of 12-staff manuscript paper. The rhythmic pattern was written in the second space of the top staff. The remaining staves were sectioned into measures corresponding with those of the rhythm, but were otherwise blank. All subjects were asked to 'use the rhythmic pattern at the top of the page and write a melody starting in the key of C major, passing through the key of F sharp major, and closing in C major.' A pen was provided and subjects were instructed to make all revisions in the measure immediately below their initial choice (see Example 11.2). They were requested not to cross out any of their work. The subjects were asked to talk aloud as they worked and to explain what they were considering at each step of the process; they were also instructed to use the piano whenever they wished. The task had a time limit of 30 minutes; subjects were not informed of this limit, but were stopped after 30 minutes had elapsed. The entire session was tape-recorded and an observer was present.

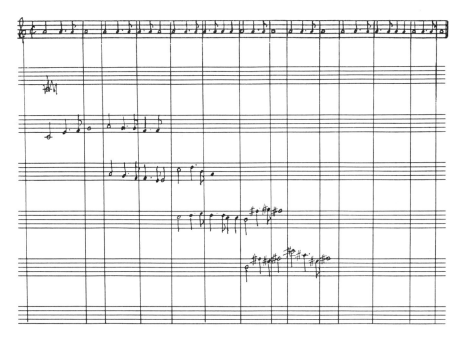

Example 11.2

Later, the second author made a transcription of each session which organized the student's activity in a chronological manner. The transcriptions were based upon the tape-recordings of the sessions, the notes of the observer, and the music manuscript pages on which the students notated their melodies and made their revisions.

Below is an excerpt from the transcript of a beginning student. The transcription excerpt begins just after this student has completed the first four measures of his melody. He has written those measures in C major.

When the student replays material already written down it is designated beneath the music as M1, M2, etc., for measure 1, measure 1, and so forth. In all examples of playing or singing, the rhythmic notation is proportional and reflects only relative durations.

Writes measure 4
Plays:

Example 11.3

11 seconds silence
Plays and hums:

Example 11.4

37 seconds silence
'Um, now I'm trying to get into F sharp somehow, smoothly.'
Plays:

Example 11.5

Writes measure 5

The sessions were analysed on the basis of categories which took into account several aspects of the composition process. These categories focused upon working procedures, rhythmic and tonal considerations, and the overall success of the activity and its final melody. The specific categories were:

(A) Size of the working unit
(B) Generation of new melodic material
(C) Integration of rhythm into the working process
(D) Use of motivic relationships
(E) Orientation to the first key
(F) Transition to the new key
(G) Return to the home key
(H) Efficiency of the modulation process
(I) How a key is defined
(J) Strategies
(K) Success of melody

The analysis was carried out by the two authors independently; a high degree of reliability was achieved. For measure (J), strategies, the transcripts were examined for evidence of strategies and both scorers had to agree on the specific strategy being used. For measure (K), success of melody, seven musicians rated the melodies independently. The definitions of each analytic category and the findings for each category are presented in the results section which follows.

Results

In this portion of the paper, we first consider general features of the working style. These features are the size of the working unit, sequence and manner in which melodic material is generated, the role of the rhythm in the process of constructing the melody, and the degree to which motivic relationships are used in the melody. After we examine the profile of working styles, we consider the issues of tonality. The tonality measures discussed include the orientation to the first key (C major), the location of the cadences (in C and F sharp), the location of the first indication of key change (in C and F sharp), and how tonalities are defined while composing this melody. Finally, after the discussion of strategies used while composing the melody, we consider the transfer of knowledge of tonality acquired through performance to the compositional task.

General working style

Size of the working unit
One of the findings from the 'novice-expert' literature suggests that the

amount of organized information at an individual's disposal is dependent, at least in part, on the level of that individual's experience (DeGroot 1965, 1966). The key word is 'organized'. The expert sees patterns of organized information where the novice sees only unrelated details. In music composition, the amount of information an individual works with at any single moment can also be an index of the level of development. Presumably, the novice will be able to work with only the immediate context or next note, while the more developmentally advanced musician will be able to chunk information into larger units and to work more efficiently—projecting further ahead and reflecting further back while at the same time holding the moment of focus in place. This makes it possible for the expert to consider immediate contextual issues and the degree to which a specific instance is forecast by earlier moments of the composition, and to develop a higher degree of motivic organization than the novice would be able to achieve. Consequently, we kept track of the size of the frame of reference within which individuals worked. We refer to this as the 'size of the working unit', which measures the area to which a subject made either verbal or behavioural reference during the task. There are five levels in this measure: (1) note-to-note, (2) measure-to-measure, (3) two-measure chunks, (4) three-measure chunks, and (5) whole phrases.

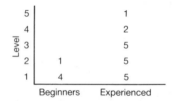

Fig. 11.1. Size of the working unit.

The size of the working unit proved to be a useful measure for distinguishing among the subjects. The scores reflect the magnitude of the differences between the first-year students and those in the more experienced group. Four of the five beginners used only the note as a working unit, while the third-year students all used two entire measures as a working unit at least once during the session. Furthermore, the more experienced subjects used much more variation in the size of the unit they employed when they constructed their melodies. At some time during the task, all of the third-year students used the next note, and one- and two-measure chunks. In addition, two of these subjects once used a three-measure unit, and one spoke in terms of an entire phrase. In contrast, the first-year students were less flexible in their ability to look ahead and to use units of various sizes. Specifically, four of the beginners usually looked only to the next note. One was able to occasionally use a whole measure as a unit of focus.

Generation of new material

The order or sequence in which a mature composer might work on a piece is largely unexplored. Obviously, one can work in many different ways. One might work on different places at once, shuttling back and forth between one area and another throughout the compositional process; another might systematically write in a front-to-back order. There is no reason to expect that one procedure is superior to another. However, one might expect to see evidence of more back-and-forth movement (more flexibility) in the experienced students, but more beginning-to-end movement (less flexibility) in the beginning students.

When we looked at the sequence in which the new material was generated we saw two different patterns. The beginners normally worked in a left-to-right order, usually playing back only within a local context. The experienced students also worked left-to-right, but when they played back their results they were careful to connect the new material to larger chunks—the previous measure or phrase—or even to the beginning.

How composers generate new ideas or the next chunk of music is also largely unexplored. Sloboda's analysis of his own compositional process is one of the few attempts to look systematically at this important issue (Sloboda 1985). We did observe the first-year students generating new ideas, but the processes of the experienced students proved to be more elusive.

The first-year students' reliance on an enactive, sensory-motor mode of generating new melodic material was striking. They would often begin by playing or writing out a melodic shape and then get stuck. Once stuck, they would abandon their plan and start to explore ways of getting from the note they last wrote down to the next one of the rhythmic pattern. Remarkably, they often did this by letting their fingers sound the notes between two goal pitches, sometimes slowly playing all the semitones between. It is immediately striking that *all* of the first-year students, but *none* of the third-year students, let their fingers lead in this way when searching for the next note or bit of melody.

It was more difficult to determine how the experienced students were generating new material. They would more often consider the next part of the rhythmic pattern, and then write out or play a fully developed bit of melody. Clearly, they were able to consider the contextual constraints and generate pitch shapes and integrate them into the rhythmic pattern, as well as reflect on the effect without committing themselves to a solution.

Integration of rhythm into the working process

The ability to integrate the given rhythm into the compositional process proved to be another useful index of difference between the two groups. When the beginners were engaged in the process of generating melody, they ignored the given rhythm entirely. On the other hand, all of the more experienced students used the given rhythm in the compositional process. In addition, when playing the completed melody at the end of the task, none of the beginners played the pitches consistently in rhythm, while the experienced students always played their melodies back in rhythm.

Use of motivic relationships

The rhythmic shape given as a control in this study suggests many possible motives and therefore allows the possibility of establishing and strengthening the formal relationship between the opening and the ending of the piece. The use of melodic motives is not only a powerful means of achieving structural unity and contrast, but their use also reflects the ability to think in larger structural chunks.

One of the beginners and four of the experienced students used the rhythmic pattern as a source of motivic material.

How a tonality is defined

The centre of the study was tonality. Measures of tonal thinking included the orientation to the first key, transition to the new key, return to the home key, the relative efficiency of the modulation process, and how a key was defined. Other topics included the degree of difficulty in changing key and the way in which notes were used to define a key in the introduction as well as during the composition of the melody.

Orientation to first key

During the first moments of the task, students were in the process of defining the problem for themselves; trying out different ways of establishing the first key and testing the distance to the second key. Five behaviours occurred during the opening:

(1) Establishing the key by repeating the tonic note of the scale;
(2) Establishing the key by extending the duration of the tonic note of the scale;
(3) Establishing the key by using tonal formula, for example, scale degree motion from 7 to 1;
(4) Establishing the key by using scalar motion;
(5) Establishing the key by using the notes of the scale to suggest long-range tonal relationships, specifically by starting on a weaker portion of the scale, thereby preparing a smoother transition to the new key.

There was a sharp distinction between the two groups on this measure.

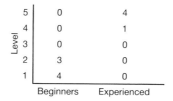

Fig. 11.2. Orientation to the first key.

Entrance of the modulation

Each student had to determine from the given rhythmic structure where critical tonal shifts had to be made in order to meet the modulation requirements of the task. The location of first indication of modulation is important because it provides an index of how the problem is interpreted, how the boundaries of key are determined, and how the moment of modulation is defined.

Six of the 10 students (three of the beginners and three of the experienced students) placed their first accidental in measure 4; no one used an accidental before measure 4. Four students placed the first accidental of their modulations after measure 4.

Most students tended to make the first move of the modulation in the fourth measure. This suggests they recognized the traditional phrase structure implicit in the rhythmic pattern.

Location of cadence in F sharp

The location of the cadence in F sharp is critical. If it occurs too early, the second key is too prominent. On the other hand, if it appears too late in the melody there is not enough time to get back smoothly to the home key of C major. The rhythmic structure suggests a cadence would be best placed at measure 8. All of the beginning students made a cadence in F sharp at measure 8. Three of the experienced students also made the cadence in this measure.

Return to the home tonic and the ending

This measurement has three levels. Level one places the moment of modulation at bar 8, and level two places the moment of modulation at bar 10, while level three indicates the modulation took place at some other point (see Fig. 11.3).

Economy when making a modulation

We expected that students who did not have strong and flexible representations of tonal structures would find it difficult to make a

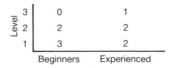

Fig. 11.3. Return to the home tonic.

modulation. They would not be able to easily and quickly create the tonal shift necessary to effect a new key. Consequently, we anticipated that the first-year students would use many more trial-and-error attempts to make a modulation than the more experienced subjects. We measured the students' efficiency by counting the number of notes played between the first written accidental and the cadence in the new key. There was a significant difference between the two groups of students.

The first transition was defined as the area between the first written accidental in the first section (C major) and the cadence goal on the key of F sharp major. The beginners played or hummed an average of 232 notes while composing this portion of their melody, while the experienced students averaged only 72 notes.

The second transition was defined as the area between the cadence on F sharp and the clear statement of C major at the end of the piece. Beginners sounded an average of 132 notes in the course of writing this section, in contrast to an average of 92 notes for the experienced students. The first-year students had great difficulty negotiating the shift of keys from C major to F sharp major, and somewhat less difficulty moving from F sharp major back to C major. Interestingly, the experienced students had somewhat more difficulty returning to C major than moving away from it.

Definition of key

There are five levels in this measurement. These levels chart the distance between between treating notes as mere collections of pitches to simultaneously considering the tonal value of each note in relation to both keys required for the task.

Level (1) Collection of notes without any specific order; key is defined by an aggregate of pitches common to the scale but not necessarily used in a way that suggested a tonal framework.

Level (2) Key defined only by local emphasis on the tonic of the scale; other notes of the scale are ignored. Focus is created by the (frequency of occurrence or) repetition of the tonic note, or by the duration of the tonic triad.

Level (3) Key defined by the use of a scheme (any of several functional chunks such as 'leading tone' function, or triad shape). This level is an extension of level (2), in which the knowledge of a triad or a scale degree function is fixed, for example, scale degree 7 is transposed as a unit with sd 1 (7–1 in C, then 7–1 in F sharp), or as a triad (1–3–5 in C [C–E–G], then in F sharp [F sharp–A sharp–C sharp]).

Level (4) Key defined by using specific transferable relationships within the context of different keys. Specifically, this includes the use of dominant-to-tonic relationships, and the use of pitches as part of small scalar fragments. This reflects an understanding of the relation of pitches to a local tonic.

Level (5) This level shows the use of single pitches to suggest different scales. A pitch may be chosen because of its relation to the local tonic *and* the target or goal tonic. A common example of this level is to start the melody on a weak scale degree, thereby heightening the likelihood of a smooth transition to the second key. Pitches are chosen which can suggest the local tonic while forecasting other tonics, scales, and scale degree functions, for example using sd 6 (A) as a starting point because it can also function as sd 3 in F sharp minor.

Figure 11.4 shows the frequency of use for each level by each group.

Level	Beginners	Experienced
5	0	1
4	0	5
3	4	5
2	5	5
1	5	5

Fig. 11.4. Definition of key.

To summarize the results of looking at working styles, clearly, there are differences between groups. It is possible to show contrasting profiles of the two groups on the basis of the differences between them on a variety of measures. The groups differed significantly in the number of notes which they used to make the transition between the two keys. There were also differences in the ability to separate the identity of a note when it had a specific function, for example, a note as a leading tone, and the function of 'leading tone' in general. The beginning students had difficulty finding the leading tone of F sharp major because they tended to confuse it with the leading tone of the scale of C major. Similarly, none of the beginning students were able to use the note 'B' to mediate between the two scales (even though it is the single common tone between the two keys). In contrast, the members of the more experienced group were easily able to find and use the common tone as a means of entering or leaving either key.

Strategies

The differences in working styles, defined by the size of working unit, the work sequence, and the integration of rhythm and pitches when composing the melody, were supported by a wide range of strategies. Several strategies have family resemblances which enable us to group them into categories.

The strategies can be arranged to form a three-step scale from the least sophisticated (level (1)) to the most sophisticated (level (3)). The less advanced strategies tend to rely only on local features or single, uncoordinated attributes, while more advanced strategies require the ability to consider moments of the task from the perspective of the structured whole.

First-level strategies

The first level contains the strategies used by the five beginning students. These are the most local of all the strategies observed, and they tend to focus on single attributes. They include the use of repetition of a single note, a heavy reliance on the use of sensory-motor or finger knowledge when finding new notes, and the use of a simple 'next-to' rule which defines the extent the beginners look ahead or back when they co-ordinate the notes on which they are currently working. That is, the beginners tended to compare what they were working on with only the immediate notes rather than phrase-length units.

One striking characteristic of this level of strategy is the reduction of the working unit to the immediate context. The field of vision and hearing appears to be restricted to the notes on either side of the one(s) being worked on at the moment. It is especially difficult to achieve a high degree of integration when working in this bit-to-bit manner. Only by ignoring the rhythmic durations of notes is it possible to weigh each note in relative isolation. Because each note occupies the same amount of attention, the effect of shorter and longer durations on the tonal weight a pitch may receive is either not realized or not taken into account during the composition process. It is easy to observe that the beginners fail to understand the tonal implications of the given rhythmic series.

Sounding a note and repeating it is an early means of either establishing a tonally weighted note, such as the tonic note of a scale, or of filling up a space of musical time. Another beginning strategy is the reliance on whatever falls under the fingers when generating new material. The uncritical acceptance of melodic shapes which appear to grow out of finger motion alone, and which appear to be unconnected to whatever has been generated during the previous chunk, is surprising.

The transcript excerpt (Examples 11.6–12) shows many characteristic behaviours of the beginners. Most important is the reliance on the finger knowledge to find new notes of the melody. It also shows the small unit within which the beginners work, and the comment at the end suggests the importance of the number of occurrences of F sharp as a means of defining the F sharp major tonality. This student has just completed writing measure 6 and is starting to explore possible ways of continuing the melody into measure 7.

Plays:

Example 11.6

Hums:

Example 11.7

8 seconds silence
Plays:

Example 11.8

18 seconds silence
Plays:

Example 11.9

12 seconds silence
Plays:

Example 11.10

9 seconds silence

Writes first part of measure 7
Plays as she continues to write measures 7 and 8:

Example II.II

'Got to get back to C again?' *(meaning C major)*
Observer: 'Yes.'
Hums:

Example II.I2

'Only two F sharps'. Gotta get more than two out of this! OK?'

Second-level strategies

Three of the experienced students used second-level strategies which feature various local rules. Unlike level (I), however, this level prescribes the use of chunks of material which are larger than individual notes. These chunks consist either of portions or scales or of triads.

The least-developed aspect of this level is the use of a descending semitone motion from a goal pitch in one measure to a goal pitch in another measure. This is similar to the sensory motor exploration of the first level. The difference between the two strategies is that the sensory motor strategy appears to have no clearly directed goal, while the descending semi-tone motion has specific boundaries forming its top and bottom pitches. Thus there is a feeling of intentional design guiding the use of this strategy.

In the example below, the G sharp in measure 9 forms the top pitch and D sharp at the end of excerpt forms the final pitch of what becomes measure 10. This experienced student plays the entire completed portion of the melody before he explores the next chunk.

Plays:

Example II.I3

6 seconds silence
Writes measure II

A slightly more elaborate strategy is the use of a specific tonal function such as the leading-tone-to-tonic motion. Successful use of this step shows that the subject can easily locate the critical scale degrees (7 and 1) in C major *and* in F sharp major. These are usually co-ordinated with a specific rhythmic motive as well, knitting the whole into a coherent melodic shape.

The most advanced of these local rules uses fragments of scales to introduce the modulation. The next example shows the use of a 'leading-tone' strategy to approach the new key and the use of scale fragments (the upper tetrachord of F sharp major: C sharp, D sharp, E sharp, and F sharp).

Plays:

Example 11.14

7 seconds silence
'E sharp is enharmonic for F natural. OK, I'll go from there maybe.'
Plays:

(M6)   M7

Example 11.15

20-seconds silence
'OK, this is what I'll do, you see?'
Writes measure 6 and 7

Third-level strategies

Two of the experienced students used strategies which were very different from those of the other students. Students at this level easily talk about their plans and strategies, and often forecast the success of an expected solution—all before sounding a note. These students were able to balance the focal and the subsidiary aspects of the task and integrate the particular shapes into a coherent and whole melody. For example, students at this level looked at the rhythmic shape, thought about the two keys, and then stated a specific plan which would take the melody from C major to F sharp major, for example, through the intermediary key of A major.

'So this is just the rhythm?' (*points to the page*)
Observer: 'Yes, that's the rhythm'.
'It's just the melody?'
Observer: 'Right.'

14 seconds silence
Writes in the clef
Plays:

Example 11.16

5 seconds silence
Plays:

Example 11.17

4 seconds silence
Plays:

Example 11.18

3 seconds silence
Plays:

Example 11.19

8 seconds silence
Plays:

Example 11.20

39 seconds silence in which she writes measures 1, 2, 3, and 4
'OK. What I'm going to do is go from C major to a minor to, um, F sharp major.'

Characteristically, individual decisions at the note-by-note level are assessed in terms of their overall effect on the design. These students' ability to maintain the most global perspective while considering the local situation is evident from the use of a hypothesis-testing model throughout the task. The model appears to have four steps, *hypotheses*, *test*, *try out in context*, and *evaluate* (accept or reject). The similarity to the TOTE (Test–Operate–Test–Exit) model described by Miller, *et al.* (1960) is obvious.

Success of melody

Is it possible that composing a successful melody is the result of pure inspiration? If this is the case, one might expect to find little correlation among the factors of experience and the most successful of these melodies. On the other hand, to the extent that writing a successful tonal melody is dependent on rules of composition, one can expect the more experienced students to write more successful melodies. In an attempt to consider these questions, we asked a group of seven professional musicians to judge the melodies. Some of the musicians were college teachers while others were freelance musicians; all had a great deal of performing experience. We asked them to place the melodies in rank order from most to least successful. The judges were not told about the students or the study, and the melodies were presented in random order. The results are interesting because they shed more light on the role of formal knowledge in music. The resulting rank order of the melodies showed a high correlation with the experience of the student (Spearman Rho, $r = 0.86$). This means that the more sophisticated the strategies used in the process of composing the melody, the more likely judges were to consider it a successful melody. This suggests that experience, including theoretical knowledge of tonality, does indeed play a role in the creation of a more successful melody.

The melodies below were judged the least successful and the most successful respectively.

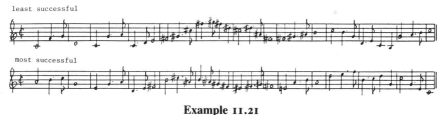

Example 11.21

Summary and discussion

Looking at the working styles and the strategies employed by members of the two groups suggests that a developmental stance combined with a problem-finding/problem-solving approach is a very useful way of investigating musical questions. Examining how a task is represented, and determining the role a representation plays in forming strategies, operations, and definitions of goals, sheds light on even such a simple task as adding notes to a rhythmic pattern.

Representation of the problem

The beginning and experienced music students' representations of the task were very different because of their distinctive knowledge states. The dimensions of their different knowledge states are seen in the particular ways members of the two groups defined keys and integrate rhythm into the composing process.

At a verbal level all the students appeared to have the problem well defined. For example, the beginning and experienced students understood the keys to be used as C major and F sharp major without difficulty. However, the meaning supporting the text was very different for the two groups. The beginning students defined keys with single notes (usually the tonic) or the tonic triad. This suggests their schema for key is limited to rather simple and static units. The notes of these units are not hierarchically integrated with other notes of the scale, but simply exist as part of a familiar collection of tones. In contrast, the experienced students relied on more dynamic and structured tonal schemata which supported the hierarchical relationships implicit in scales and scalar fragments. They were able to 'lift out' overlapping portions of different scales, co-ordinating and integrating them into a tonal blend which linked the two.

Similarly, the difference rhythm played in the representation of the task was striking. Although the rhythm was specified for everyone, only the third-year students used it when constructing their melodies. The beginning students appeared not to include rhythm in their representation of the task, since they focused exclusively on the pitches of the melody. The beginners even ignored the rhythm when playing back their final version, as if slowly testing each note as they played the entire melody through. Again in contrast to the beginners, the experienced students used the rhythm at every stage of the task, making it clear that their concept of melody included rhythm *as well as* pitch.

There was a striking difference between the groups in their choice of when to edit the melody. Members of the third-year group characteristically edited measures and phrases of the melody immediately, while they were composing. This reflects their ability to work on precise moments within a larger framework as evidenced by their not needing to listen when they had finished working and not wanting to make revisions once they had completed the melody. This was very different from the editing behaviour of the beginning students. Characteristically, they did not assess the effect of their melodic accretions until the final performance of the melody. They usually played the melody the last time as though they were listening carefully to the effect of the whole shape. After that performance, they would often pick up the pen again and make 'corrections'. Usually, only a few notes were changed and, confident of their work, they usually did not perform the entire melody a second time to check their revisions.

In summary, members of the two groups see the task differently. Beginners do not have many ways to define a tonality, whereas the more sophisticated musicians employ very different ways of establishing key centres. The beginners fail to see rhythm as a central or crucial factor in constructing a tonality or designing a tonal melody. This leads them to an unsatisfactory definition of key, because they fail to realize the importance of placing more important notes of the key on longer and/or more accented moments of the rhythmic series. In sharp contrast, experienced subjects were keenly aware of the role rhythm plays in contributing to the tonal weight of a note, both during the composition process and during the playing of the final melody.

Defining the limits of the problem of making a modulation around the use of appropriate triads is very different from defining the problem as involving the use of scales. While the triad definition has the virtue of being simple, that focus tends to make melodies which are abrupt in their shifts. The scale definition does not place a limit on the nature of melodic materials (one can use triads and stepwise scalar motions), and at the same time allows abrupt as well as smooth moments of transition. Seeing the problem of establishing a key as requiring units of two or three notes of the scale (for example, scale degrees 7 and 1, or a triad) is very different from interpreting it as based on a concept of a collection of seven pitches which exist in specific hierarchical tension.

Clearly, having alternative representations of the problem is an advantage. It was possible to see the task essentially as a problem of linking tonic triads, making a harmonic progression, or locating a specific tonic note, scalar fragment, or scale. The beginners characteristically had fewer alternative representations, while the experienced subjects not only had a wider range of representations, but were able to move among them, selecting an approach which seemed appropriate for a given moment.

Representation of the problem and strategies employed

Each representation of the problem defines and limits the range of operations used to arrive at solutions. For the problem solver, the formulation of a plan of action or strategy depends on how the problem is understood and represented. For the researcher, understanding the dimensions within which the problem solver is working makes it possible to observe and evaluate the set of actions or operations which the problem solver hopes will lead to a solution of the problem.

The task we presented was open ended in so far as the moment of modulation was not defined. An algorithmic or rule-governed approach, even though it might lead to a solution, was not used by anyone. On the other hand, there were a wide variety of heuristic approaches to the problem. The most local strategies included the use of finger patterns and semitone chromatic pitch motion, the identification of a specific tonal relation such as the leading tone, and the use of a tone common to both keys as a pivot point. More advanced strategies included the use of melodic shapes, contours, and motives (sometimes in melodic sequence), as well as the hypothesis–test–incorporate–evaluate model. Finally, the most advanced and long-range strategies included the hypothesis-testing operation in conjunction with verbal statement of means, and the ability to plan future areas of focus.

Characteristically, the beginners were unable to design or construct a strategy except at the most local level. Consequently, they usually added notes to their melody without a long-range plan or design in mind. If they began with a plan, it was usually only temporary since they were often unable to transform it into a flexible heuristic attitude. Because of this, their attempts either looked as though there was no plan at all, or like perseveration, since they would use the same unsuccessful strategy over and over. In contrast, the most experienced students were able to use means-ends analysis, and even use a generate-test model.

Two levels of tonal thinking: enactive vs. reflective processes

First-year students, the beginners, were generally unable to reflect on the task without enactively sounding out each step of a solution. Their reliance on their fingers when finding the next notes of their melody was particularly striking. Their knowledge of tonality appeared to have not yet been integrated into a flexible working system. They were aware of individual notes or triads but not able to use them in larger functional contexts. Their goals emerged as they worked. They were in constant conflict between an explicit local context within which they were working and the implicit global context imposed by the task definition. It was symptomatic of this conflict that they were unable to reflect on and evaluate the focal moment in terms of the whole product.

These students also tended to work from front to back in note-to-note or one-measure units and with little regard for the rhythmic shape of the melody either during construction or during the playback at the end of the session. They were unable to talk about their strategies or goals until after they had finished solving a specific problem. They were unable to assess the effect of choices they made during the process of writing the melody. They also had trouble keeping the context in focus while they were making additional bits of melody. Similarly, they seemed to have a limited awareness of the final shape of their melody since they were frequently surprised when they played their melody at the end of the session. They used one of three strategies: using the leading-tone-to-tonic relationship as a means of entering a key; using the root-position triad to either stand for a key or as a reference point for a key; and relying on finger movement over the keyboard as a means of exploring for new notes and expanding the melody.

Third-year students, the experienced group, were able to reflect on the dimensions of the problem and solve much of it before they committed themselves to a specific version on paper. Two of them had to be requested to play their final melodies. Their tonal knowledge was integrated into a rich and flexible working system. They had an understanding of tonality which included awareness of how scale degrees functioned and how even distant key areas could be related. They were able to define their methods and their goals in advance of starting to work on them. They were able to work on a local problem while evaluating it in terms of the whole.

Like the beginning students, they also worked from front to back, but the experienced students more often worked in larger chunks (normally one-, two-, and three-measure units). They were able to talk about their strategies and goals in advance of the immediate working context. In addition, they quickly integrated the pitches into the rhythmic pattern provided at the top of the page. Since they used significantly fewer notes (and relied less on trial and error) they appeared to be relatively sure of the effect of their choices while they were constructing the melody. When they played their melody at the end of the session, they appeared to be satisfied with the result. This suggests they already knew how it was going to sound. They were able to plan an approach to the problem and adjust it to changing contexts as they worked through the task. Significantly, they were able to make sections of melody without losing the context of the whole melodic shape. Two in this group used a clear hypothesis-testing model when they worked. Specifically, they would generate a melodic fragment and test it out in isolation of its context. If it satisfied their criteria, they would integrate it into the already composed section by playing it and evaluating it. On the basis of its effect within the context of the whole shape, they would either accept it and integrate it into the melodic line, or throw it out and start again.

One final question remains. On the basis of this study, what is the relation between perceptual knowledge of tonality and the knowledge of tonality required for production? The results of this study strongly suggest that the composition of a tonal melody requires a qualitatively different understanding of tonality than does the perception of tonality. Surprisingly, it appears that even the years of practice involved in studying an instrument fail to provide the breadth and depth of knowledge required for a tonal composition task like the one in this study. It seems that problem solving in a domain like music is fundamentally different from problem solving in a domain like chess. In chess, one is either a novice or an expert. In music, unlike chess, one can be both expert and novice at the same time, depending on whether the task is a performance task or a composition task, a perception task or a production task. The musicians in this study were all gifted performers. Only the older group approached the level of tonal knowledge which was necessary for the successful solution of the melody-writing task. That group had received two additional years of intensive training in the charged musical environment of a conservatory.

In light of this, we see there is a great deal of difference in the knowledge which supports each of the working styles described in the opening of this chapter, especially when we are considering less than fully mature composers. While a master composer may appear at times like a beginner, for example, proceeding on a note-to-note level or making revisions after a 'final' playing, on the basis of this study it is likely that the master composer has a much richer representation of the task and has strategic procedures which are more flexible than perhaps even the relatively advanced student. More than that, the results of this study indicate some of the milestones occurring along the developmental path which leads from beginning to advanced levels of tonal knowledge. We see that the definition of a task like writing a melody is very different for musicians at different levels of development. We see that these differences play an important role not only in the definition and goals of the task, but also in the strategies employed and in the quality of the results.

Acknowledgements

This research was supported in part by grants from the Carnegie Corporation, Rockefeller Foundation, and the Spencer Foundation. The authors wish to thank members of the Thursday Night Group and especially Erin Phelps and Joan Meyaard for their assistance.

References

Bamberger, J. (1986). Cognitive issues in the development of musically gifted children. In *Conceptions of giftedness* (ed. R. J. Sternberg and J. E. Davidson), pp. 388–413. Cambridge University Press, Cambridge.
Bartlett, F. C. (1958). *Thinking: an experimental and social study*. Basic Books, New York.
DeGroot, A. D. (1965). *Thought and choice in chess*. Mouton, The Hague.

DeGroot, A. D. (1966). Perception and memory versus thought: some old ideas and recent findings. *Problem solving: research, method and theory* (ed. B. Kleinmunte). Wiley, New York.

Cuddy, L. L. and Lyons, H. I. (1981). Musical pattern recognition: a comparison of listening to and studying tonal structures and tonal ambiguities. *Psychomusicology* 1(2), 15–33.

Dowling, W. J. and Fujitani, D. S. (1971). Contour, interval and pitch recognition in memory for melodies. *Journal of the Acoustical Society of America* 49, 524–31.

Frances, R. (1958). *La perception de la musique*, pp. 81–90. Vrin, Paris.

Johnson-Laird, P. N. and Wason, P. C. (1977). *Thinking: readings in cognitive science*. Cambridge University Press, Cambridge.

Krumhansl, C. L. (1979). The psychological representation of musical pitch in a tonal context. *Cognitive Psychology* 11, 346–74.

Krumhansl, C. L., Bharucha, J., and Castellano, M. A. (1982). Key distance effects on perceived harmonic structure in music. *Perception and Psychophysics* 31, 75–85.

Miller, G. A., Galanter, E., and Pribram, K. (1960). *Plans and the structure of behavior*. Holt, Rinehart and Winston, New York.

Newell, A., and Simon, H. A. (1972). *Human problem solving*. Prentice-Hall, Englewood Cliffs, NJ.

Perkins, D. N. (1981). *The mind's best work*. Harvard University Press, Cambridge, Mass.

Simon, H. A. (1979). *Models of thought*. Yale University Press, New Haven.

Sloboda, J. (1985). *The musical mind: the cognitive psychology of music*. Clarendon press, Oxford

Sloboda, J. and Edworthy, J. (1981). Attending to two melodies at once: the effect of key relatedness. *Psychology of Music* 9, 39–43.

Zenatti, A. (1975). Melodic memory tests: a comparison of normal children and mental defectives. *Journal of Research in Music Education* 23, 41–52.

Appendix (Chapter 8)

Example 8.11. Conservatory student, 24 years old.

Form: A A$_v$^{5} B C
     A A$_v$^{5} B$_v$ C$_v$
Tonality: pentatonic

Example 8.12. Music pupil, 13 years old.

Form: A⁵ A B A$_v$
     A⁵ A B A$_v$

Tonality: minor + pentaton old style, folk-song like

Example 8.13. Peasant, 47-year-old-man.

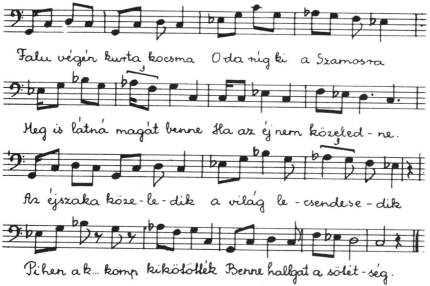

Form: A B B$_v$ C
     A B$_{v2}$ $_v$B C

Tonality: in dome-structure C-minor, E flat major, E flat major, C minor

Example 8.14. Industrial worker, 30 years old.

Form: A B C A_v

A_v A_v^3 D A_v

Tonality: minor in composed folk song style example for tonality minor

Example 8.15. Pupil, 13 years old.

Form: A A_{2v} A A_{2v}

A_v A_2 A B

Tonality: major pentachord in 'non-Hungarian intonations', i.e. hit song style

Example 8.16. Peasant, 52-year-old woman.

Example 8.17. Apprentice, 17-year-old boy.

Example 8.18. Grammar school pupil, 17 years old.

Author index

Subject index

action plan theory in motor control 133
agogic accent 19
articulation 37–41
  and expression 19–21
  indication 38–9
  synthesized sequence experiments 39, 40
artificial intelligence and improvisation
    150–2
  knowledge representation 151–2
  problem reduction 150–1
  search techniques 150
automaticity and skill development 139–40

Baroque style 22
Bethoven piano sonata note values 37, 38
Boulez, P. *Le Marteau sans Maître*, structure
    of 231–3, 241
  and grammars, musical 233, 234

children, musical representations by 195–230
  and cognitive processes 201–2
  and context, musical 218–20
    rhythm/pitch 222–6, 227–8
    symbols, choice of 220–2
  developing notations 208–18
    and developing performance 215–18
    for song 212–15
    symbol system sequence 211–12
  development of 200–1
  first notations 203–9
    abstract 204–6
    combination/elaboration 208–9
    pictorial 204
    rebus 206, 207
    text 206, 207, 208
  research design 202–3
  three-dimensional view 198–203
    cognitive shift in perception 198–9
    performance ability 199
  see also melody construction by children;
    tonal structure and early learning
compositional systems, cognitive constraints
    on 231–59
  comprehensibility, aesthetic value of
    254–7
    complexity/complicatedness 255–6

    compositional/listening alliance 256–7
  grammar, compositional/listening 233–7
    gap between 234, 235–6
    natural/artificial 235
  listening theory 237–43
    compositional constraints 244–51
    Le Marteau sans Maître, structure of
      231–3, 241
  serialism, cognitive capacity of 251–4
    consonance/dissonance avoidance 253–4
    permutational structure 252–3
    and pitch space 254
composition study, novice/expert 263–84
  the experiment
    conditions 264–7
    task 263–4
  key definition 272–4
  modulation, economy in 271–2
  strategy levels 274–9
  success of melodies 279
  summary and discussion 279–84
    problem representation 280–1
    strategies 281–2
    tonal thinking 282–3
    tonality, composition/perception of
      283–4
  tonality definition 270–1
  working styles
    working units 267–9
    new material genertion 269
    rhythm integration 269–70
    motivic relationships 270
comprehensibility, aesthetic value of 254–7
  complexity/complicatedness 255–6
  compositional/listenign alliance 256–7
computer synthesis, *see* synthesis, computer
conductor and synchronization 86–8
consonance/dissonance
  and octave division 245–6
  and serialism 253–4
creativity studies 179–94
  composing ability 180
  conclusions 193–4
  experimental procedure
    creativity assessment 180–3
    discussion 183–4